A PIAGETIAN MODEL OF
CHARACTER STRUCTURE

A PIAGETIAN MODEL
OF CHARACTER STRUCTURE

A. J. Malerstein, M.D.

Associate Clinical Professor
University of California, San Francisco

Mary Ahern, M.S.W., Ph.D.

Lecturer in Psychiatric Social Work
University of California, San Francisco

HUMAN SCIENCES PRESS, INC.
72 FIFTH AVENUE,
NEW YORK, N.Y. 10011

Grateful acknowledgement is made for permission to reprint copyrighted material from:

The Moral Judgment of the Child by Jean Piaget, translated by Marjorie Gabain. Published by The Free Press, A Division of Macmillan Publishing Company, Inc., 1965.

Play, Dreams, and Imitation in Childhood by Jean Piaget, translated by C. Gattegno and F. M. Hodgson. Published by W. W. Norton & Company, Inc., copyright 1951 (First printed by Norton Library, 1962).

Copyright © 1982 by A. J. Malerstein and Mary Ahern
Published by Human Sciences Press, Inc.
72 Fifth Avenue, New York, New York 10011

Printed in the United States of America
23456789 987654321

Library of Congress Cataloging in Publication Data

Malerstein, Abraham J.
A Piagetian model of character structure.

Bibliography: p. 235
Includes index.
1. Character. 2. Psychology, Pathological. 3. Piaget, Jean, 1896–1980. I. Ahern, Mary. II. Title.
BF818.M35   155.2'6   LC   81-6305
ISBN 0-89885-002-9   AACR2

CONTENTS

INTRODUCTION

Our cognitive model of character structure is the budding of a coherent and structural general psychology based on Piaget's psychological theory. The model provides a framework for including psychodynamics, clinical findings, and knowledge of content, e.g., oedipal conflict. It embraces normal and abnormal function and fits current knowledge of personality and traits. It helps explain certain descriptive psychiatric findings and, partly because of its structural base, appears more likely to interdigitate with the biologic substrate.

In the course of explaining development of character structure, we will propose a concept of superego formation which differs to some extent from either Freud's or Piaget's. Making use of Piaget's observations, we will also propose a different dating to the origins of traits such as distrust and dependency than is suggested by psychoanalytic theory. We believe that both these modifications are significant corrections. Our concept of character structure, although originally conceived from, and usually diagnosed by complex clinical derivatives, is sim-

ple, and accounted for by social cognitive style and basic investment. Such basic components suggest simple parameters for
investigation and for application to treatment.

Our study of character structure did not begin with any
expectation that the findings and some of the concepts of Freud
and Piaget might interrelate. Rather, our study grew out of
efforts to understand patients as we practiced and taught psychotherapy. Like many other clinicians, we were profoundly
ignorant of Piaget's work. In our practice and teaching, we
drew heavily on our understanding of the psychoanalytic model
as well as the findings of psychoanalysis and psychoanalytically
oriented psychotherapy. Accordingly, we anticipate that our
work will be of most interest to, and is directed primarily
toward, psychotherapists of psychoanalytic persuasion. Other
clinicians, however, may find Piaget's system offers them a
more acceptable body of constructs, especially practitioners
who found Freud's ideas too fanciful (particularly his energic
concepts) or too far removed from the biologic, making the
eventual bridging between the psychologic and biologic domains appear hopeless. Academicians who are interested in a
marriage of psychoanalytic theory and findings with Piagetian
theory will find here a system for accomplishing this.

Efforts to refine our understanding of dynamic classificatory designations, such as borderline syndrome, and to understand which treatment interventions helped our patients
spawned our investigation of character structure. We went
through a number of confused gropings, at times thinking that
obsessive-compulsive personality was a character structure or
at other times not precisely differentiating the types of social
cognition found in the character syndromes. Our confusion
regarding the borderline mirrored that in the literature, sometimes referring to preschizophrenia, sometimes to behavior disorder. Stepwise, we grasped the essence of character structure,
that is, the most stable aspects of a person as a social being, as
opposed to less abiding or less selective qualities, such as personality traits.

We first considered writing about our conceptualizations when teaching at Langley Porter Institute, University of California San Francisco. Our task at that time was selection of patients for students, providing each student with a balanced sample of patients and each patient with an appropriate treatment program. We found we selected on the basis of character structure of the patients. Of the hundreds of patients we saw or were presented to us, we could usually classify each as having one of three character structures: the intuitive, the operational, or the symbolic.

These terms were borrowed from Piaget several years later. Initially, we tried to use preschizophrenic, borderline (including behavior disorder or narcissistic personality) and neurotic (that is, someone who was an optimal case for psychoanalysis). These classificatory designations could probably have been retained except for two reasons. First, although initially our character syndromes were dissected out in the clinical setting, because we think of the character structure as normal, it was important to us that any new names not bring with them a connotation of the pathologic nor a pejorative taint. Second, the social cognition of each type of character structure parallels the cognition found in three of Piaget's stages of cognitive development. Since the clinical terms bear no relationship to Piagetian psychology, we chose ones that did.

Our understanding of character structure was heavily influenced by the ideas of psychoanalytic authors, particularly Erikson's (1950) conceptualization of the interrelationship between culture, child-rearing practices, and phases of development of the child; the concepts of Freud (1953a) and Reich (1949) on obsessive characteristics; and Deutsch's (1942) idea of the "as-if" personality that gave birth to the concept of borderline personality organizations, made more precise by such authors as Kernberg (1970) and Zetzel (1971). Weiss's (1967) paper on the integration of defenses contributed to our thinking about the obsessive. Anna Freud's (1946) recognition of a given person's preference for certain defense mechanisms and shunning of others was of aid in enabling us to differentiate the character structures.

For some years we had been discontent with the energic theory of psychoanalysis: that the psyche is a closed energic system under pressure always seeking discharge and that the development, function, and structure of the psyche may be explained by deployments of libinal and aggressive energy. Any notion that cognitive structures derived from hierarchies of cathexes and countercathexes seemed unlikely to us. Furthermore, concepts of primary and secondary autonomous ego functions did little but delay the long overdue overhaul of psychoanalytic theory. In our view, this delay was basically a disservice. We became impatient with the mental gymnastics displayed in use of concepts such as bound, unbound, neutralized, or deneutralized energy, efforts to bend perfectly reasonable observations into nineteenth century concepts of closed, physical systems.

It was in this abiding state of disequilibrium that we encountered Piaget's work. Not unlike other psychoanalytically oriented psychotherapists, we thought that reality testing, a function of identity formation, together with basic trust and dependency, were issues of the first year of life. We then assumed, when treating or diagnosing a patient who had a symbolic character structure or an intuitive one, that is, a patient who had major conflicts involving trust, reality testing, and dependency, that the period of special difficulty for him or her had been the first year of life. In preparation for presenting our particular delineation of character structure, we reviewed the work of psychologists who studied early childhood development. In this review, we were startled to find that Piaget had described a style of thinking about things (and people) at age 2 to 4 which we were finding in what we now call our symbolic character. Similarly, the thought processes of the 4- to 7-year-old, as described by Piaget, corresponded to those of whom we now call our intuitive character; and, finally, the 8- to 11-year-old's thinking was like that of whom we now call our operational character. Impelled by our psychoanalytic bias, we had attributed the type of thought processes exhibited by each of the different types of adult to an origin much earlier in childhood than was seen regularly in the normal child investigated by Piaget. This was very confusing.

Over the next few years, we resolved the dilemma for ourselves, deciding that Piaget's findings date a later origin to our syndromes and that the very rich clinical findings of psychoanalysis may be best integrated by using Piaget's theoretical model. Piaget, a student of cognitive development, provides us with a foundation and framework, a general model of the psyche's system for organizing data, which includes cognition in the social sphere.

Bringing psychiatry into the mainstream of Piaget is a major goal of this book. Other less holistic attempts have been made to integrate Piaget's work with the findings and propositions of psychoanalysis or psychodynamics. Maier (1965) compared Piaget's developmental psychology with Eriksons. Wolff (1960) pointed up parallels between psychoanalytic concepts and Piagetian ones during the first two years of life, while more recently Basch (1977) has described parallels between Freud's topographic model and Piaget's periods of cognitive development. Ainsworth (1969) has attempted to understand child development by integrating Bowlby's ethologic concepts with those of other schools of psychology. In her integration, she clearly makes room for Piaget's findings and concepts. Lidz (1973) has made significant use of Piaget's theory in an effort to clarify the family interaction factors in schizophrenia. Slipp (1973), Sameroff and Zax (1978), as well as Blatt and Wild (1976) have brought in Piaget's concepts in trying to understand schizophrenia. Piaget (1923, 1962a, 1962b, 1968, and 1973) himself attempted to bridge his work and that of psychoanalysis. Hanford (1975) stressed the potential of Piagetian concepts as a means of understanding clinical factors in adults. Through use of several Piagetian concepts, Friedman (1978) has conceptualized the effective components in psychoanalytic

treatment. Appel (1977) brought considerable clinical sophisti-
cation into her Piagetian-oriented investigation of children's
development of understanding of mothers' efforts to socialize
their children. Loevinger (1976) comes closest to our attempt
at a holistic integration of psychodynamic psychiatry into Piagetian psychology. We will extend Piaget's theory and
findings, derived from his study of cognition in the child, into
a sphere which is foreign territory, normal and abnormal psychodynamic psychology.

Chapter 1

THE IMPORTANCE OF A PIAGETIAN
THEORETICAL FRAMEWORK

The adage that there are "acres of diamonds in your own backyard" holds, provided you have the genius of a Freud or a Piaget to see the diamonds. The subjects Freud and Piaget observed, the data they gathered, the kinds of instrumentation they employed were available to anyone. The fact that each could exploit such homely data: patients' verbalizations and self-observation in the case of Freud and simple experiments with children, for example, hiding a shiny object, in the case of Piaget, attest to their genius and their skill as observers as well as their ability to adhere to a scientific code or model when approaching data. Their commitment to scientific principle allowed them to forsake the traditional garb of their fellow scientists and recognize factors that must necessarily be obscured by large group, random samplings; statistical analyses; or by microscopic, physical, or chemical analyses. Neither relied on so-called hard data. It should be recognized that in studying the group or in studying the organic substrate itself, one is removing oneself an additional step from the raw data. As tricky as observation of behavior and communication is, it is as close to the psychological organism as we can get as yet. Freud's and Piaget's instrumentation was primarily their own senses and their uncommon intellects coupled with great integrity. Surely errors and limitations are to be found in their work. We anticipate, however, that most of the observations of both men will hold and that the essence of Piaget's theory may prove final. Both Freud and Piaget were committed to basic scientific concepts of their time which they applied to data that their contemporaries disregarded. Freud observed commonplace, usually overlooked behavior in himself, friends, and patients. From this behavior (dreams, parapraxes, neurotic symptoms, and later contiguity of associations) and committed to the concepts of determinism, that if we know all the antecedents we can explain what we observe, even psychological phenomena, he was forced to accept a dynamic unconscious as well as to take a developmental point of view. For instance, when one failed to remember an associate's name, Freud (1943) concluded this forgetting was not usually just static in the system, but might be the result of an unconscious antipathy one had toward the person whose name was forgotten or due to associations one had to a specific name. When Breuer fled in the face of his discomforts caused by the patient's transference behavior in treatment, Freud adhered to his deterministic principle and was able to treat transference as another piece of behavior subject to its own laws which could then be investigated. So Freud's adhering to a theoretical principle was fundamental to his achievements. Subsequently, his postulation of a dynamic unconscious and his energic and structural concepts had profound effects on both theory and practice such that ideas of his and other psychoanalysts are invoked automatically by psychotherapists of all persuasions and often used with little awareness of their origins.

Now, however, we think Freudian metapsychology is lacking. One major limitation in Freud's conceptualizations derives from his adherence to a theoretical concept based on the physics model of his time, which dealt with closed power systems such as hydraulic or electrostatic systems. This type of conceptualization, applied to understanding psychological functions, led to both theoretical and practical problems. A convoluted metapsychology was evolved in an effort to explain structures deriving from libidinal or aggressive energy. Additionally, certain clinical errors resulted from this theoretical model. The current physics model of information systems controlling power systems was unavailable to Freud. More importantly, Freud did not assimilate into his scientific understanding a concept of open, biologic systems, including an understanding of embryology.

Piaget, on the other hand, steeped in a knowledge of biology and embryology from his earlier work with mollusks, was able to bring his biologic bias to bear when he formulated his theoretical model. We believe his "digestive" model of the psyche was fundamental in his being able to formulate and interpret his experiments with children. Interestingly enough, just as Freud was able to exploit the principle of determinism while dealing with quite homely data, so Piaget using his biologic model was able to see into the basic ideational development of the child through such simple experiments as placing the child's bottle in various locations and watching the child's behavior. Some of our most recent psychological theorists have drawn on information models of modern day physics. We do not have high expectations for these models in helping us to understand psychology. The beauty of Piaget's theory is that it is biologically rooted. We believe this biologic rootedness of Piaget's model increases the likelihood that his model will one day be integrated into our understanding of brain function and structure.

Just as with Piaget and Freud, so with other clinicians and theoreticians, the theoretical model employed influences both practice and subsequent development of theory. When applied assiduously a theoretical model opens up new vistas for understanding, but also opportunities for practical application in treatment or prevention. Psychoanalysis opened up the entire area of psychotherapy as well as provided a wealth of new knowledge. In our eagerness, however, psychoanalytic treatment was applied indiscriminately, had its deleterious effects in some conditions, for example, prepsychotics, and was powerless in others, for example, psychopaths. It was the same with penicillin that was overprescribed initially. Gradually, we learn the indications, contraindications, and limitations of any new treatment. In the same vein, to the extent that a theoretical model is limited, so errors in application may follow. For example, the psychoanalytic concept that the psyche is a closed, energic system under pressure led to an erroneous assumption that removal of a symptom, the symptom being conceptualized as an open discharge valve for the psyche, would invariably result in the appearance of another symptom elsewhere, that is, another effort at discharge. Thus, theory had direct impact on therapy, psychoanalysts contending that, without genetic insight, that is a conscious understanding of early childhood antecedents with attendant discharge, and working through, symptom removal would result in development of new symptoms. Another example of theory adversely affecting clinical function is illustrated by the training analyst who, when confronted with the fact that schizophrenic patients have sex lives and experience orgasm said, "But just think of the quality of their orgasms." Thus, he implied that their orgasms were inferior somehow. Apparently, he had drawn on psychosexual developmental theory, including the notion that genital love is the ultimate stage in psychosexual development and the concept that schizophrenics are arrested at, or regressed to, a primitive psychosexual stage. He then concluded that schizophrenics could not possibly have high quality orgasms. So the theoretical framework employed may influence practical treatment issues and day-to-day clinical assumptions and attitudes. This is aside from any misinterpretation of concepts as occurs in the fringe groups who see "letting it all hang out" as equivalent to psychoanalytic treatment and then view this either as a panacea or an anathema.

The theoretical model used affects subsequent theory. For instance, psychoanalytic theoreticians (Hartman, Kris, and Lowenstein, 1964; Rapaport, 1967) have attempted to keep the energic model while trying to explain organic givens and structural concepts. They have kept Freud's neutralized, deneutralized, fused, defused, bound and unbound energy concepts, and added concepts of primary and secondary autonomous ego function or hierarchical cathectic and countercathectic structures. Their theory has become unwieldy, overloaded with abstruse jargon, forcing an energic model to accommodate developmental and neurophysiologic findings.

Influenced by Freud's energic model of the psyche plus the psychoanalytic concept of retroflexed rage as the cause of depression, Spitz (1946) suggested that aggression turned against the self caused depression in infants. He had initially discovered that children who had minimal human contact suffered a severe depression which he named *anaclitic* depression. He then reasoned that because of their confinement to their cribs the children had no outlet for their aggression, which was then turned against the self. That is, the aggressive energy became converted to depression.

Spitz (1965) used the fact that infants develop person-object representations prior to thing-object representations to imply that good thing-reality testing developed out of good person-reality testing. This position fits the standard psychoanalytic concept of development of perception of reality. We assume it was this concept that influenced Spitz in the theoretical position he took. His position is likely in error as we will point out.

The theory embraced is significant both practically and in further growth of understanding. Up until now the most coherent explanatory system for dynamic psychiatry has been the psychoanalytic one. It has provided a basis for most of our understanding of psychodynamics. Psychoanalysis is an exceptional investigative tool, an entrance into the psyche, which resulted in major findings. In no way do we wish to minimize the findings of Freud and psychoanalysis or the value that psychoanalysis has had as an investigative tool. Certainly, our work is derivative of the findings and constructs of psychoanalysis. *Nevertheless, we believe that Piaget's theoretical model has major advantages over Freud's model and should replace it. Piaget's model is open-ended, biologically-based, structural, and more holistic. We think Piaget's model fits our current findings better than Freud's and hopefully will foster future improved practice and understanding.*

Like other biologic structures, the psychological structure, as conceived by Piaget, is open-ended. It requires some nutrient for maintenance, will atrophy without it, will respond differently to some extent to different nutrient, but does not become the nutrient. In its development, a biologic structure is respondent to the environment to some extent, but will assimilate the largest whole of the environment that the structure, in accordance with its state, is ready to assimilate. The structure has its own timetable of development. Each structure evolves by small steps from previous structures, reorganizing itself in stages, the final outcome being quite dissimilar from its beginnings; just as in all other embryologic developmental systems.

When or where Piaget's model will fail to serve us is uncertain. Case (1974) felt that the Piagetian model's strong tie to structure was limiting and proposed a functionally oriented model that derived in part from a computer model. Perhaps Piaget's model will be lacking in certain ways when brain microstructure is better understood, e.g., the relationship of affective valences to site-specific biochemistry (Snyder, 1978) or where and how data are stored, be it as a hologram (Pribram, et al, 1974). Perhaps when the function and interrelationships between different substructures of the brain, such as right and left hemispheres or limbic system and cortex is better understood, some defects in Piaget's model will be obvious. At this point, however, Piaget's model dissects out primary divisions of psychological function. We think that it is doubtful that Piaget's basic concepts will become obsolete unless there is a major breakthrough in our understanding of biology, perhaps only if a better understanding of embryology is attained. By the same token, keeping the Piagetian model in mind may assist investigators in their exploration of brain microstructure or brain structure interrelationships.

There is a good possibility that Piaget's model will one day integrate with the understanding of biologic structure. Piaget conceptualizes construction of representation of an object out of multi-integrations and differentiations of input viewed from a multitude of angles and relationships. This concept that an engram is constructed through many interrelated avenues fits with the experiments of Lashley (1950) in which he was unable to excise a memory engram. Such experiments suggest that memory engrams are diffusely located or multiply encoded if not a function of the brain as a whole. In Piaget's system, information is contained in the interrelationship. Generally speaking, the greater the interrelationship (if not overdone), the more stable the content. One point or several point localization of recorded data is irrelevant in such a system.

Piaget's emphasis on activity in learning and his description of the general configuration sensitivity (as we will note in body imitations of object movement, e.g., the opening and closing, in Chapter 3) of the sensorimotor apparatus both fit with our increased understanding of sensory organs being change detectors (Johanssen, 1975) rather than being cameralike. Previously, it was thought that the retina was like a photographic plate and that, once focused by the lens, the image which fell on the retina was transmitted to the central nervous system. Now it is realized that the eye responds to changes in light and that these changes are interpreted centrally. Both this new concept of sensory organ function and Piaget's system fit with a neurologic apparatus that integrates the multiple, multirelated patterns of stimulation into constructs, a sensory system which takes into account (constructs its image out of) proprioceptive impulses from eye and neck muscles along with changes in retinal impulses.

We assume that Piaget's concepts will lead to increased understanding of brain damage in children and adults. One puzzling clinical finding in adults has been that acute organic brain syndromes may or may not present with paranoid or acute schizophrenic symptoms as well as impaired intellectual function, while schizophrenics or paranoids do not present with impaired intellectual function. The view we put forward in this book holds that social cognition, although somewhat autonomous, is a subfunction of general cognition. In keeping with this view, it follows that someone who has brain damage may present with a disturbance in social cognition. At the same time, we would not expect the reverse to be true. We would not expect that a person with a thought disorder, a basic disturbance in social cognition, which is merely a subfunction of general cognition, to present with symptoms of an organic brain syndrome, that is, intellectual deficits. It is early to predict the impact of Piaget's theoretical model on our understanding of brain function. However, we think it will be substantial.

Clearly, adoption of a new theoretical framework will have impact on subsequent clinical and theoretical considerations just as it did with Freud and Piaget. A fundamental aspect to Piaget's theory is that the schemes are quasi-biologic structures. A biologic structure requires input for maintenance, is expected to be vulnerable to input deprivation, but is not just a reflection of the input. Such a structure or scheme abides and has characteristic expressions, if not subject to deprivation (as may occur in a concentration camp, in isolation at the North Pole, or in classic psychoanalysis). Analogously, deprivation or chemical assault may be expected to damage the mature organ, as shock may cause kidney shutdown. Once the kidney is restored, however, it functions like a kidney, not like a liver. So under assault mature substructures of the psyche could be expected to dysfunction or fail to function. With restored health, they may regain function to some extent, but it is not likely that there will be very efficient structure substitution, one class of structure replacing another. Generally the liver will not do the job of the kidney. Carrying this analogy further, reintegration following orthodox psychoanalysis (which facilitates transference neurosis through regression) would be expected to take place in a somewhat loosened structure, but one which remains essentially the same in overall design. The person may become a looser obsessive, but he is still an obsessive or a person may become a less flamboyant and defended hysteric, but he is still an hysteric. We are aware that we are reifying the model, when we use it in this manner. We think reification has utility, however, since if we push the model to its limits we may be clear about some of the assumptions that may operate out of our awareness as we proceed to use the model.

If the psyche is made up of evolving "biologic" structures, then it is likely that there are stages or steady states that occur in the mature organism and that these states are basic limitations to growth or alteration.

We have not as yet been successful in causing change of one character structure to another in our adult patients. We do not think this is because our technique is defective or that lack of intensity of therapy is the explanation.* In keeping with our theoretical position, we think our failure to cause character structure change is due to limitations set by the biologic apparatus or the equilibrated cognitive structures. It is precisely this kind of position, influenced by theory, that is the strength

*Heavily influenced by Piaget, Weiner (1975) had his psychotherapy patients solve cognitive tasks using selected puzzles. As the patient attempted to solve a puzzle, he was asked to free associate much as he would to a dream. Weiner reports that incorporating this parameter into psychoanalytic psychotherapy stimulated particularly rich early memories and provided a vehicle for cognitive restructuring in the affectual and intellectual spheres. We doubt that cognitive restructuring of the kind we are referring to here can be effected through this means although we can see the usefulness of sometimes introducing a cognitive task as a stimulus for certain types of exploration.

of a good theory and the weakness of a bad one. One must be mindful that psychoanalytic energic theory predicted that symptom removal was not good treatment and in doing so deprived some patients of help. Nevertheless, both on the basis of experience (thus far) and theory, conversion of one of our types of character structure into another appears unlikely. We assume that an equilibrium has begun to be established, shortly after the close of the 5- to 7-year old stage and that at some point this balance gets set into one of the three character structures.*

When we say "set" we do not mean a psychological structure becomes set like concrete. We think of it more as occurs with a developing biological structure which may be fluid for a long period of time, but at some juncture reaches a point of no return. We think at some point the character organization becomes relatively fixed in form and function.

The embryologic nature of Piaget's model makes us think of the developing psychological apparatus in a totally different manner than we had. We now think of it as a structure that reorganizes itself as it grows, that in the Concrete Operational Period basic decisions are made, inclusions and exclusions or dissociation of some things from others occur. The child's experiences of his social world during the period from age 2 to 7, then, must be balanced out within an integrated structure. At that time, the organism reaches a new state of total reorganization much like when the neural tube forms in an embryo. There are times when embryologic structures are sufficiently plastic that an eye can be induced to grow in an aberrant location. This kind of plasticity, however, is lost for most biologic structures very early. Psychological function retains considerable plasticity much longer, that is, well after birth. Nevertheless, we think it is not likely that plasticity persists indefinitely; that is,

*Luria (1976) suggests that change of both general and social cognitive structures to more mature ones occurs in illiterate peasants when they learn to read and are exposed to modern culture. We, like Cole (Luria's editor), think that the mature structures were likely present from the outset, but were used differently by the illiterate peasants.

that the human animal can learn all things at all times. We believe that there are times when it is too early and times when it is too late to learn certain things.

Theory affects practice and practice affects theory. It is much like an equilibrium or balance, with a change in one forcing a change in the other. When theory is not supportive of practice, then in time clinicians abandon the theory or press for a modification of theory.

Chapter 2

CHARACTER STRUCTURE

To know who a person is, primarily, we must know his *charac-*
ter structure, his most basic and abiding intrapsychic organiza-
tion as a social being: his primary concerns and his system for
processing data involving person relationships. He may process
information about things, that is, chairs, tables, and so on (or
people as things), differently than he does his world of social
relationships and feelings. Hand in hand with his social cognition are his basic concerns or investments whether they center
around function, narcissistic supplies, or attachment. When we
say basic investment we mean the ultimate guiding influence or
motivations. If the person's basic investment is in attachment
to another human being then all his efforts eventually serve his
need to attach. His use of charm to elicit narcissistic supplies,
his giving or sharing with others, his abiding by codes are not
ends in themselves, but on close examination can be seen to
secure his sense of feeling attached to another person. A person
whose basic investment is in attachment will value and experience each of the therapist's (or any other associate's) interven-

tions in terms of whether an attachment is made, sustained, or broken.

Our view of character is very similar to Hogan's (1973). He defined character as not what one does, but the recurring motives and dispositions that give stability to one's social conduct. He saw character structure as a more basic organization than personality and more allied with moral and social behavior. At the same time, he regarded moral and social behavior as not particularly distinct from each other and as irrational, but evolutionarily adaptive.

We see character structure as being more integral to the person and more stable than personality, although both tend to be abiding functions. We think of personality as similar to a cloak that is worn over the character structure. With some persons, the cloak is loose and easily shed. With others, it is ill-fitting. With still others, the cloak is so tightly worn and such a good fit that it can hardly be distinguished from character structure. Personality is more evident to the observer and to the person himself than is character structure. We observe at least a dozen personality types, while we find only three character structure types.

There is no agreement in the literature on the use of the terms character and personality which often are used interchangeably. In 1937, Allport listed over 50 different definitions of personality. The definition he chose, "the dynamic organization within the individual of those psychophysical systems that determine his unique adjustments to his environment" (Hall and Lindzey, 1957, p. 262) includes both personality and character as we view them. Our use of personality roughly corresponds to that in the psychiatric diagnostic system (for example, obsessive-compulsive or shizoid personality). Compared to personality, character structure is the person's social core, his more general system of organization as a social being. We postulate that character structure is always present and operating in the adult, while personality as an organized system of function in some individuals is almost always in operation;

in others, while available and in that sense abiding, may be called into play more or less contingent on the setting. For example, some hysterical personalities at times may or may not show their hysterical traits. Others manifest their traits at all times. We think character structure forms during latency. Personality formation appears more complex in its origins. It may have very early roots, for example, traits derived from toilet training, and yet depend upon both structural and content changes which take place as late as adolescence.

In a particular character structure, major concerns are identity diffusion, fear of a symbiotic relationship, and a desire for one. The solution may be formation of a schizoid personality. The schizoid solution handles the wish for and fear of merging with another person and handles identity diffusion through use of physical and psychological distancing maneuvers. In this instance, the personality is a solution to character involvements or dilemmas. It is an integral part of the character structure. In other instances, the personality is not fully integrated into the character structure. Some persons who have hysterical features may readily set these aside when issues of function are important.

We are committed to diagnosis as a necessity for treatment. We do not conceive of persons as all being the same or as facets of a multidimensional continuum of mixes, composed of a little of this or more of that. Hence, we do not think of treatment as a little uncovering and a little support any more than we think of treatment as a blanket application of one technique to all persons, regardless of who they are. All persons are the same in the sense of being entitled to respect as persons and as individuals who use the approaches they have developed to address life. Beyond this given, however, they cannot be treated alike. Fundamental to our view is the concept that there are, in fact, some basic syndromes and that understanding of these syndromes helps us to formulate a rational approach that can be applied to those who have the syndromes.

A clinical diagnosis is not an additive process, neither does it rest on elimination of all possible alternatives. An experienced clinician makes a diagnosis on the basis of how well things fit together. The body of the mature organism is a well-coordinated whole. Organs and parts are not attached at random or summed. Likewise, the psyche of a person is not a disjunctive aggregate but, over the years, has developed into an organized, integrated, abiding system of approaches. Although influenced by his setting a person tends to do certain things and not to do others. He has at his disposal a certain array of defense mechanisms. These defense mechanisms tend to go together in clusters. Where we find one or two, we will usually find the other defenses of the cluster. These mechanisms will have a certain coherence with each other as well as with the other functions of a person's psyche. For instance, when a person is overly concerned with control of his functioning, very likely we will find that he uses obsessive-compulsive defenses (e.g., undoing or intellectualization); moreover, he will give a history of over-controlling parents. In contrast, we find that someone who has oral-narcissistic concerns opts for use of projection or denial and often has a history of deprivation or disruption in his early life.

Character diagnosis usually may be made early in the interviews, frequently in the first interview, because we need only a sample of the person's behavior, any sample being part of the coordinated whole. The diagnosis is sometimes made on the basis of primary criteria: style of social cognition or basic investments. Even in an unguided, nonjudgmental setting in which the patient is generally motivated to reveal himself, the fundamental signs of character structure are not evident constantly. We see them in the overall flavor of an hour, or in a special instance of handling a piece of data. Generally there will only be two or three clues during an hour or several hours. Although character structure is likely always in operation, embedded in every sentence, it is not detectable, it is not on the surface. Most often the diagnosis is made on derivatives or secondary criteria. It is unpredictable which particular characteristics a patient will present clearly to the interviewer in any one interview, so the entire syndrome must be kept in mind. Every type of information available is used—type of defense mechanisms employed, content and symbolism of concerns, contiguity of associations, the patient's style of relating to the therapist, the therapist's thoughts and feelings, and his knowledge of other patients and of the literature. All of these are only as good as the therapist's perceptive instrument. But assuming that his perceptive ability is satisfactory, he will find that data from all these sources will (almost by definition) fit the particular character type of a given person. Typically, any three or four samples of information, sometimes just one, will predict the general types of data that will appear eventually along each dimension.

We wish to emphasize that in this model we are not postulating an arrest in development, but rather a branching. As with all biologic development, decision points occur, branching takes place. Pruning, training, and other experiences may influence further growth and global appearance. Short of amputation, however, the branches once made are abiding and determine part of the function of a structural organization. In the uncovering psychotherapeutic interview we glimpse this basic branching.

In adults, we find three character structures: the operational, the intuitive, and the symbolic. Generally, the operational character processes social data like a concrete operational child in his embrace of classification and ordering in his abiding codes. Hand in hand are his concern with and investment in function and control of function, his involvement with social roles and codes, for example, whether he or others are good parents, democrats, fascists, etc. His superego is autonomous; what he believes is right or wrong is largely uninfluenced by setting or affect state. Generally, life choices, friends, lovers, and jobs, are in tune with long-term or abiding attributes or pay offs. In such choices is balanced off a friend's slovenliness against the friend's loyalty or honesty. In such styles of choosing, is exhibited ability to use hierarchies and classification much as a concrete operational child may order and sort physical objects in accord with intensity of color and shape.

An intuitive character is more interested in narcissistic supplies, in getting, having, and being. He or she judges social values on the basis of the most striking appearance at a given time. To an intuitive, what looks good at the moment is good, and what looks bad at the moment is bad. He has a heteronomous superego, a superego-precursor. His boundaries of self-valuation and object-valuation are not fixed. He may feel inferior in the presence of someone he regards as inferior. He will often choose a lover or a friend based on the person's appearance or how the person makes him feel for the time being. This is much like the intuitive stage child who thinks that he or she has more lemonade if it comes to the brim of a glass or that a sausage is bigger if it is elongated.

Symbolic characters are involved with identity and attachment. They tend to see themselves and others in terms of parts. Their boundaries between self and object are blurred. When on a committee or a job an symbolic character's direction may rest on whatever is going wrong. He may feel responsible for what went wrong before he was a member of the committee and define his goal as correcting whatever the current wrong is. Defined as a member of an organization, he may feel centered and whole. Losing that attachment, he may feel lost and question his existence and what is real. His cognition parallels the symbolic-stage child's who may define the self by a part, for example, a garment.

Symbolic characters, in addition to using part to part reasoning and being focused on attachment and identity, may to a varying extent manifest the cognition and investments of either an operational or an intuitive or some combinations of the two. So their presentation may be quite complex.

We will give a more detailed description of the three character structures including an example of each in Chapters 5,6, and 7. Before doing so, we will briefly review some of Piaget's work, principally to enable us to demonstrate the isomorphism between each character type and corresponding stages of cognitive development that he described. In our review all four periods of Piaget's cognitive development will be described, but we will emphasize the Concrete Operational Period and the two stages of the Preoperational Period. The Sensorimotor Period, the first two years of life, does not appear to contribute directly to character structure formation, although some tones of social function may be set during this first developmental period. In contrast, we suggest that the experiences of the Preoperational and Concrete Operational Periods are the primary contributors that give shape to character structure, a social cognitive structure which is formed during the Concrete Operational Period. We will detail our position in Chapter 8 in our discussion of superego formation. We propose that during the Concrete Operational Period the child's social cognitive system opts for one of three available structural reorganizations, the one which best embraces his groupings of understandings of his social world and himself as a social being.

In Chapter 9, we will examine how this relatively set form of character structure becomes part of social cognition generally during Piaget's final phase of cognitive development, the Formal Operational Period. We will also suggest the role of formal operations in personality configurations.

At that point a somewhat peculiar thing happens. We seem to come full circle. We borrowed from Piaget his classifications of cognitive stages, derived largely from studies in the physical domain. We did this to organize and clarify our findings in the social domain. Then, it appears that the particular configurations we found in our study in the social domain, in turn, shed light on earlier findings made in the physical domain. That is, our constructs may explain the finding that whole groups of adults fail to demonstrate formal operational function. Heretofore, these findings have been seen as defects or aberrations in Piaget's system. If our explanation of our social cognitive findings may be applied to physical cognitive findings, then our work in the social cognitive domain makes a contribution to the understanding of genetic epistemology generally, Piaget's primary involvement.

Chapter 3

PIAGET'S DEVELOPMENTAL PHASES BEGINNING WITH THE SENSORIMOTOR PERIOD

Application of Piaget's findings and theory to understanding emotional life, especially adult emotional life, has been neglected; partly because of the difficulty inherent in reading Piaget's books and, until recently, the absence of any satisfactory interpretations or clarifications of his works in English. Thus, psychotherapists are only beginning to become acquainted with his findings and theory.* Additionally, the tendency of psychotherapists to separate emotional development and disorders from cognitive function, the object of Piaget's study, accounts somewhat for their disinclination to learn more about Piagetian psychology. Finally, the emphasis on thought process in psychotherapy is relatively recent. This focus prepares the clinician to recognize parallels between adult thought processes and children's thought processes at certain developmental stages

*For the beginning student of Piaget we suggest Ginsburg and Opper (1969) followed by Flavell (1963) and then Piaget's *Play, Dreams and Imitation in Childhood.*

(Basch, 1977; Lidz, 1973; Malerstein & Ahern, 1979; Sameroff & Zax, 1978). We think the particular organization of character structure that we propose permits psychodynamic findings to be assimilated into Piaget's theoretical system. Accordingly, his work should become increasingly important to psychotherapists.

In his study of cognition from birth to adolescence (beginning with reflexes such as sucking and grasping and culminating in hypotheticodeductive reasoning of the adolescent), Piaget was able to infer the child's psychological experiences at each phase. He divided cognitive development into four major periods: the Sensorimotor Period (the first 2 years of life), the Preoperational Period (from age 2 to 7), the Concrete Operational Period (from age 8 to 11), and the Formal Operational Period (beginning at age twelve). Table 3-1 summarizes the tasks and some typical behaviors of the developmental periods; including those of the two stages of the Preoperational Period: the Preconceptual or Symbolic Stage (from age 2 to 4) and the Intuitive Stage (from age 5 to 7). We are interested most in the Concrete Operational Period and the two stages of the Preoperational Period because the style of thinking of each of these phases of development parallels the style of thinking of each of our character types. Accordingly, all of Chapter 4 is devoted to the Preoperational and Operational Periods while we restrict ourselves to a very brief review of the Sensorimotor Period at the end of this chapter.

All age ranges for stages or periods are approximate and apply to children raised in an urban culture similar to Geneva, where Piaget worked. There is some variation in the onset of a given period or stage in children from Geneva-like cultures and there may be considerable delay in the onset of certain periods in children from nonliterate cultures. With minor variations, however, children progress through each period and stage in order; they do not skip stages or periods. Unless they are in transition from one stage to the next, they do not mix them. They may, however, be at one stage for one function

Table 3-1 Tasks of Cognitive Development

Phase of development	Tasks
Sensorimotor Period (0–2 yr) Six stages, beginning with modifiable reflexes.	To construct objects, self, and symbols; differentiation of thought and perception.
Preoperational Period (2–7 yr) 1. Symbolic or Preconceptual Stage (2–4 years) One slug on the path is the same as another encountered later. Lucienne in a bathing suit is not the same person as Lucienne in her street clothes. Jacqueline in a photo is not the same person as Jacqueline herself.	To separate objects, self, and symbols; to understand what is essential and nonessential to an object and to the self.
2. Intuitive Stage (5–7 yr) High in a glass or full to the brim is more. A big ink blot is a more serious crime than a little blot, regardless of intent. Rules of marbles are regarded as sacred, but then are broken when playing the game. A majority of daisies is regarded as more than (all of) the flowers.	To construct values or attributes of objects and events including moral values as abstracts, separate from one's immediate perception of them; to coordinate different perspectives.
Concrete Operational Period (8–11 yr) Understands values and attributes with objects present. Has integrated surface discrepant variables into abiding attributes and values (including those which form character structure).	To understand values and attributes without objects being present.
Formal Operational Period (12 yr and over) Attributes and values are autonomous, split from objects. Can do hypothetical-deductive reasoning. Full separation of value from object (including self and other social objects).	

while they lag in development of another function. For instance, at age 7, a child may have reached the Concrete Operational Period with regard to judgment of quantities of substances; that is, he or she understands that a piece of clay is the same amount regardless of how it is shaped. Yet, he or she still may be at the Intuitive Stage of the Preoperational Period for judgment of weights. For instance, the fact that altering the shape of a given item will not change its weight will not be understood. Later he or she will judge weights in accordance with concrete operational concepts. In essence, a gradual unfolding of stages within periods takes place; the stages have some (biologic) limits on how soon they may be reached, with some functions unfolding more slowly than others, and the speed varying from one child to another. Nonetheless, one stage of a function feeds into and allows for the development of the next.

To provide an overall framework, we will give a schematic view of the tasks of each period and include certain definitions essential to a grasp of Piaget's system. (Our use of tasks refers to cognitive developments or reorganizations, not to performance on Piaget's experimental problems, sometimes referred to as tasks.) Presumably the child's psyche is undifferentiated at birth. He has no concept of self as differentiated from object. The task of the Sensorimotor Period is to develop concepts of objects as existing separate from the self. In the Preconceptual or Symbolic Stage of the Preoperational Period, the child has concepts of objects as somewhat separate from himself and other objects, but not completely so, since he is uncertain whether a part of an object (including a part of himself as an object) defines the object as a different object. For example, Jacqueline (Piaget's daughter) did not know that her sister was the same person when she was wearing different clothes (Piaget, 1962a). Jacqueline also confused a symbol (for example, a photograph of an object) with an object itself. The task of the Symbolic Stage is to construct concepts of stable objects, to get to understand the essence of an object (what truly defines it), and to know that a change in a part of an object does not make it a different object. In the Intuitive Stage, when the child has reasonably stable objects and understands their essence, his task is construction of the essence of certain attributes of objects. He must develop an understanding of attributes such as quantity, weight, color intensity, and so on, and in terms of these to learn to understand the meaning of more, less, or the same. He must learn that a given amount of lemonade is not greater in a narrow glass than in a wide one; in the Intuitive Stage he thinks there is more lemonade in the narrow glass. He grasps the essence of attributes of objects when he enters the Concrete Operational Period, but he can only conceptualize such attributes while the objects are in front of him. He cannot deal with attributes strictly in his thinking until the Formal Operational Period. Then he can deal with a problem such as, "If Virginia has darker hair than Mary and Mary has lighter hair than Jane, which one has the lightest hair?" without having three such dolls placed before him. The Formal Operational Period is probably Piaget's most controversial developmental phase; some researchers question its existence and others assert that cognition develops beyond this period. Based on the tests in use, many people never attain formal operational reasoning, and Piaget (1972) suggested that one tends to develop formal operational reasoning only in one's spheres of specialization, for example, in one's work.

THE YOUNG CHILD'S EXPERIENCE OF THE WORLD

Before we review the stages of development, consider how the young child experiences the world. Around four months of age, a child follows a moving white ball with his head and eyes until the ball disappears from sight. He does not know what a moving white ball is, as you and I conceive of moving, of white, or of a ball. Rather he experiences the ball as an intrapsychic reflection of nerve impulses. (However, integrated by the brain and the peripheral sensory nervous system). These impulses derive not only from the nerve cells of the parts of the retina on which the image (and changes of the image) of the ball falls, but from proprioceptive nerve cells attached to the eye muscles as the eyes follow the ball, as well as from proprioceptive nerve cells attached to the neck muscles as the head follows the ball, plus any internal fragmentary intrapsychic reflection of the coordinated motor nerve cell firings to the eye muscles or the neck muscles directing their movement.

To the 4-month-old child, the organized result of these various inputs (including proprioceptive firings and whatever recognition of motor output is possible at this stage, pretty much as a whole) is the moving white ball. Piaget calls this intrapsychic organization a *scheme.* (Most of the English translations of Piaget's texts have translated his term *schéme* as *schema.* Since Piaget has begun to use *schema* to mean an approximate figurative representation, we will use only the term *scheme* in this book.)

At this point, extraneous aspects of the environment or factors within the child himself are likely all part of his moving white ball. If he is in a crib, his sensations and motor action toward the crib may be experienced as part of the ball. His father's moving the ball, the child's being satiated from a feeding may be part of his scheme of the ball if this occurs when the ball passes by. All of these things are the moving ball to him. Later, out of this kind of experiencing of the ball, he constructs, by stages, a concept of moving white balls (one that roughly corresponds to what other human beings, wired together similarly, agree is a moving white ball). In part by the fact that the ball moves in different directions and different motor and sensory nerve firings occur, in part by changes in size of the image on the retina, and so on, by 18 months of age he differentiates (and integrates) the moving white ball as a thing separate from, but related to, the stimuli from movement of eyes and neck or presence or absence of father, being in or out of the crib, being satiated or not. The stages of this differentiation will be described shortly. One can imagine that if the child sees balls only in the presence of his father, then at the age of 18 months, when he has a concept of a ball as separate from himself, stimuli related to the father's presence will be inseparable from his construct of balls as objects.

Even though in time we all agree to some extent on what a moving white ball is, one point to be made from the foregoing is that each person's world is unique in its construction, each of us having had different states and experiences as we learned to construct our worlds.

Fundamental to Piaget's work is his concept that the child *actively constructs* his world. He is not a passive receptacle to be filled or a blank slate to be recorded upon by input thrust upon him. The child depends to some extent on the environment for nutrients or aliments, for example, balls and accompanying settings, to build his world. However, he makes use of, that is, assimilates, these nutrients as he is able, given his past development and the stage he is at.

A current term for *nutrient* or *aliment* might be *data input.* However, keeping terms like aliment that imply an analogy of psychological process with digestive processes comes much closer to the kind of processing that appears to take place in the psyche. Consonant with this kind of conceptualization of the development of the intellectual organ are the definitions that follow. Piaget carefully chose his own terms to conceptualize the psychology of the child. For a full understanding of Piaget's thinking these terms must be kept in mind.

The *scheme* is the basic unit or building block of psychic structure. For those who are accustomed to think in biologic terms, it is helpful to think of schemes as similar to cells, and schemes that are more differentiated and highly interrelated, as similar to organs, for example, the kidney or kidney tubule. Piaget uses scheme to refer to a hypothetical, organized, holistic unit of the psyche that corresponds to an event (the child's interaction with the world), for instance, the sucking scheme. At a given time, the sucking scheme will be a coordinated, intrapsychic structure reflecting arrays of stimuli having to do with sucking. Within the parameters allowed by the maturing neurophysiologic apparatus, the sucking scheme includes the total intrapsychic reflections of the motor impulses to muscles of the face, mouth, tongue, etc., involved in sucking as well as that of the sensory system involved, e.g., proprioception temperature, and pressure. It includes the more or less organized array of nervous system stimuli related to affect states of hunger and satiation or body warmth from the mother, not just sensations from lips, mouth, and muscles. All this input is *nutrient* or *aliment* for the sucking scheme.

The child may have differentiated subschemes, for instance, sucking for practice and sucking when hungry, etc. Such differentiated subschemes are postulated from the infant's behavior at the end of the first month. At that point, the infant when hungry, if offered a finger to suck, quickly extrudes the finger. When he is not hungry, however, he will suck a finger for awhile.

The scheme, much like any other biologic unit, requires nutrient or aliment to sustain itself. For the schemes of the psyche the aliment is a form of stimulation or input. However, the scheme is not taken over by the nutrient any more than we become a carrot when we eat a carrot, even though we may have to eat carrots or something similar in order to maintain certain structures. The scheme selectively takes in what it can use in accordance with its state of development. It discards or ignores what it cannot make its own. For example, if you give an infant a toy truck, he will suck it, not roll it on the floor or play truck driver. The scheme actively taking into itself nutrient is called *assimilation.*

At the same time, a child's schemes are somewhat modified by the aliment assimilated. The intrapsychic reflection, the sucking scheme, modifies to some extent, depending on whether the block is soft or hard, smooth or rough. That is, different arrays of stimuli as triggered by these properties of the blocks impinge on, and are taken into, the sucking scheme. The modification that occurs in the scheme as a result of the aliment is called *accommodation* by Piaget. We can infer such modifications because we can observe the child modify his mouth to the shape of the block or become more efficient in his sucking movements. Those schemes, thus modified by accommodation, then, are altered units which will assimilate new types of aliment.

Through *assimilation* and *accommodation* of the *aliment* the *schemes* adapt. Piaget's terminology stresses that he sees the psyche as made up of active, holistic, evolving biologic structures, developed as they use (interact with) the environmental matrix. So we have a concept of the psyche that is analogous to a digestive system. A scheme, like other biologic structures, requires aliment for maintenance and development. However, it is *not* a passive receptacle. The scheme actively processes the total nutrient, takes in the largest wholes it can assimilate, and eliminates parts that it cannot. Yet, in taking in the nutrient the scheme is to some extent modified by it. The scheme accommodates to the nutrient. As we noted, when one eats a carrot, one does not become a carrot. One chews it up and processes it, takes in parts that can be assimilated and eliminates other parts of it. Within the constraints of the body physiology and its frame, one's body grows and modifies on the basis of eating its carrots.

At first blush, this system appears primitive and inelegant for something so grand as the human psyche, but if we consider the models we have been using, for example, Freud's, which is essentially a closed energy system (e.g., electrostatic), or, more recently, the computer models that are high-speed counters that can be made to control power systems, we need not apologize. With Piaget's digestive model, we have a biologic model, not one based on inorganic physics. We have the fact that the systems of the model function in a holistic manner. The model is fully integrated with embryologic concepts. The model provides for an internal time clock and stages as all developing biologic units have. The developing psyche does its own growing but needs aliment and is able to adapt. The scheme is an open system, not a closed one. We have every chance, one day, of bridging the gap between intrapsychic function and brain neurophysiology through the use of Piaget's model. Such a possibility appears out of the question with a closed energy system such as Freud's and very unlikely with the current electronic models which have particulate registration loci as meaningful items.

THE SENSORIMOTOR PERIOD

The Sensorimotor Period is not central to character structure. Accordingly, we will only sketch this period. We base this sketch on Piaget's companion books (1954, 1962a, 1963) on this period (principally his *Play, Dreams and Imitation in Childhood*), which contain numerous detailed observations of his own children, and demonstrate his brilliance as observer, experimenter, and theoretician as well as his precision and patience. As we show how each of Piaget's stages builds upon or is a slight extension of the previous one, observations and concepts of psychoanalytically oriented investigators of child development will be addressed, particularly the findings and interpretations of Mahler and Spitz. Generally speaking, their findings supplement or repeat Piaget's, while their interpretations of their findings are often at odds with his.

The Sensorimotor Period from birth to 18 months is divided into six stages. Stepwise, by extension, integrations, and differentiations, drawing on maturation and experience, the child constructs his world, beginning with schemes of reflexes, moving from self–object undifferentiation to the sixth stage in which he has schemes of the self and object that are relatively separate entities. At the same time, hand in hand he differentiates percept from thought as well as symbols.

Characteristic of the period following the Sensorimotor Period is the child's use and further refinement of symbols.

Piaget distinguished between *symbols* and *signs*. In his definition, a *symbol* is a part of an object (or event) or something that in some way resembles the object and which the child uses to represent the object. A symbol has an intrinsic relationship to the object. To Piaget, a word is not a symbol but a sign, an arbitrary representation of an object. A word is chosen by the culture and need have no inherent relationship to the object it represents.

Over the course of the first month, Piaget's Stage 1, a child, practicing his reflexes, becomes better coordinated, sucks a bit more efficiently, shapes his mouth to the nipple, grasps a bit better, etc. At times, without external stimuli, he sucks or opens and closes his fist. As already noted, at the close of the first month a child, when hungry, will rapidly extrude a finger.

Both Mahler (1968) and Spitz (1965) stressed that not only is the outside world nonexistent to the child, but that he has a high stimulus barrier to external stimuli. Spitz emphasized the importance of the barrier (supplemented in part by the mother's quick response to her child's needs and his tendency to sleep much of the time) in protecting the child from a flood of unorganized (in his state) and likely stressful stimulation from the external world. Mahler stated that the child is in a normal, absolute autistic shell which cracks around the 3rd or 4th week of life.

Spitz observed that between the 8th and 14th day of life, a child, if held horizontally, when hungry, will turn his head toward the chest of either a man or a woman. Also, he corroborated Piaget's finding that before the end of the month, a hungry child recognizes food (unless he is distracted).

This recognition of food- and nonfood-hungry states evidences beginning intelligent adaptation and some differentiation of the schemes of sucking. Nevertheless, we have no reason to assume that the child has any notion of himself or of external objects nor could we expect him to distinguish action, perception, or mental image (thought). In Freudian theory, it should be remembered that ability to perceive, then hallucinate the breast was a given at birth.*

The next two stages are characterized by *reciprocal assimilation* of one scheme to another, for example, sucking to grasping and grasping to sucking. Stage 2, 1 to 3 months, extends Stage 1's practice of reflexes. For example, when Laurent happened to encounter the edge of his blanket with his palm, he repeated his movements—reaching, grasping, and letting go—again and again for 15 minutes at a time, showing how the schemes of grasping and striking assimilate each other. He also sucked as soon as he was placed in the nursing position. His sucking scheme accommodates to position schemes. A few days after the beginning of the second month at feeding time a child will be quieted by an approaching adult (Spitz 1965). (This would be a bit premature if he is responding to visual or auditory cues.)

In Stage 3, 4 to 7 months, when Jacqueline, for example, inadvertently made a sound by rubbing a piece of paper on wicker, she repeated her motion again and again, listening to the sound. This is in the same form as Laurent's grasping and letting go of Stage 1, but instead of being confined to proximal sensory aliment, Jacqueline is also focused on distance sensory stimulation, that is, hearing. Likewise, when Lucienne struck her crib with her foot, if an object such as a suspended doll bounced, she repeated her movement again and again while watching the bouncing of the doll. Watching or listening stimulates striking; the striking stimulates the watching or listening. At this stage, the child has no concept of any causal connection

---

*Freudian theory proposed that the child having experienced pleasure sucking at the breast, when hungry, then invoked his past visual image of the breast, perception being a given. The child learns to differentiate this hallucination of the breast from perception of the breast on the basis of the hallucination being less gratifying. At the point that perception is differentiated from hallucination, hallucination becomes mental image or thought.

or separateness between his schemes. When Piaget stopped drumming on a tin box, Laurent went through his various procedures, shaking, striking, etc., and waited for the drumming noise to resume.

Around the 50th day, Spitz (1965) observed that the child followed the adult with his eyes, particularly watching the adult's face. It was as if the child were readying himself for the smiling response that occurs at 2 or 3 months of age. Spitz showed that the child will smile at a moving mask, provided the pattern on the mask corresponds roughly to the configuration of the nose and eyes. Spitz called the smiling response the first major indicator of development of object relations and saw it as indicating a major shift in development. Spitz implied that smiling is a built-in and specific response to the human face. Piaget reported the smiling response to familiar sounds around age 6 weeks. Accordingly, Piaget regarded smiling as a built-in response to recognition (recognitory assimilation, the same patterns of stimuli are assimilated into schemes that assimilated them before) of any (not unpleasant) configuration. That is, the smiling response is not a response to a face pattern specifically. If Piaget is correct, then the eye-nose-movement configuration (á la Spitz) is merely the minimal data required for recognition of the face by the child at 2 to 3 months of age. Blind babies smiling as early as sighted ones (Fraiberg, 1968; Freedman, 1974) supports Piaget's position. While the smile is a genetic given and likely serves survival through eliciting attachment behavior, it need not be more human-specific oriented than a signaling of pleasure and recognition.

Mahler (Mahler, Pine & Bergman, 1975) called the 2nd to 5th month the period of normal symbiosis. She postulated the height of symbiosis in the fourth or fifth month, mother and child in a common dual unity. Intrapsychically, "All is me and not me" or "pleasure and out there." Included in this intrapsychic "me" or self is all stimulation coming from mother that is somehow pleasant. So for Mahler the child during Piaget's Stage 2 has differentiated from absolute autism of the first month by developing a division of patterns of stimulation into good feeling-me and bad feeling-not-me.

In Stage 3, each scheme accommodates to the other. The child varies the vigor and frequency of his actions. For example, he varies his striking a rattle, thus varying its motion and sound. All the while, he closely attends to the object as it moves or makes noise. He tries all the procedures in his repertoire when any novel situation presents or to make a spectacle last, including those over which he has no control, for example, the drumming noise caused by Piaget. (The particular mechanisms preferred by a particular child vary; hence, the content of schemes is highly idiosyncratic.) When a child had practiced an activity several times at length, such as causing an object suspended by a string to swing, two interesting variants took place. Instead of striking the object, the child either made only an abbreviated striking movement, a motor recognition or self-imitation of striking activity, or he swayed his hand imitating the swinging motion of the object.

Countless assimilations and accommodations of one scheme to another prepare the child for Stage 4, 8 to 12 months, in which schemes are not just assimilated to each other, but one scheme becomes an index for another. The index scheme allows the child to imitate things he cannot see as well as sounds he has never made before. He may use a sound to find his mouth or the sight of his mother's hat to anticipate his mother's departure. Intent becomes clearly evident and partially differentiated from act. The child appears to study the object, moving it closer or farther away. Unable to reach a doll, a child may grasp his father's hand indicating to father that he wants him to cause the doll to swing. He may strike a pillow to get a watch when his access is partially obstructed by the pillow.

While all we can observe is the child's behavior, we may infer that, if he can order striking the pillow with grasping the watch, he then has an intrapsychic ordering of schemes, something he did not have before. Previously he had no awareness that rubbing paper on wicker caused noise. It was rather that he rubbed while he listened. One scheme excited the other in Stages 2 and 3. In Stage 4, one scheme is used as a means or intermediary to another. The child evidenced wish or intent and beginning distinction between self and object when he purposefully attempts to get an object or attempts to induce an action. In the next stage, Stage 5, that is, after 12 months, a child will learn to obtain a watch by pulling toward himself the pillow on which a watch rests. That is, he learns to use an inanimate object as an instrument after he learns to use a person object as an instrument. Some separation of self and object is necessary for wish or intent to exist. A child must have some idea that he is over here and the object is over there for him to have the notion of wanting the object. It is conceivable he could desire a different state, but again he must have some recognition of two different states or conditions of the self.

In Stage 3, when a child saw the experimenter hide an object, only if part (an index scheme) of the object was visible or the shape was evident, as when a toy is under a handkerchief or if his hand grazed the object did the child continue his search for the object. In stage 4, he continued his search even when the object was completely hidden. However if the child had recovered the object successfully several times under a pillow on one side of him and he watched the experimenter hide the object under a pillow on the other side of him, the child searched under the pillow where he found it before. During Stage 4, the object is successful-action-bound, not recent-receptor-bound as in the next stage.

Spitz (1965) regarded stranger anxiety or eighth-month anxiety—the child's crying when a stranger approaches—as the second major indicator of development of object relations. The 8th-month anxiety indicates the child distinguishes strangers from his mother, that is, he differentiates different person objects. (It is not surprising he can distinguish different person objects since, as noted, a Stage-4 child distinguishes between various thing objects to some extent in his use of index schemes, that is, he distinguishes the pillow from the watch).

Spitz repeatedly made the point that person relationships precede thing relationships. For example, the 4-month-old cries if his mother leaves while it is not until he is 6 months of age that he cries when a toy he likes is taken away from him. Spitz reported that a child does not have a favorite toy until 10 months while he clearly has a favorite person, mother, at 8 months. As Piaget pointed out, all of his own findings supported this order of development. For example, in Stage 4, the child used his parent's hand as an instrument while only in the next stage did he use things, for example, cushions and sticks, as instruments. DeCarie (1965) and Bell (1970) confirmed thing object development's lagging behind person object development. Spitz, however, appeared to conclude that good thing relationships depended on good person relationships. Piaget (1973) asserted that person relationships develop first because a person is more interesting to the child and that a child learns his mother as an object using the same mechanisms he uses to learn about things as objects.

Bowlby (1969) suggested that stranger anxiety occurs earlier than 8 months and that fear of new things is probably the cause of stranger anxiety, not separation (from mother) anxiety. While not integral to our thesis, we prefer Bowlby's position that the eighth-month anxiety is not fear of loss of mother but fear of the strange or unfamiliar and is part of a built-in, biologically adaptive mechanism, part of attachment behavior. The cries of the helpless 8-month-old signal mother to seek him when he would be at risk in the face of the unfamiliar. It is, of course, important that this mechanism, fear of strangeness, not be operative from the very beginning of life. Otherwise, the child could not assimilate the input that then becomes the nexus of the familiar. It is reasonable that there be an early period in which a child is very poorly defended against imprinting, and so on, as he constructs the familiar within the constraints of his sensorimotor apparatus, including the constraints set by the schemes he has already constructed.

For our purposes, it is irrelevant whether eighth-month anxiety signals fear of separation or fear of the novel. It is only necessary to note that eighth-month anxiety indicates the child distinguishes mother from other persons. Although the child lags in his differentiation between various thing objects, this differentiation occurs at approximately the same age (Stage 4) as his differentiation between person objects.

Mahler's (1968) findings do not conflict with Piaget's although she places greater emphasis on the interaction between mother and child; focuses more on vicissitudes of affect, for example, the child's sense of potency; and explains her observations in terms of shifts of libidinal energy. Mahler's separation-individuation phase begins around the sixth month when the child–mother symbiotic relationship starts to fade. The separation-individuation phase lasts until the third year. Mahler reports that at about 6 months, prior to stranger anxiety at 8 months, a child can be observed to check his mother's face against a stranger's face. At 9 to 12 months, there is a "massive shift" in a child's psyche with the development of locomotion and hence physical separation and return. At this stage although his conceptualization is in terms of part-objects and part-self, this is an advance over his absolute symbiosis. He now has a beginning notion of self and object as separate.

The timing of this differentiation essentially agrees with Piaget's timetable since the means scheme of striking a close object to get a distant object or pressing an adult's finger to persuade him to get a distant object both imply some separation of self from object. Mahler's use of the terms *part-self* and *part-object* stresses that, while begun, the child's differentiation between self and object is very limited at this time. These part-objects may disappear when the object fails to please the child. The symbiosis, now disrupted largely by locomotion and beginning individuation, cause the impact of mother and child on each other to become less direct and to be replaced by (1) mirroring—the child imitating the mother, and (2) shaping— the mother coaxing out certain behavior and disregarding or shunning other behavior, her raising a child who will fit her systems. Mahler hopes that mother is reliable since the child certainly remains very much in need of her while he shifts his focus from the symbiotic orbit to the autonomous ego functions; for example, locomotion and perception, as he ventures out. His self esteem, his notion that he can trust himself and where he goes must be protected. The mother's task is to spare his sense of omnipotence by seeing that he does not get into trouble. From 10 to 16 months, the child is checking his mother and strangers, presumably using locomotion as an aid to checking as he used looking for checking earlier.

Piaget's Stage 5 is an extension of Stage 4 and is much like when the child was in Stage 3, he varied the striking of a rattle as he listened. Now the child, however, has a beginning separation of self from object and can presumably assign variations to it to some extent as he studies relationships of one object or another including himself as an object. He subordinates his activities to the qualities of the object. Accommodation weighs heavily in this stage. After a chance action on an object leading to a novel result, the child experiments on the object until he can repeat the novel event. If he flips a box by inadvertently pressing on its edge, he presses here and there until he discovers where to press on the box to cause it to flip again. After that he flips the box pretty much at will. If he drops a bread crumb and watches it fall, he may drop one crumb here and another there, studying the falling of crumbs. He uses instruments to pull an object toward himself. For example, Piaget placed a watch on a cushion with a second cushion partially under the first one, but somewhat nearer the child. After seeing that moving the second cushion did not bring the watch toward him, the child immediately reached past the second cushion for the first and pulled the first cushion toward himself with the watch on it. He learned which things go through a given size hole.

When he could not open a container himself, he held it out for his parent to open. He pointed with his finger toward objects he could not reach.

If he saw one hide an object at B, his having successfully found it at A, he immediately searched at B. His notion of an object is "perception"-(i.e., recent-receptor) bound, no longer successful-action-bound (as at the end of Stage 4). The object exists where he sees it (last acted on it with his eyes) disappear, not where he last acted upon it with his hand (even if he has successfully acted on it at A). He appears to be thinking ahead, experimenting in his mind. Each step, however, must be confirmed by "perception." This confirmation is not necessary in the next stage.

In all of the above reactions he is constructing more of a separation between his self-representations and object-representations, placing more reliance on distance perceptual activity allied to the object as he studies the relationship, the interface between self and object, his action on one object compared to another.

In Stage 6, 18 months to 2 years, the culmination of the Sensorimotor Period, the child is able to do new activities without going through overt intermediate ones, that is, without behavioral groping. Presumably, he goes through intermediate (perhaps very abbreviated) steps in his conscious or unconscious thinking. When a stool he was leaning against started to slide, he immediately moved it against a couch to steady it. The intermediate experiences of Stage 5 were not in evidence. When Piaget made a warming movement, the usual hugging and unhugging one's body with one's arms, his child, never having gone through this procedure before, immediately imitated his movements without use of any intermediate steps. In addition to immediate imitation, the child also evidences deferred imitation, that is, imitation in the absence of the model. For example, Jacqueline imitated in abbreviated form (stamping her feet lightly and with little negative affect) a temper tantrum she had witnessed the day before. In Stage 6, a child searches for an object behind a second screen. When he has seen it disappear behind the first screen, e.g., a blanket, but does not see one place the object under a second screen, e.g., a cushion covered by the blanket, failing to find the object behind the first screen, he looks under the second.

Both deferred imitation and search behind a second screen indicate the child has a mental image of the object that is separate from his perception of it. His thinking and/or memory of an object or event is distinct from perception of it. The existence of an object is memory-bound, not action- or recent-receptor-bound. The object has a life of its own. The child through his constructions has achieved object permanence.

Piaget speaks of thought as beginning at this stage. Thought as separate from perception is clearly possible now. In Stage 5, a child looks for a watch behind a screen, but will not look for a watch behind a second screen. So, if he has thought, his thought of a watch is not separate from his perception of one. He does not know whether the image he has is inside or outside (is a thought or a perception) is part of the self representation or part of the object representation. He essentially is hallucinating.* In the next stage he looks for the watch behind a second screen. He now has a thought; that is, he has a mental image, separate from perception. It should be recognized that there is no percept until there is thought; prior to that, perception and thought are undifferentiated, percept not being distinguished from what is inside. (We will not recapitulate here Piaget's concept of symbol formation, based on his study of the interplay of imitation and play [1962a]).

---

*The position that thought and percept are differentiated from each other in Stage 6, and that prior to Stage 6 the child hallucinates, is our own, not Piaget's. Piaget places perception in Stage 5 and does not use hallucination in his conceptualization of cognitive development.

At the conclusion of Stage 6, the child has constructed thought, perception, symbols, and achieved some separation of self from object. After 18 months, symbols are available to the child although, as will be seen in the next chapter, it is not until after age 4 that a child clearly differentiates between symbol or sign and the object it represents.

Chapter 4

THE PREOPERATIONAL AND CONCRETE OPERATIONAL PERIODS

As mentioned in Chapter 2, Piaget's two stages of the Preoperational Period, the Symbolic (from age 2 to 4) and the Intuitive (from age 5 to 7) Stages, and their culmination, the Concrete Operational Period (from age 8 to 11) are of special interest to us, since the concept of character structure formation we propose postulates that the child adopts a style of social cognitive processing that parallels the thought-processing system used in one of these three phases of cognitive development.

During the Preoperational Period, given the achievements of the Sensorimotor Period as a base, the child constructs a system for handling attributes, (e.g., amount, color, morality, etc.,) of objects and events. Much as the child over the course of the first 18 months constructs understandings of an object that are more abiding than his action on an object (including his visual action on it), from age 2 to 7 he begins to abstract certain properties or attributes of objects and their relationships to each other that are more stable than any particular appearance of objects. For instance, an Intuitive-Stage child thinks if his juice is in a narrow glass, thereby rising higher or to the brim, he has more to drink. When concrete-operational, he has constructed a more coordinated concept of quantity; he knows he has the same amount to drink whether his juice is in a narrow glass or a wide one. Similarly, when he is concrete-operational, he knows a group of squares have abiding properties different from a group of discs. He can classify objects on the basis of shape or shape and color at the same time. A 3-year-old fails to abstract, that is, construct these relationships as abiding similarities and differences, classes and subclasses of shared or not-shared properties. Rather, a 3-year-old organizes these objects into super-objects, a house or a design. Such a pictorial organization is not an abiding quality or attribute of these objects as are their similarities or their differences. By age 7 or 8, in the Concrete Operational Period, a child understands the basic dimensions of attributes. He understands classification, including exclusion and inclusion, and seriation. He can classify objects on the basis of color, shape, size, or other attributes. He can order a series on the basis of size, shade of color, etc.

The Symbolic Stage of the Preoperational Period

The Symbolic Stage basically extends Stage 6 of the Sensorimotor Period. While, during Stage 6, the 18-month-old managed to construct representations, that is, symbols, and had some separation between self and object, it is clear that until 4 or later he confuses symbols with objects and self as well as one object with another, including the self. For instance, when the 2- to 4-year-old crouches holding a pen, he thinks he is writing a letter (Maier, 1965). In this instance, the symbol is equivalent to the entire event. Likewise, the 2- to 4-year-old does not distinguish a word, a sign, from the thing it represents. Jacqueline (age 2) wanted a dress from another room (Piaget, 1962a, p. 231). Both parents refused to get it for her, explaining to her that it was too cold to go into that room. She said she wanted to fetch it for herself. After a long silence she said, "Not too cold." [When asked,] "Where?" [she replied,] "in the room." [When asked why it wasn't too cold,] she said, "Get dress." At this age, there is no clear-cut distinction between word or fantasy and reality. Sequence of action and wish fulfillment dominate. If it is too cold to go into the room, just say, "It is not cold." Idea, word, and wish run rough shod over reality when Piaget's daughter says, "Not cold."

When Jacqueline was almost 3 she wanted an orange and was told that oranges were green, that is, unripe (Piaget, 1962a, p. 231). When she encountered some camomile tea that was yellow, she said, "Camomile isn't green. It's yellow already. Give me some oranges!" Aside from wish-fulfillment, she reasoned if yellow is ripeness and camomile is yellow, then other things such as oranges must be ripe. There is a failure in differentiation between symbols and objects and between qualities belonging to one object and not to the other. A symbol or condition applicable to one situation may be applied to a totally different situation. If one thing is yellow, everything is yellow. If yellow exists, it exists everywhere.

The 2-to 4-year-old's reasoning is transductive, that is, he reasons from particular to particular. If one thing is similar to another, has a common property, it is the same as the other. On the other hand, if the youngster focuses on a part or aspect of the object that has changed, then the object or event is a different one to him. As mentioned earlier, Jacqueline, when she was 2½ failed to recognize her sister who was wearing a new bathing suit and cap, until she changed to her usual clothes. A change in clothing, an alteration in part of an object, makes the object a different one. In contrast, at the same age Jacqueline announced that a slug was the same one as a slug seen 10 yards behind her on her walk. Two objects that are similar are the same; part and whole are not distinguished in the thinking of the 2-to 4-year-old. The dress is not distinguished from the person. Similarity in appearance is enough for two different objects to be the same. The slugs 10 yards apart are the same. Having played in Uncle Alfred's garden, Jacqueline (at 2) referred to other gardens as Uncle Alfred's. Or, she reasoned that because she had not taken a nap, it was not afternoon. When she was almost 3 she asserted that a picture was of a dog although actually it was of a cat. When asked why, she said it was grey.

Jacqueline was accustomed to encountering a hunchback on her walk (Piaget, 1962a, p. 231). She had been told that his hump was due to his being ill. She responded, "Poor boy, he's ill, he has a hump." On one occasion when she was two, she wished to see him but was informed he had influenza. She responded, "Ill in bed." The next day, when on a walk she inquired if he was still ill in bed. When informed that he was not, she said, "He hasn't a big hump now!" This type of reasoning is in the service of the wish, but also it is clear that one type of illness, the hunchback, is not separate from the symbol for influenza. She has no class of illness with subclasses, reasoning is from the particular to the particular.

The 2-to 4-year-old evidences a richness and fluidity of imagery that is at times lovely and certainly free. When Jacqueline was 3 ½, she likened the ripples made and moved in the sand by the movement of the lake water to a girl's hair being combed. Also, Jacqueline in her play endowed a small box with the attributes of a cat as she played at having the cat run along the wall. While there is a beauty and freedom to the use of these symbols, one must also note the child is content with minimal resemblance between a symbol (object played with) and the events or objects it represents. The fluidity is not some special gift any more than a child calling his summer home Pickinberry Place is poetry. It is a reflection of the style of conceptualization used by the 2-to 4-year-old. He goes from particle to particle whether it is in his play, his reasoning, his use of symbols, his identity of objects or part objects.

Just as the child in the Symbolic Stage may have separate representations of an external object, he also has not unified his concepts of himself. When Jacqueline (age 2) came home she said she was going to see "Daddy, Odette, and Jacqueline in the glass" as if she were a different person in the mirror than she was otherwise even though she already recognized herself very well in the mirror (Piaget, 1962a, p. 224). Likewise, she attributed a reality to photographs of herself. She became frightened when she saw a picture of herself being carried on a mountain walk, although she noted that Jacqueline in the photograph was not frightened. She also theorized that her little sister could close her eyes when she is big Jacqueline on a mountain walk as in the picture. When she was about 2½ looking at a picture of herself when she was younger, she said it was she when she was her little sister. When she was 3 she said a daddy is a man who "has lots of Luciennes and lots of Jacquelines." Luciennes are "little girls and Jacquelines are big girls" (Piaget, 1962a, p. 225).

A 2-to 4-year-old has no clear single, identity of self that includes the self in time past and is separate from other similar objects or from symbols of self.

Mahler (1975), although aware of Piaget's work, apparently failed to take into account some of Piaget's findings. Basically, there is no disagreement between her work and Piaget's, but she asserted there is. She acknowledged that by 18 months or so, the child has object permanence as demonstrated by Piaget. She stressed, however, that until 3 (in one instance Mahler [1968] stated that object constancy may begin as late as 3½) or older the child does not have libidinal object constancy, that is, he does not have a single image of his mother regardless of his affect state. After 3 he is able to have an image, an object representation of his mother that has, or includes, good and bad qualities rather than a good mother image separate from a bad mother image. Likewise, only after 3 does his self-representation include both good and bad qualties. He does not have separate good and bad selves. Finally, his self-image is separate from his mother image; whereas, prior to 3 this is not so.

Piaget's picture of object relations at this age may be seen by the following quotation from *Play, Dreams and Imitation in Childhood* (p. 226):

> On the one hand, the particular objects involved in the child's thought have less individuality, i.e., they are less identical with themselves, than in the later stages. For instance (Obs. 106)*sic,* a particular garden was identified with another: J. refused to accept the identity of her sister L. when she was wearing a bathing-suit and then said, "it's Lucienne again," when she was wearing her dress again; J. separated herself, according to the images she saw of herself, into "J. in the glass," "J. doing that," and "J. in the photo." In a word, the same individual can be composed of distinct persons, according to the clothes worn or the images presented in a mirror or photograph. In the same way, L. thought that her elder sister J. had been a Lucienne, and that little girls were Luciennes before becoming Jacquelines. The essential character of these beings is thus not their identity through time, but the distinct successive stages through which they pass in changing character.
>
> But on other hand, classes are less comprehensive than they will be later, a class being a kind of typical individual reproduced in several copies. Slugs (obs. 107)*sic,* are all "the slug" reappearing in various forms. . . .
>
> These two characteristics, absences of individual identity and of general class, are in reality one and the same. It is becasue a stable general class does not exist, that the individual elements, not being assembled within the framework of a real whole, partake directly of one another without permanent individuality, and it is the lack of individuality in the parts which prevents the whole from becoming an inclusive class. Thus as it is still halfway between the individual and the general, the child's preconcept constitutes a kind of "participation" . . .

As can be seen, the 2-to 4-year-old has object and self-representations that are multiple and sometimes fused depending on part to part relationships.

So, for the 2-to 4-year-old to have separate images of mother depending on his affect state, that is, to have a bad mother image separate from a good mother image (or to incorporate good things into a self image and project bad qualities onto outside objects) is in keeping with the lack of separation between objects including the self, plus the child's facility for allowing fantasy to be as real as reality. That is basically what Mahler asserts, that good and bad mother are not fused, that the child does not have libidinal object constancy. So, Mahler's object constancy is a special case of Piaget's more general understanding of 2- to 4-year-old cognition.

Interestingly enough, if there is a timing conflict between the two authors concerning the development of object constancy, it is that Piaget's data suggest that the child does not attain object constancy until into the 4th year, while Mahler dates object constancy to 3 (or as late as 3½). One must realize, however, that Piaget is talking about object relations as including thing-objects, while Mahler is concerned only with development of stable person-objects, notably the mother and the self. As already pointed out, thing-cognition lags behind a person-cognition at every stage of normal development. (It should be kept in mind that Piaget's measures are all made on person-as-thing-cognition, as in the example of the child's use of the parent's finger as an instrument before he attempts to use a stick, and Mahler's measure is a global one, just good and bad.) A lag of six months to a year is considerable, but not out of reason. While a lag is never as much as a year in the earlier stages, a lag of as much as a year at age 4 is proportionately not greater than a stage (4 months) at 12 months. For example, at Stage 4 of the Sensorimotor Period, the child can use the parent's finger as a tool and only at Stage 5 of the Sensorimotor Period can he use a stick or a pillow as a tool.

So, both Mahler and Piaget, using different theoretical systems—one concerned with the child's emotional life, the other with his cognition—concluded that while the 2-year-old's acquisition of object-representation and self-representation has begun, it is not fully differentiated until after 3 or 4 years of age.

Piaget's observations and conceptualizations encompass more than the relationship between mother and child. They point up consistent undifferentiation during the Symbolic Stage, manifest in the boundaries between symbols, objects, signs, and self whether the objects are human or not, while Mahler confines her study to cognition of social relationships.

THE INTUITIVE STAGE OF THE PREOPERATIONAL PERIOD: PASSAGE INTO THE CONCRETE OPERATIONAL PERIOD

Having developed stable, separate constructs of self, external objects, and parts of objects including symbols or attributes, the goal of the Intuitive Stage (from age 5 to 7) is construction of attributes or values which in the Concrete Operational Period will embrace an understanding of classification and seriation. Values or attributes of objects or events are concepts such as fast and slow, long and short, big and small, good and bad, heavy and light, etc. In the Intuitive Stage, the child has only a global or impressionistic grasp of such attributes. His conceptualization of a value or attribute is bound to his immediate view. For instance, if a 5- to 7-year-old sees a car finish first in a race, to him, that car is the fastest car regardless of the course it took, the job that is finished first is the easiest job (Maier, 1965). A straight line that extends beyond a wavy line is to him the longer one (Inhelder, Sinclair, & Bovet, 1974). The same amount of juice in a glass in which it comes to the brim is more. One may count out some beads with the child, such that the child agrees that the resulting two rows of beads paired side by side are equal. If one then bunches each row, the child will insist that the pile which looks bigger to him has more beads in it.

He takes the cover for the book; what looks bigger is bigger; full to the brim is more. Rather than reasoning from the particular to the particular, as the 2- to 4-year-old does, he now reasons from the conclusion, the end stage or his view, to the premise in a single jump. The outcome justifies the logic applied. The outcome had to happen. Likewise, in the sphere of good and bad, that is, morality, the child, who makes a big ink blot when trying to help Daddy, is viewed as naughtier than the child who makes a small blot when playing with Daddy's ink well (Piaget, 1965a). The apparent result, the thing that is in view, is the thing that counts to the 5- to 7-year-old.

It is important to know the techniques used in posing the problems to the child. The experimenter uses words and contexts that are meaningful to the child. The experimenter talks about sausages, pancakes, sweets, and juice. The child is asked when he gets this or that bunch of sweets whether he is happy or sad. "Is it fun?" "Is this just as much to eat?" An excellent example of the style of interviewing and the type of responses given by the child is presented in Inhelder, Sinclair, and Bovet's (1974) book.

A 5-year-old prefers a hamburger patty that appears larger to him, the one with the larger diameter, because he focuses on its diameter. He does not take into account its thinness or that it came from the same sized meat ball as a plump patty. Even though he will acknowledge and remember that both the plump and flattened patties took their origin from equal sized meat balls a moment ago, he believes now that the flatter patty is more. He will be happier with that one; to him it is better and more. Initially, he is quite certain of his position. Six months or a year later he may be puzzled by the fact that each patty came from an equal sized meat ball, or by the fact that while one patty is wider, it is also thinner. At the conclusion of this stage, after age 7 or so, he will be able to coordinate these dimensions, these points of view, that is, thickness, diameter, and present and past appearance. He will contend that nothing was added or taken away; hence, it could not have changed in amount. He will have constructed a concept of quantity that is more abiding than his immediate point of view, his current perception. He will have developed concepts of qualities, values or attributes of objects and events, that are stable in the face of different vantage points, that coordinate different points of view.

When a child passes from the Intuitive Stage of the Preoperational Period, a revolution takes place in his egocentrism. Egocentrism, basic to Piaget's concepts, is thought to diminish stepwise. When born, a child is egocentric just as he is undifferentiated. All he can center on is what he knows and what he does. When he passes from the Preoperational Period, however, his point of view is no longer the only point of view. During the Symbolic Stage, his point of view was undifferentiated from himself and from external objects. For example, the room was not cold when Piaget's daughter did not want it to be. Sharp was part of a particular scissors and obedience part of Daddy. During the Intuitive Stage the child's point of view is separate from the object or the event or wish as such. But once he centers on an aspect, for example, once he is fixed on the diameter of the hamburger patty, he cannot shift or if he can be induced to shift, he cannot coordinate the two different aspects. If he views model of three mountains and is asked to indicate how the mountains would look were he or another in a different position, he thinks the view would be unchanged (Piaget, 1937). It should be kept in mind that Piaget does not use the term "egocentric" to mean selfish but but merely to indicate that the child is centered on himself and what he is able to understand from his point of view. The child starts out unable to perceive an outside (or inside) world, let alone an outside opinion or point of view. Nevertheless, starting out entirely egocentric, he is also egocentric in his perception of needs and desires. What is good for him is good for the world. Hence, egocentrism includes selfishness, although it is much more than selfishness. Since he cannot coordinate his current view with his previous point of view, he really has no concept of his own past or long-term point of view, just what he is seeing now.

Modification of egocentrism with development parallels Freud's vicissitudes of narcissism: primary narcissism to secondary narcissism, and finally altruism. However, Piaget's concept is broader and does not postulate any particular linkage to shifts in libidinal energy as does Freud's. Rather, in Piaget's psychology, there is a gradual, albeit stepwise, reduction in egocentrism as the child passes from complete undifferentiation between self and objects, comparable to primary narcissism, through stagewise differentiation between self and objects. This includes the symbolic stage since the child still does not clearly differentiate between one object and another (including the self) or an object and its attributes, that is, part objects. From 5 to 7 in the stage we are now describing, he is unable to separate his current point of view, his interest of the moment, from object or essence of self. He judges an attribute such as amount by a dimension that impresses him most, for example, height, the impact an appearance has on him. This is a general formulation of secondary narcissism. In the Concrete Operational Period, from age 8 to 11, the child's various perceptions of objects, such as height and width or current and past appearance become merely coordinates of his construct of an attribute. He can coordinate his view of a hamburger from above with his view of it from the side and/or his view of it in the past as a meat ball, concluding that its quantity, the attribute in question, remains unchanged. Quantity is not tied to one appearance. So the child is no longer locked into his view of the moment, that is, "centered" in Piaget's terms. He may take into account another('s) point of view. He has the beginning orientation necessary for altruism.

Returning to the Intuitive Stage, from age 5 to 7, the child differentiates between objects, even though, or more likely because his schemes of the objects have become much richer, have assimilated a great deal more to themselves as well as accommodated to many different events. In his play, the 5-year-old comprehends more what a sheriff really is and what he actually does. In the Symbolic Stage when he wore a badge, he thought he was the sheriff (Maier, 1965). Now, he plays at being sheriff to capture the sheriff's values or the status which the sheriff represents. The child distinguishes the sheriff from the badge, that is, the symbol is understood as different from the thing or the action. Also, the child differentiates more between himself and any role he is playing. At the same time, the child now requires that the objects with which he plays be more like the real objects they represent. His play cat must look more like a cat. Generally, words are separate from things; just as symbols are separate from things.

The intuitive-stage child's inability to coordinate different points of view, to decenter, also makes it impossible for him to comprehend fully class and subclass conceptions. He cannot swing back and forth in his thinking between the whole and the part, keeping in mind the relationship, the quality or value. He cannot keep in mind that blue squares and red sqares are part of the class of squares. If given some blue discs, blue squares, and red squares and asked to put the ones together that belong together, the 5-year-old may cull red and blue squares for a time, but then if the last item placed in the set is a blue square, he may now include blue discs in his collection. If a child younger than 7 or 8 years is given a bunch of artificial flowers made up of ten daisies and two or three roses, while he has no trouble stating that there are more daisies than roses, he will contend that there are more daisies than flowers. He does not really understand the concept of "more" as an operational construct. "More" to him is the largest amount he is struck by. He sees a predominance of daisies, so there are more daisies. He does not comprehend class and subclass, that the class always includes its subclasses and is greater than any one subclass. If given eight primroses and eight other flowers, he will know that primroses are flowers but assert that there are more primroses than flowers or the same amount of flowers as primroses, (indicating) that there are eight of one and eight of the other (Inhelder and Piaget, 1969).

The concept of a series or order involves keeping in mind the overall attribute or value while one focuses on the relationship between the items of the series. For instance, in arranging sticks of different lengths, according to increasing size, one must keep in mind the overall task, the idea of a range of sizes extending from smallest to largest, at the same time as one examines each stick with reference to another. This involves coordinating different points of view. A child much younger than 5 is able to order three items in terms of size and knows that three objects are more than two. However, he does not have a concept of a total series in mind as well as where each item fits with its neighbors. If a 5-year-old is asked to arrange a series of ten sticks according to their size, he may say he can, and then arrange them—A, B, C, D, H, F, E, G, J, I (where A is smallest and I is largest and where the increments between sizes is small but visible) (Piaget, 1965b). He gets an approximate order that lasts for awhile, much like his sorting of squares and discs. Or, if shown how to make a staircase of sticks, he may arrange the sticks so that the top of each stick is higher than the next, but the sticks are ordered randomly according to length.

It is much like in the Symbolic Stage when he makes a figure or design, if requested to sort circles and squares. He appears to assimilate the whole scene to his system or schemes. He sees a major aspect of the forest first, a part of the overall configuration, the appearance of the staircase, but does not fully understand the idea of a size series. Further, if with difficulty or with a bit of assistance, a 5-year-old has been able to order a set of sticks, he is unable successfully to place intermediate sized sticks properly within the series.* He cannot swing back and forth between the concept of the whole, that is order, and relationship between the parts.

It is not until after 6 or 7 years of age that he has a fully organized intrapsychic concept of series. (It may be noted that

*For Piaget, a true grasp of seriation or classification must include the essential nuances. This is particularly important to us, since we contend that what appears to be a "higher" level of achievement is not so in certain circumstances and that small evidence of "lower" level function may invalidate predominant or average function.

he usually grasps order before he understands classification.) Then he starts with a plan, for example, begins with the smallest and unaided goes about ordering the sticks, coordinating inter-relations of the individual sticks as he goes along. At this point he has a construct of order including the relationship between parts within the order. He no longer is confined to one view or one relationship at a time.

Various techniques have been used by the Piagetians to facilitate passage of a child's thought processes through the Intuitive Stage into the Concrete Operational Period (Inhelder, Sinclair, & Bovet, 1974). Two factors remain consistent in these studies. One is that the order of substages remains unchanged. Two, the major factor in ability to progress is a child's level of development, hence his readiness to take a next step and not any particular technique employed to facilitate learning.

Interestingly, 7- to 8-year-old, unschooled Algerian children consistently were able to judge liquid poured into differently shaped glasses as continuing to be equal in amount. Usually one expects children from underdeveloped countries to lag in their cognitive understandings. These children appeared to be as advanced in cognitive development as Genevans. In contrast to Genevans, however, the Algerian children were unable to explain their judgment. Also, when asked to predict how high a given amount of liquid will rise in variously shaped glasses, the Algerian children progressed more slowly than Genevans who predicted successfully at about the same age as they recognized that pouring from one container to another does not alter the quantity. Further, older Algerian children appeared to have regressed since they judged quantity by this dimension or that, much as a younger Genevan child does. Finally, not until age 10 or 11 were the Algerian children again able to judge the given amount of liquid poured into differently shaped glasses as equal. They were also able then to explain their judgment.

The point is twofold. One is that in different cultures one may find discordance in level of performance on different tasks.

Two, although one may find an example of premature performance, this performance does not likely rest on a genuine underlying mental structure (i.e., operational thinking) attested to by the facts that (1) the children's performance levels varied on different, but comparable tasks; (2) the children were unable to explain their performance; and (3) they later regressed and then passed through a phase they apparently skipped before regaining their performance level. The argument is that if the underlying basic structure were fully developed, the child should be able to justify his performance and his performance should occur across various situations and be more lasting.

These studies (Inhelder, Sinclair, & Bovet, 1974) support the idea that true understanding of values or attributes such as quantity or length rests upon a mental organization. The mental organization or structure is not the result of a linear progression but is based on a stepwise unfolding preparation for organized input which, to be assimilated, requires new structure formation that establishes a new equilibrium. These studies also confirm that the organization is relatively stable.

Unless otherwise indicated, the following review of Piaget's study of moral development is drawn from his book, *The Moral Judgment of the Child.* Piaget proposed that development of moral codes is a product of the Preoperational Period, its development parallelling the style of all other thought processes for this period. While he found stages in development of rules which corresponded to the stages of intellectual development, he was particularly careful to point out that the stages in development of morality could be expected to be accelerated or delayed as a function of the child's cultural background. He stressed that the stages are not as discrete as in other developmental phenomena. We quote the following excerpts from pages 84 and 85.

> For instance, after having tried to describe the child's mentality as distinct from the adult's we have found ourselved obliged to include it in our descriptions of the adult mind in so far as the

adult still remains a child. This happens particularly in the case of moral psychology, since certain features of child morality always appear to be closely connected with a situation that from the first predominates in childhood. . . . There exist in the child certain attitudes and beliefs which intellectual development will more and more tend to eliminate: there are others which will acquire more and more importance. The latter are not simply derived from the former but are partly antagonistic to them. The two sets of phenomena are to be met both in the child and in the adult, but one set predominates in the one, the other in the other. It is, we may say, simply a question of the proportions in which they are mixed; so long as we remember that every difference of proportion is also a difference of general quality, for the spirit is one and undivided.

Prior to age 4, during the Symbolic Stage, the child's moral concepts are part of an object. As "sharp" is part of a particular scissors or the clothes worn by a child are a part of the particular child, so obedience is part of the parent. Not until into the Intuitive Stage does a child split off concepts of right and wrong from the object or action. Yet, "right" and "wrong" are not operational, but tied to their appearance in a given situation. Just as an intuitive-stage child cannot classify blond girls and brunette girls or red squares and blue squares into conglomerate entities, so he cannot differentiate a lie from an error; that is, differentiate a willful misdeed from a misdeed with no malice intended. To him, a lie is what does not agree with the truth, independent of the subject's intention. A 6-year-old says a lie is a bad word. When told two stories; one in which a youngster deliberately deceived his mother regarding his grades, the other in which a child said he was frightened by a dog as big as a cow; he asserted the latter is the bigger lie, explaining that it is a less likely possibility. In failing to discriminate between a lie and an error, a child does not take into account the person's intent, that is, the other person's point of view.

At the same time, as mentioned earlier, to an intuitive-stage child, the amount of damage caused rather than intent, determines the seriousness of a crime. When Piaget told children two stories, one in which a youngster, in attempting to aid his father, spilled ink and made a big blot; the other in which the child played with father's ink bottle and made a small blot, 7-year-olds asserted the one who made the big blot was naughtier. The 10-year-olds took into account the motives of the transgressor when judging guilt.

A 7-year-old's judgment of evil is a correlate of the amount of damage done. It is based on the the end stage or conclusion much like his assertion that the car that finishes the race first is the fastest car.

The same kind of reasoning, that is, reasoning from the end stage, is manifest in the child's belief in "immanent justice," a belief that if a bad thing happens to you, you must be bad and if a good thing happens to you, you are good. For example, when told about a boy who, after stealing some apples, stepped on a rotten bridge plank and fell into the water, 6-year-olds responded that the bridge broke because the boy in the story ate the apples. A typical response was that the boy in the story would not have fallen into the water if he had not done wrong. Another response was that he fell into the water to punish him. Eight or nine-year-olds typically explain that the bridge plank was worn out, that the child in the story would have fallen in if he had not stolen the apples, and/or there is no relationship between the board and the transgression. Their concept of justice is separate from the mischievous act, or from the mechanics involved in the defective bridge. Punishment is not any longer meted out in some animistic, personalized, egocentric manner, reasoned from the end stage.

Although some of the children's responses could be interpreted as their belief in immanent rewards, all of Piaget's (1965a) stories involved immanent justice in the form of punishment. Kohlberg (1963a) tested children with stories in which disobedience to a rule or an adult was followed by a reward, and other stories in which obedience was followed by punishment.

Four-year-olds defined goodness or badness according to the reward or punishment rather than whether the child had misbehaved. Somewhat older children were puzzled while 7-year-olds defined right and wrong in terms of whether the child behaved or misbehaved.

It is clear that the intuitive-stage child's moral judgment parallels his judgment of the physical world. He judges the extremity of a crime based on what he sees, that is, the extent of the damage, just as he judges quantity based on the dimension on which he is focused. He is unable to take into account intent any more than he can take into account a different position for viewing a mountain scene (Piaget, 1937). Similarly, he sees punishment meted out in a highly personal, egocentric manner as a function of the transgression that is in view. In the next period, the Concrete Operational Period, he can take into account intent, separating mishap from willful transgression.

Piaget's understanding of moral development drew heavily on his studies of children playing marbles. Still in the Symbolic Stage, the 2- to 4-year-old will play with marbles in two ways, either in symbolic play or in ritualistic play with pleasure of repeating. In symbolic play, a marble may become an egg in a nest. When two children at this age play together, each will be busy assimilating the marbles to his own favorite symbolic schemes. In ritualistic play, the child may drop the marbles from a given height onto some object. Ritualistic play involves some motor rules, although these rules are much less sophisticated than those in a game of marbles. The child is unaware of any obligatory rules.

Between 3 and 5 years of age, a child picks up some of the rules of marbles as played in his neighborhood. He and a playmate of the same age will play marbles together contentedly, each not watching the other and neither unifying his rules with the other for the duration of even one game: "he longs" "to feel himself a member of the very honorable fraternity" (Piaget, 1965a, p. 41). He imitates the rule he observes but quickly assimilates it to his own schemes at the level of knowledge he has developed. He may declare he wins whenever he knocks one marble out of the square. His understanding of winning is much like his understanding of quantity at this stage, confined to an intuition of the moment, the one success.

Sometime after 3 years of age and until about 9, he believes that the rules are sacred, untouchable, and passed down by prestigious adults. Nevertheless, if the experimenter changes a rule by suggesting they use a circle, not a square, a 4- or 5-year-old does not object and plays using a circle. If asked, however, he would assert that marbles may be played only using a square. Similarly, in his own play, he changes the rules as he goes along. When a 5 ½-year old child was asked if a younger child may be permitted to shoot from in front of the shooting line, as was ordinarily allowed, he insisted that this would not be fair: "Because God would make the little boy's shot not reach the marbles and the big boy's shot would reach them" (Piaget, 1965a, p. 58).

At around 7 or 8, he becomes able to play marbles according to the rules that are used in his community. He may not know all of the rules used in his neighborhood as he will at age 11. However, now the game is a social activity between two peers. During the previous stage, the child attempted to be a part of the respected group, the marble players, and to that extent his effort to play was social. However, his primary investment was in how being a member of the chosen fraternity of marble players reflected on him, not so after six, when his interest is in cooperating in a cohesive social activity with a prescribed set of rules.

After age 10, he no longer sees the rules as having always been the same, as having been made up by adults, and as something that cannot be changed if all the participants agree. He will say that the rules have likely varied from time to time and that the rules are made up by children. After 11 a child has mastered the rules and is sometimes more interested in the rules than the game. He has legal discussions involving the rules, recognizing their arbitrary nature, and their potential for flexibility.

It is not surprising that Piaget postulated that the child constructs his concepts of morality and justice out of his contact with playmates who according to Piaget are not as considerate as a child's parents and who present discrepant systems of behavior to the child. The child is confronted with the multiple dimensions involved in the playmates' differing intentions. Able to take into account different points of view, he coordinates the differing intents in his concepts of morality much as he does various appearances of length and width in his concept of quantity. In Chapter 8 we will discuss Piaget's conceptualization of the factors involved in superego development, including some disagreement we have with his theory.

To recapitulate, at 5 to 7 years generally a child has separated objects from each other and symbols from objects. He has notions of order, more, equality, or goodness and badness. But these attributes of objects and actions are not yet understood by him as being even more abiding constructs than the appearances of action or objects. To him the attributes are not clearly separate from his particular perception of the action or object from his vantage point now. He is appearance-bound.

In the Concrete Operational Period, beginning after 7 or so, a child understands seriation, order, and degree, or amount. He truly understands more, less, and equal as abiding attributes in spite of transformations of appearances of objects. His seriation is a smooth function rather than dichotomous (or trichotomous) as in the 5- to 7-year-old. He can do addition or subtraction, that is, inclusion and exclusion. He is capable of handling multiplicative functions; that is, he can classify in accord with a product of two attributes, for example, blond boys, brunette boys, blond girls, and brunette girls.

Moral judgment in the Concrete Operational Period is consonant with these developments. A concrete operational child can adhere to a set of codes, he has a cluster of attributes split off from his own action or his perception of other's actions, and he can separate the act from the intent and degree from absolute. Now he can separate the world of concrete objects from intent and drops the concept of immanent justice.

Our description of the child's thought-processing phases enables us in the following chapters to show the parallel between the cognition of each of the three character types and the cognition of the Symbolic Stage, the Intuitive Stage, or the Concrete Operational Period.

Chapter 5

INTUITIVE CHARACTER

By discussing the intuitive character first, in a way we are presenting the character structures out of order since the intuitive character's social cognition parallels the 5-to 7-old's, while the operational's social cognition corresponds to a later phase of cognition, and the symbolic's social cognition corresponds in a significant way to an earlier phase. We chose this order of presentation because the operational is easier to understand once one knows the distinguishing features of the intuitive and because knowing the operational's and intuitive's characteristics facilitates seeing similarities and differences between them and the characteristics of the symbolic.

No psychoanalytic or psychiatric term in general use precisely corresponds to our delineation of the intuitive character syndrome. The old usage of character disorder connoted something close. If one includes, however, obsessive-compulsive personality as a type of character disorder, as is commonly done, then character disorder would be a completely unsuitable designation for intuitive character since an obsessive-compulsive personality is probably never an intuitive character. Gunderson and Singer's (1975) distillation of the variables found in the literature on the borderline resulted in a group of characteristics that is broad enough to include most of our intuitive characters as well as most of our symbolic characters. Hence, we avoided the term *borderline* for the intuitive or symbolic. While the intuitive character bears a close resemblance to narcisisstic or impulsive personalities, not all narcissistic or impulsive personalities have intuitive character structure. Further, a personality type other than narcissistic or impulsive may have an intuitive character structure. Because each of the established clinical designations was either too broad or too narrow, and because the social cognition of our intuitive character corresponds to the cognition of the intuitive-stage child, we chose Piaget's term *intuitive.*

We repeat, *the essence of a person's character structure is his basic style of social cognition plus a not entirely separable factor, his basic investment.* The style of cognition that typifies a particular character structure is confined to data handling in the social, motivational, and affective spheres. It does not extend to thinking and perception related to nonperson things, except as they have social value.

The intuitive character, whose overriding investment is in *narcissistic supplies: in getting, having, and being,* makes use of end-stage reasoning as he addresses his social world. His understandings are impressionistic and global not particulate or graded.

He is undifferentiated in the sphere of values or attributes, not in the sphere of identity of self or object. He or the external object representation is black or white—all good or all bad. He lacks seriation and does not think in degrees. His classifying lacks precision. His cognition in the social domain is like that of the intuitive-stage child, ungraded and impressionistic, based on what strikes him at the moment.

A major part of our discussion of social cognition will focus on superego function because, defined as the cluster of codes that range in valence from convention to extreme moral good or bad, the superego is coincident with much of social cognitive function. This view of the superego is supported by the fact that one culture's sacrilege is another's convention and by Damon's (1977) observation that convention and morality are undifferentiated in the young child.

The intuitive character's superego is heteronomous, not autonomous. The outside tells the intuitive if he has done wrong. Long-term good does not count, only what looks good now. His valuations do not exist separate from the present. They are in flux as a function of the setting. He has no clear demarcation between his valuation of the self and his valuation of the object.

The intuitive character, like the intuitive-stage child, subscribes to the concept of immanent justice, "You get what you deserve and you deserve what you get. If a good thing happens to you, you must be good. If a bad thing happens to you, you must be bad. If you have been good, good things will happen to you; if bad, bad things will happen to you." An intuitive character accused of stealing may feel guilty, even though he has not stolen anything. An intuitive character who has prospered feels he is a good person. If not in good circumstances he believes he is a bad person. If something does not show, it does not count. If he commits a misdeed and is not caught, he is not guilty. If he talks about a defect he has, it is somehow "more real." The social value or attribute is not abstract, that is, abiding and separate from the concrete instance. Judgmental function is outside the self, automatic, and immanent. This is no different than the intuitive-stage youngster who feels, for example, that if a small child is permitted to shoot marbles from in front of the line, his shooter will not be allowed to hit the target marble or if a child falls into the water it is because he stole apples earlier (Piaget, 1965a).

The permeability of an intuitive's intrapsychic boundaries applies to his affects as well and not to just morality and convention. His affects may be unbounded both in terms of shifting from one object to another, including the self, and in terms of intensity, lacking in gradation or seriation. His affects tend to be dichotomous, on or off. If an intuitive character becomes aware of a defect in himself, ordinarily he defends against this perception. He may rationalize or may project blame for his condition onto someone else. However, when, as sometimes occurs, an intuitive fails to defend himself against perceiving himself as flawed, he responds in a global fashion that he is extremely flawed. His unmodulated superego function parallels the harsh moral judgments made by an intuitive-stage child and evidences overinclusion and lack of gradation. The boundary between his part-self deficiency valuation and whole-self-valuation is breached. If depressed, an intuitive's depression is profound. He does not feel bad about the incident; instead, he feels worthless. An intuitive character's experiencing a defect as total also applies to his judgment of others. Once aware of a weakness in the other person, an intuitive character may be impelled to discard that person. Correspondingly, if paid a compliment, an intuitive may be awash with good feeling, even though he may distrust the compliment. He moves from the specific to the general with an all-encompassing affectual response, a blurring of judgmental boundaries. His valuation is total, both lacks gradation and is all-inclusive like a 5- to 7-year-old who lacks seriation and does not fully understand classification.

Not only does self-valuation lack compartmentalization, but self- and object-valuation are not clearly held separate. An intuitive may see a weakness or strength of another person not as confined to that person, but reflecting upon him. When in association with a person he regards as inferior, he may feel shabby. Similarly, if he is in association with someone he regards as refined or elegant, he may feel good about himself. The physical surroundings, for example, a nice home, may have the same effect. The mark or quality of the setting rubs off on him; there is a failure in separation of the "values" or "attributes" of the object representation from those of the self-representation, a diffusion of boundaries within the ego, the value of one diffusing into the value of the other. Sometimes, rather than feeling good in a pleasant setting or when in association with someone who is good, he feels the opposite. Elegance causes him to feel shabby, refinement leaves him feeling coarse. Esteem or lack of esteem sweeps over self-representation and object-representation. (In the same manner anger may sweep across him and his objects.)

The intuitive character treats intangibles as if they were tangible and in short supply. For instance, he responds as if there were not enough approbation to go around. If someone else receives approval, he feels deprived. If he is complimented, he may feel that he has taken it away from someone else. A source of gratification is seen as finite, as if approval were a piece of pie and there was only so much of it. This is a failure in abstraction—in the sense of the attribute being treated as if it were an object—as well as in seriation and class inclusion. There is no true concept of approbation as an operational value that exists in all degrees and is essentially inexhaustible. There is a failure to use the overall concept of series; just the relationship between two or three neighbors in a series is used. There is no concept of approbation (of people) as a superordinate class that includes approbation of both others and the self. To the intuitive, approbation of one wipes out the other. Like the intuitive-stage child only the view of the moment truly matters.

Almost invariably, we elicit a history of the intuitive character's having experienced significant neglect as a young child. The neglect may result from a parental deficiency or from the child's needs outstripping the ability of an average set of parents to meet them. It may result from the child's being physically ill and frequently hospitalized or from the actual or psychological absence of the parent for any reason, e.g., size of family, demands placed due to illness of other family members, parental depression, etc. Nevertheless, whether the information is elicited from the patient or from an outsider, though it varies in degree, a history of absent, changing, or narcissistic mothering or erratic family life becomes evident in almost all cases.

We think that lack of protective, reliable caretaking experience during the first 5 to 7 years of life leads to the intuitive character's stabilized adaptation to life as he has known it. He has no delusion that people care. He had better get what he can from them, and he had better get it now. There is no point in his delaying gratification; waiting has not paid off consistently enough. He has little faith in the future or the promised return. He had better believe in what he can see and touch right now. So it is not surprising that he is end-stage oriented and interested in narcissistic supplies. Neither is it a surprise that he would distrust people and tend to be untrustworthy and impulsive.

Intuitive characters' distrust is manifest throughout their relationships, including the psychotherapeutic one. Those who had had extended prior psychiatric treatment sometimes failed to mention this fact until very late in treatment with us. This was not just because of their humiliation at having had to be treated, but rather out of fear that we might prejudge them. For the same reason such patients may not mention that they are in psychiatric treatment when consulting an internist about a psychosomatic illness.

Untrustworthiness of the intuitive is integral to both lack of abiding codes and need for immediate gratification. The range of untrustworthiness manifest by various persons who are intuitive characters is broad. It may show as ease in making up "little white lies," for example, the excuses made with facility when one is late for appointments or fails to meet other obligations. In more flagrant form, it may show as opportunistic behavior of the (stereotype of) used car salesmen or of upwardly mobile members of middle management. It is found in full flower in antisocial behavior of criminals.

Consonant with being impulse-ridden, intuitive characters often lead chaotic lives with much moving around. They usually are unable to delay gratification, have little tolerance for pain, are particularly vulnerable to deprivation or loss, and will move to avoid it. They are likely to reach for any object that promises gratification whether it is a material object such as a car or house they may be unable to afford or perhaps a charming, but dishonest associate. Because of their impulse to choose appearance even though they are often manipulators themselves, they are vulnerable to manipulation by other manipulators. They have little faith in the future and are usually unable to learn from the past. Only the pleasure or pain of the now really matters.

Having felt they missed out as children, they have major dependency problems. Focused only on what is coming to them, they see all relationships as sources of supply and accordingly tend to use people. As narcissistic supplies are not readily available in an adult world, they are particularly apt to be disappointed and frequently become depressed. Also, because of their tending to take the first appealing thing that comes along or to take flight from any situation that is causing temporary discomfort, they are repeatedly disappointed, especially in the long run. They tend to have low self-esteem and are very sensitive to criticism. Depending upon external supplies to bolster their sense of worth, they are focused on what they are and what they have, not on what they do or how they function.

It must be understood that impulsivity and dependency, while usually present, may not be obvious. Impulsivity is seldom actually manifest in overt behavior. (Consider that the most hardened criminals are not often engaged in impulsive acts.) Most intuitive characters will not be dishonest whenever they are not watched and certainly many are dishonest symbolically only. The impulsivity or moving about need not be geographical. For example, one professor announced different plans for his department from one day to the next. Also, an intuitive character may be able to delay gratification in the service of upward mobility and get immediate gratification in telling (or thinking) how well he carried off his latest manipulation. Within a large organization, an intuitive character often uses the system effectively; plays politics for power, prestige, and personal gain. Bursten (1972), in his descriptions of the manipulative personality, points up the broad range of manifest behavior, and the adaptive value of such behavior. We do not agree with Bursten that the central mechanism of this group is manipulation, and we see their parenting experience a bit differently. However, we clearly are describing the same person as he. Sometimes an intuitive character manifests enlightened self-interest. The world, his peers, the finance company, and his business associates force him to learn. The other takers are his conscience, as it were. In all cases, however, his conscience is significantly external.

Whenever possible, the intuitive character deals with matters as outside himself. He prefers action over thinking, will act out and often uses manipulation. He projects, externalizes, denies, and rationalizes. Most intuitive characters do not use conversion; but when conversion is used, most often (in our practice) it is used by a person who is an intuitive character.

Considering his tendency toward impulsivity and dependency, his problems with trust and his typical defenses, it is not surprising that the pathological prototype of the intuitive character is the person with a behavior disorder or with a narcissistic personality. As we have indicated, however, the relationship is not one-to-one since some behavior disorders and narcissists have symbolic character structures and since many intuitives would not be classified as having a personality disorder. Nevertheless, presence of narcissistic or impulsive traits suggest the person is an intuitive.

The intuitive character's goals in treatment are narcissistic, oriented to the present, and global. Much like an intuitive-stage child, his own, ungraded view is all he seems to embrace. In some cases, there is no defensive disguise to his presentation for treatment. He makes his global request of the therapist: "All I want is to be happy." When he has some defensive disguise, still his efforts in therapy may ignore inner and outer rules in pursuit of narcissistic supplies or avoidance of pain to try to achieve his global goal of happiness. He is not interested particularly in improving his function in one sphere or another and has little involvement with function or long-range goals.

Insight is not his goal. Typically, he will report the week's events, since his primary motive is to get interest, affection, or concern from the therapist. He takes attempts by the therapist to give him an insight as an indication of the therapist's liking him or hating him, that is, whether the insight makes him feel good or bad. Basically, he does not take insight in as information. Typically, he is very sensitive to any affective response of the therapist. The intuitive character, however, is often able to hide this sensitivity. In the game of therapy, as in other life games, he is less involved in the game itself than he is in the effects on his self-esteem. He is much like the intuitive-stage marble player who is less interested in how to play marbles than he is in seeing himself as a member of the illustrious group of marble players (Piaget, 1965a).

AN EXAMPLE OF AN INTUITIVE CHARACTER AND THE COGNITION OF THE INTUITIVE-STAGE CHILD

Mrs. R., a typical intuitive character, had a social cognitive style which paralleled the cognition of the intuitive-stage child. She was an exceptionally attractive and intelligent woman who looked younger than her chronologic age. She had been married several times and was considering divorce at the time she developed anxiety attacks and became phobic of sharp instruments. She and her husband were very much alike, "had nothing until we had each other." They were at times capable of great compassion and understanding of each other; at other times each was completely intolerant of the other. Their relationship was explosively intense. They separated many times. In addition to emotional ties, Mr. and Mrs. R. had common economic goals that were being attained and that bound them together. Parallel to the entrapping quality of her marriage, Mrs. R. felt trapped at work. Until this time of her life, if she became dissatisfied with a job, she merely walked out. Sometimes she went out to lunch and never returned. She knew all she had to do in order to get another job was, during the interview, to raise her skirt a bit exposing her legs. However, she thought because she was aging she could not continue to get away with this. She had had two previous anxiety attacks, also centering around being trapped. Closely associated with her anxiety was anger that she felt (and was required to control) toward the person with whom she was trapped.

Her childhood was characterized by economic and emotional deprivation. Father had a small pension for a psychogenic illness. He was hypochrondriacal and rarely left the house. He thought of daily work as beneath him. Mother was seldom home and knew very little of Mrs. R.'s activities or interests as she was growing up. Even though she was a good student, both parents urged her to quit school in order to work.

After her father died, Mrs. R.'s mother lived with her and her husband. To avoid acknowledging an error, mother would lie or somehow obfuscate the situation. She advised the patient to lie to her psychotherapist about her expenditures in order to get the therapist to reduce her fee. She also advised the patient not to tell the therapist about her upsetting dreams. When requested to do a household task, if the request was not precise, Mrs. R.'s mother would fail to carry out the task. She regarded housework as demeaning. Mrs. R. and her mother each seemed bent on squeezing caretaking out of the other; both were unsuccessful.

Mrs. R.'s end-stage, narcissistic orientation was manifest in all her relationships, including her approach to therapy. She began her first psychotherapy interview by saying she wanted to determine whether the therapist was suitable. She then unloaded verbally, leaving little opportunity for the therapist to intervene. Having lost sight of her initial, stated goal, she did not query the therapist at all. She was much like the intuitive-stage child, losing sight of the rules once he is actively playing or forgetting his criteria for culling out blue squares. Similarly, she rarely came on time for her appointments; yet she was reluctant to leave. Her therapeutic focus was on the end stage. She filled her hours with talking about intervening current events, rarely connecting one hour with another or focusing on a problem in order to understand it. She would mention and to some extent work on a problem such as anxiety provided it had troubled her in the past day or so. Most often she brought up a problem as one other thing that was bad about her week. "You can't imagine what kind of week I had, Doctor." Long-term goals had little meaning for her. At times, as with other relationships, from one interview to the next, she said she was going to quit psychotherapy, sometimes because she felt better, sometimes because she felt worse.

Mrs. R. usually became involved with men (and friends) who, like herself, presented a very attractive surface; men who were handsome and "exuded confidence," usually men who were younger than she. One professional man, a blind date, she dropped immediately although she had determined that he was a good person and a good prospect. She dropped him because he was several years older than she and was only of average height (Mrs. R. herself was not tall). She felt young, attractive, and good when dating a younger man. Likewise, with girl-friends, glamour, glibness, and superficial affability had a primary draw for Mrs. R. She suffered repeated disappointments at the hands of these associates, always being surprised and often outraged by their erratic or irresponsible behavior.

Her style of interpersonal object choice, that is, choosing surface glitter instead of substance, was the same as a 5-year-old's preferring two nickels to a dime or the lemonade that rises high in a narrow drinking glass. Mrs. R. was never able to coordinate any clues that could spell unreliability on the part of this pretty person whose presence she felt reflected well on her. Both Mrs. R. and the 5- to 7-year-old choose the cover for the book. She, like the intuitive-stage child, was unable to coordinate compensating dimensions or present appearance with past history within an abiding attribute. Evidenced in this type of object choice is an undifferentiation, a defect in reality testing, but involving *only values and attributes of objects, not involving objects per se.*

Once disappointed in persons who initially seemed so wonderful, Mrs. R. thought of them as unmitigated scoundrels. She did not respond in degrees; her judgmental responses were all or nothing. This parallels the preoperational child of 5 who has no concept of seriation or range in dealing with physical attributes and whose condemnation of a transgression is extreme. Mrs. R.'s social cognition operated in black or white terms. To her, a person was either a hero or a scoundrel. While many of these glittery people were irresponsible and erratic, they were not irresponsible or erratic all of the time nor without redeeming qualities. Their behavior was not inhuman or impossible to understand or tolerate. Certainly, they sampled a wide range of irresponsibility. Nevertheless, Mrs. R.'s response toward any one of them was not tempered but essentially on or off. She could verbalize that a person was both good and bad, but these verbalizations had no real meaning for her.

Aside from understanding gradation or degree, there is a multiplicatory function in the understanding that a person is made up of good and bad qualities, and in reaching a true composite or on-balance picture of them as human beings, e.g. "He may not be young, but he is rich and reliable." It is like constructing a unit or subclass of blond girls or blue squares, a task the concrete-operational child can do, but the intuitive-stage child cannot. In her social relationships, Mrs. R. could not do this.

On two occasions during therapy, Mrs. R. attempted to have relationships with relatively reliable men. It may not be coincidental that both of these attempts were made when she was functioning fairly stably and when she felt good about herself. Both men were moderately successful in business and were divorced, but devoted to their children. Each spent time with his children, attended their school functions, etc. When Mr. A. was away at such a function or when he had to carry out other obligations and be away from Mrs. R., she experienced a "sick, scared feeling in her stomach." She asserted that they could not possibly get along. Referring to herself, she said, "It's like giving a baby a bottle and snatching it away." She could see intellectually that Mr. A.'s reliability in terms of business and toward his children portended an abiding characteristic of reliability that she might expect in her own relationship with him. Emotionally and in her behavior, however, she only responded to his carrying out his other commitments and his absenting himself from her as his giving to another, depriving her, and rendering her sick and scared. It is the same as the intuitive-stage child who cannot see that quantity is something more stable and abiding than height in a container; Mrs. R. could not see concern, reliability, or security as anything more than what she had or did not have at the moment. She said she felt judged as "bad" by Mr. A. "because he is unavailable." Very much inclined to manipulate people, she was constantly worried about being manipulated. She was less likely to be used by Mr. A. than by most of her associates. Nevertheless, she worried that he might use her. His possible using her thereby making her feel "cheap" and his unavailability rendering the judgment that she is a bad person are examples of her belief in immanent justice, that if a bad thing happens to you, you must be bad. This is much like a 5- to 7-year-old asserting that the little boy would not have fallen into the water if he had not stolen any apples. Mrs. R.'s discovery that Mr. A. had a whole, relatively full life before meeting her was upsetting, as if somehow she were being deprived, as if these memories were tangible and in short supply. Similarly, she was very hurt and angry when her daughter gave more gifts to her mother-in-law or to Mrs. R.'s ex-husband than she gave to Mrs. R. She had no abstract, abiding concept of someone's being invested in her. Investment for Mrs. R. was tangible and in the present. Parallel to the 5- to 7-year old, Mrs. R. focused on one dimension, for example, Mr. A.'s past or the gift to someone else. She could not shift to the present or—more importantly—coordinate past with present in an operational concept of being cared about.

In the above examples, her response was also global or dichotomous. It did not take into account degrees of investment. Similarly, when Mr. A. flirted with another woman, he became all "bad" to her, completely untrustworthy, just using her. At another time when she was with a different lover, she discovered that he was a bit dull when he was out of his own setting. She saw him then as a "nothing." She ordinarily greatly admired her boss and strove to measure up to his expectations. Nevertheless, she completely discredited him when he was awkward in one social circumstance and at another time in a situation when he and another office worker shared a private joke, that is, excluded her. Mrs. R. expected her doctors to be all-caring, omnipotent, and omniscient. She was "depressed" when she discovered they had flaws. With regard to herself also, her valuation was global and dichotomous. For example, when she was minimally overweight, she called herself a "pig" and talked about herself as if she were obese. A single offhand criticism by her boss so crushed her that she started to look for another job. A compliment by him elicited a similar positive, though temporary, global affective response in her. It is worth noting that as a rule, in spite of their intensity, none of these responses were evident to an outside observer. She suppressed virtually all direct external manifestations of these feelings.

In each of these instances, she had no modulated responses; each response was total. She failed to coordinate past relations with present ones. Focused on one aspect, she saw no other. She failed to construct abiding abstract qualities of persons. She only responded to a relationship as it was at the moment. She was not unlike the 5-year-old who, having poured a given quantity of liquid into a differently shaped container no longer believes it to be the same amount. The child fails to coordinate the compensating changes in dimensions or to use the knowledge that he can reverse the process; that is, that he can pour the liquid back into the original container. He has not yet managed to coordinate these dimensions and the possibility of reversibility, integral to the more abiding concept of quantity. Mrs. R. failed to construct social values that transcended the immediate situation in her focus. Furthermore, in these types of transactions, Mrs. R. failed to take into account degree or range just as the 5-year-old is unable to comprehend relationships in an ordered series.

She had an affair with Mr. L., a man who claimed he had little sexual experience. His clumsiness sexually and his general reliability in business and toward his children suggested he was truthful in his claim. He was on a very busy schedule and always worked before he played. Mrs. R. was smitten with him. He called her when he could. If he missed her on one telephone call and failed to make a follow-up call, she felt great pain. She saw him as uncaring and casual. On one occasion, she protested that he never took her out, that she wanted a whole evening together and implied that having sexual relations in her home was not the right setting for various reasons. Accordingly, he arranged for them to have dinner out and for them to go to a hotel for the night. During the evening she made several remarks to bolster her self-esteem. For example, she mentioned a younger man who found her attractive. Also, she implied that just going to bed with someone is not enough. Finally, she dawdled over her drink as she tried to savour every minute of their time together. Because of his sexual ignorance and his conflicts regarding sexual matters, he misinterpreted her remarks and dawdling. He thought she did not want to go to bed with him, but was just going along to please him. He offered to skip that part of the evening. She was humiliated and all was disaster from that point on.

In spite of knowing of his sexual inexperience and his attitude toward sexuality—essentially that women put up with sex and that men impose sex upon them—plus his conscientiousness generally, she nevertheless saw him as uncaring, casual, and conniving. She felt that he had deliberately set her up, never intending to go to the hotel, that he just used her and that all his wooing of her was for business purposes. There was considerable history to their relationship to demonstrate that this was not so. In one instance she had caught him in an effort to cover up his inattention to a detail. He at no other time misled her. Nevertheless, she rationalized that one attempt to deceive her into his being generally untrustworthy. Her recall of his having made some ambiguous reference to a woman in his past now proved that he was a Don Juan. Aside from the fact that all of these qualities which she attributed to him were projections and rationalizations, they were also examples of reasoning from the end stage. 'I have been hurt, he must have wanted to hurt me. He must have planned it all along. He is a bad person.' This reasoning parallels the intuitive-stage child's, that the fastest car is the one that arrived first or the task that is finished first is the one that is easiest. Rationalization is by definition reasoning from the end stage. It is as if she were to say, "He hurt me: He meant to. He is untrustworthy. He uses people sexually. Remember how he referred to that woman and how I caught him in that little business coverup. He is a cheat and a liar." In the face of her hurt, she was completely unable to integrate or counterbalance all the months of data she had accumulated on his reliability in all major things in his life including his behavior toward her. She was unable to use his history or their history (except to bolster what was in front of her). In essence, her stance was the same as the intuitive-stage child who pours two equivalent quantities of lemonade into differently shaped containers and asserts one is more. Even though he just said they were equal and though he may even agree, "yes, they were equal," now he asserts there is more in the narrow glass, and will not be convinced by the experimenter's counter suggestions.

When Mrs. R. was reminded by her therapist of Mr. L.'s behavior which substantiated his conscientiousness and of the fact that he did not take advantage of people, she became confused for a bit, but went back to emphasizing how tricky he was. A child, somewhat along in the Intuitive Stage, will become bewildered when you say, "But didn't you just say the amounts were the same when they were in these other glasses?" A few months earlier the child will simply say, "They changed."

Mrs. R. had little ability to see things from the other person's point of view; isomorphic to an intuitive-stage child who does not take into account the other person's intent in moral issues or the other person's perception when looking at a set of mountains from a different location. Mrs. R. could not use the information that Mr. L. was inexperienced sexually, had somewhat antiquated sexual notions, and was trying his best to please her. All she centered on was that she was not pleased. Any reasoning which she could muster she bent to support her egocentric position.

Her inability to coordinate history in her social word applied to herself as well as Mr. L. After attending a party at which she was very popular, she aptly commented, "It's too bad I can't take it [the popularity] home." She was crushed on one occasion when her employer, whose high regard for her had been demonstrated repeatedly, offhandedly said to her, "You ought to get a sugar daddy." Only the end stage, only what she held in her cup at the time, only her current perception had any real significance to her. She felt worthless if she were at home for a weekend with no activity or dates. At the moment her cup was empty. Likewise, as pointed out, her usual choices for friends and lovers were young, pretty, and glamorous. The shiny and the pretty had worth to her; appearance, not substance (future or sustained payoff) counted.

Similarly, being around defective, ugly people or in ugly, shabby settings was very uncomfortable for her. She was taken over by a feeling of repugnance. One way or another she had to rid herself of the situation. Mrs. R. was highly critical of anyone who manifested negative characteristics which she herself once had. She had multiple rationalizations for her harsh attitude toward an alcoholic friend and her husband who drank heavily. She had been an uncontrolled drinker herself when she was younger. A brash, loud, young woman in her office reminded Mrs. R. of herself at the same age. She had the impulse to shove her fist down the woman's throat. Mrs. R.'s moral judgments were total, intense condemnations. She nearly discarded a long time friend because this friend had partially abandoned her young child and was a poor money manager. Both behaviors Mrs. R. had been guilty of years before. At the moment, Mrs. R. had no recognition of the long history of their friendship with each other, of redeeming qualities of her friend, or of the fact that it is human to have some negative characteristics. She had little ability to evaluate her friend as being a composite of good and bad qualities, as some of the qualities being more serious or less serious, a matter of degree of goodness or badness. Similarly, she was ready to discard a friend who defended herself for being late by expressing sarcasm toward Mrs. R's usual lateness. It was a personal, psychological triumph for Mrs. R. when she managed not to reject this friend and was able to view her as an acceptable or understandable human being with certain foibles. In this instance, with help, she was able to respond not like a 5-year-old; that is, she responded in terms of degree, not "all or nothing, on or off."

As noted, Mrs. R. was late for almost all appointments. She had an impressive facility with externalizations and rationalizations explaining away her lateness time after time, as if she had never been late before. When special concessions were given to her at work, allowing her to come in at a regular late hour, she was resentful when her employer complained about her being late for the later beginning time. Yet she spoke of her being 5 minutes late as if it were a major crime. This behavior is isomorphic to the 5-year-old marbles player's who says the rules are God-given, cannot be broken, and then proceeds to break them at every turn.

A major contribution to her habitual lateness was her trying to fit everything she could into the time she had before any of her appointments. For the number of activities she assigned to fit into this interval, everything would have to take place without a hitch, without a delay. A bus would have to show up when she needed it. Mrs. R. would have to find everything she was looking for. Once having made her list of activities in her mind, she would not forgo any of them although she realized she could not do them in the allotted time. In her lateness, there was often a quality of trying to wring every possible thing out of the time remaining before going to the next engagement. In her morning ablutions, eating, bathing, reading the newspaper, exercising, and so on, she could brook no deprivation before going off to work. She was regularly late. On rare occasions when everything fell together in the remaining time, she congratulated herself mightily. Her schedule for a trip involving a vacation, a visit with friends, coordination of other events or interests she had arranged, perhaps could have worked if she had a private taxi and airplane at her disposal. When it appeared as if all her required external events would fall into place for her, she was extremely pleased with herself. Valuation of self was total, current, and external.

After awhile she recognized that her expectations from a relationship were for "constant stroking," and constant reassurance of love. She had no ability to store such experiences and often they were just appetizers to her. Her responses were total, that is, she felt good or bad. She had no history she could use (hence, no future).

She, like the intuitive-stage child, subscribed to the notion of immanent justice, that is, one gets what one deserves and deserves what one gets. If a good thing happens to you, you must be good; if a bad thing happens to you, you must be bad. We have already cited several examples of this, for instance, her response when all of her schedule fitted. Some other examples follow. One morning while standing on a corner waiting for a trolley, she heard that the delay had been caused by an accident down the street. She became awash with guilt. When her mother or an associate at work accused her of things she did not do, she felt guilty as if she had. Similarly, she was ashamed of her symptoms and of seeing a psychiatrist; if one has difficulties or defects, then one is a bad person. When a child fell down the stairs in her home and sustained a fracture, she felt guilty. Her symptoms, her divorce record, and her losing things made her feel that she was bad. She felt all the worse if these "defects" were known to others. If she felt an unmet need, and especially if she displayed it, she felt cheap and inferior. With one man for whom she felt strongly, when she thought he might not feel similarly toward her, she regarded herself as cheap and called herself a "whore." She was envious of the affection given to others. She was worried when she talked to her mother that she was depriving her husband. Generally, when she was in association with a good person, she felt like a good person. At times, the opposite occurred; that is, she felt inferior in the presence of someone good, depending on what she was centered on at the moment. Her mother believed in the "evil eye"—that one should not mention anything good one has or it will be taken away. Mrs. R. could not tolerate hearing about this belief since she was uncertain whether there were such a phenomenon.

She also felt that in order to function, her "tank had to be full all of the time"; that is, that good things must be happening to her for her to go on. To some extent this was true. One time, when she flew to meet a lover, she did not hesitate and experienced no particular anxiety about the flight as she had in the past. She commented that her "fears disappeared when she was loved." She felt "confident." Because she was admired and regarded highly by her boss, she worked very well and even pursued interests such as music appreciation to which he introduced her. When she had a German boyfriend, she enrolled in a German class which she dropped immediately when they broke up. For her to work on a distant goal for herself, that is, to think in terms of what she wanted to have, to be, or to do one or two years hence was alien to her. To have an interest in studying a course just to learn a subject was almost beyond consideration. The payoff generally had to be in sight and tangible. With the exception of tennis, she pursued no hobbies or interests except when in association with someone else. However, she had a direction which was in terms of narcissistic and immediate goals: fixing herself, getting her sleep, being preoccupied with her body, wanting to be loved. While she had little direction in terms of achieving or doing, her direction was clear in terms of getting and receiving.

Her defenses were strong, and although projection and introjection were often employed, they were used only in the sphere of affects, that is, placing the blame outside or rarely taking it in. Unlike a symbolic character, no true confusion between object and self or part and whole objects occurred. While her goal was to belong to Mr. A., her wish to belong was in order to get, to be loved, to be taken care of, not in order to be attached or completed. In the moral sphere, she reasoned from part to whole. For instance, when she made an error at work, she was almost certain she would be fired by her boss even though she had ample history that he would not behave this way (although she might) and that he had high regard for her. Any transductive reasoning she showed was confined to processing affects and moral values, not things.

Largely, her superego was an external one. She arrived at her tennis club on time because she would get no partner or an inferior one if she arrived late. She was motivated by shame, more than guilt. Lying was done with facility and was no problem for her as she rationalized it as "good business." Being caught, being shamed were very painful for her. If she said something out loud (to another), "it was more real" to her. The moment valued herself, her friend, or the situation in which she was involved. She did not have an abiding system of values that coordinated past and present, that predicted the future, and that could be invoked to judge herself or to judge others or situations. Her self-condemnations for having defects were tied to the moment and severe, yet she could easily violate her codes as mentioned earlier.

Other intuitive characters are more or less impulsive, more or less narcissistic, more or less trustworthy, more or less demanding or dependent. But all of these factors are significant foci for them. Each intuitive makes evident the typical defense mechanisms he or she uses, although he or she may prefer one mechanism over another. The intuitive's belief in immanent justice or fate is there if sought. His self-centered, global response to situations is there and betrayed by action, though disguised. He judges by what he sees now, that is, he is end-stage oriented. He does not coordinate different aspects of a social relationship. In other words, an intuitive's thinking and behavior in his social world—the world of affect and persons —is the same as the Intuitive-Stage child's system of thinking generally, thinking in both the world of things and persons.

Chapter 6

OPERATIONAL CHARACTER

In deciding what type of character structure a person has, manifestation of the symbolic syndrome takes precedence over the other two, while signs of the intuitive syndrome take precedence over those of the operational syndrome. Absence of the earmarks of either the intuitive or the symbolic weighs heavily when classifying someone as an operational character. Most of what we have to say about the operational's characteristics will address how he differs from the intuitive because there is little or no overlap between the operational and the intuitive.

Many psychotherapists would regard the operational character, the inverse of the intuitive, as the good analysand. Most of us have thought of the operational character as the norm of western culture. This is probably not true. In terms of incidence among our patients, this certainly is not the case.

The differences between the social cognition of the intuitive and that of the operational are in both superego function and the handling of affects. As we noted, the intuitive has a heteronomous superego, that is, the social rules he abides by and is invested in are very much influenced by the state of his self and the state of his setting. In contrast, the operational character has an autonomous superego, a system of moral do's and don'ts which is essentially separate from object representations, self-representations, affects, and impulses. His system is relatively stable regardless of his current affect state or setting. His moral codes function relatively automatically, that is, unconsciously, and deal with a range of goodness and badness that is applied to abstract ideals and prohibitions. In other words, he has operational cognition in the moral sphere. Similarly, he processes affects in degrees, not absolutes, and his affects do not sweep across the boundaries between one object and another (including the self).

While the intuitive is invested in narcissistic supplies, the operational is invested in function and control of function in his involvement with social roles and codes. He is invested in his function in such roles, for example, democrat or fascist, mother or daughter, banker or plumber, etc. That which he regards as honorable or dishonorable is relatively stable. If he regards generosity as a desirable characteristic (it could be parsimony just as well), he expects it in himself as well as in someone else. He continues to value it whether he is generous in a given instance or not. He is basically invested in the code itself, in what he regards as right or wrong, as an abstract principle that applies generally, now or later, to himself or others. Just because he is in a different environment, he does not change what he regards as valuable even though it may be in his best interests at the time to do so. If he values generosity, he is involved with it in the abstract. His involvement is not time-, concrete instance-, or person-bound. He is not centered on one dimension in the affectual sphere just as the concrete operational child is no longer centered on one dimension in the physical sphere, for example, one view of a set of mountains or the height of juice in a glass.

An operational character does not function merely on the basis of enlightened self-interest; usually he does not make a conscious decision that it is to his advantage in the long run to delay gratification at this moment for more certain or greater gratification in the future. The decision is more automatic. Even if his behavior is in his long-term interest, which it tends to be, his major conscious or unconscious involvement is in adherence to his code. On occasions, he may believe in and act upon certain principles that are not in his own best interest in the short run or even in the long run, although the latter is generally not true. Such actions may be in his best interest in terms of his own internal economy; that is, if he forsook his code, he might anticipate experiencing considerable guilt. In this restricted sense, that is, to avoid guilt, he may be seen as acting in accord with enlightened self-interest. Standard, current rewards of life or avoidance of pain, at least some of the time and to some degree, however, may be ignored or bypassed by him as he does what he believes to be honorable.

While his moral transgressions do not ordinarily escape him, the operational character's moral perception is graded, takes into account degrees or range, and is particulate, not global as the intuitive character's is. His moral perception is integrated, coordinating different factors. He sees some transgressions as worse than others.

In his embrace of his own rules and roles is involved coordinated use of graded, multiplicative hierarchies of goodnesses and badnesses as well as class and subclass in the social sphere. All such systems for handling values or attributes, in the physical let alone in social spheres, are not constructed by a child prior to the Concrete Operational Period. The adult operational character's codes parallel the rules of the concrete operational-stage marble player who asserts that to sneak a shot at someone's especially valuable marble without a proper warning would be unfair (Piaget, 1965a). This type of code will be discussed more fully in Chapter 8.

A psychotherapist who is an operational character who is committed to truthfulness, may have difficulty in automatically telling a half truth to a patient who asks to know the truth about himself but who needs to be deceived a bit. (We do not wish to imply that an operational character's codes are inflexible. This is more often true of certain symbolic characters [Chapter 7].) An operational character may be able to go against his code fairly effectively when the situation calls for it, but generally not without some awareness of conflict. His superego function embraces a hierarchy of different values. When valuing his own behavior, a psychotherapist who is an operational character could be expected to approve of himself were he to lie to a patient who needed this. While a bit conflicted about lying, he would be able to integrate and balance off, more or less automatically, the greater good for the patient against the therapist's codes which oppose lying. Nevertheless, if he did yield to his code to tell the truth, he could be expected to feel quite guilty about breaching his implicit contract with his patient. It would not escape him that he had broken his more basic code, the one that to him involves a greater moral good. Nevertheless, he probably would not judge himself as totally callous to patients' needs and basically self-serving. His self-condemnation would be graded, not global. He would see himself as faulty in a particular instance. Inherent in this adherence to an overriding code or role, i.e. treating the patient in accordance with the patient's need, is the code's dissociation from any concrete act. The code is a whole that is greater than any of its parts and part of a graded system. Use of such a code presumes the ability to conceptualize an entire series, much like a concrete-operational child who starts with the smallest stick and orders a series.* He must be able to keep in mind the entire series and at the same time the relationship of each stick with each of his neighbors. A rigorous embrace of class and subclass is required throughout.

An operational character is often so culture- and mores-bound that it may be difficult to differentiate factors that are basic to operational character structure from those that are

*Also implied in this example is use of formal operational cognition. This will be addressed in Chapter 9.

largely a function of western culture. Usually, he truly believes in the goodness of fairness and honesty. He is invested in the rituals and beliefs of his culture or subculture as things in themselves, for example, the value of education, science, democracy, fascism, etc. He is invested in playing the game by the rules, just as a concrete-operational marble player is. His beliefs and rituals need not be virtuous, except in terms of his family and subculture.

Any number of these concepts may be important to him. In contrast to the intuitive character who may talk about investment in these rituals or beliefs in order to gain some end, such talk by an operational character usually reflects an autonomous investment. Generally, he abides by, and is invested in, the stated rules of the culture. (We say the "stated rules" because the prevailing operational rules of our culture appear to be different from the stated ones.) An operational character may be so involved with principles or with cultural values that he is out of touch with his own or other people's feelings and needs. He will not ordinarily deliberately manipulate people. In pursuit of his principles, however, an operational character may be somewhat oblivious to the person before him. Hence, though concerned with principles, he may be immoral on balance or in certain instances.

Certain social roles lend themselves to obtaining narcissistic supplies, for example, positions of power, prestige, or wealth. So one may expect intuitives to be overrepresented in such positions. In contrast, shoemakers and accountants more likely will be operationals. However, operationals may certainly be interested in power, prestige, and wealth, and intuitives may repair shoes for a living. The difference lies less in the position and its attributes themselves than in their meaning to the person. The operational will be interested in the position itself or the process or the final achievement as such, while the intuitive's involvement will be primarily in the effects the position and its attributes (for example, power) have on his self-esteem;

for instance, to be part of an esteemed group. Also, the power and prestige motives of the operational are more particularized and articulated to his specific unconscious personal goals, usually oedipal goals, for example, defeating or equaling one parent, gaining the love of the other. The intuitive's goals are more global, his need for narcissistic supplies, derivative of what he did not get from his caretakers.

Basic to the operational character structure, consistent with his involvement with abiding principles and not separate from his having an autonomous superego, is his concern with function and control of function. His involvement with function and control of function parallels an intuitive character's concern with narcissistic supplies. Sometimes an operational character focuses more on product than on function or control of function, sometimes vice versa. His function may be inhibited or at times out of control, but function and control of function are abiding, authentic issues for him. He is potentially able to develop and carry out long-term goals. Coordinate to this is a balancing off or coordination of varying dimensions, an understanding of social factors that parallel recognizing that a view from this side looks different from that side or that a current view may differ from the past, yet all views are part of an abiding appraisal of the attribute in question. This understanding of attributes—such as being trustworthy, trusting, approved of, in control, etc., and whether, in terms of self or other —is isomorphic to concrete-operational function in the physical sphere. Some operationals' long-term goals may be so consuming that they miss much of everyday life. If their planning becomes an end in itself, with emphasis on a final yield, they are in effect as short-sighted as intuitive characters who have little ability or inclination to plan. One point to be drawn is that operationality does not itself imply better adjustment or even better reality testing necessarily.

Generally speaking, an operational character's basic self-esteem is not as vulnerable as an intuitive character's. Certain operational characters may be self-effacing, but this is of no great import and is a defensive facade, their being anxious or conflicted about feeling or appearing too confident. An operational character's expectation of himself in terms of his codes may be intense, but such expectation is a part function. When he fails to meet his expectation, he condemns only part of the self; his basic sense of worth remains intact. In contrast, the intuitive character has a basic low self-esteem and when unable to bring his defenses to bear, is subject to global self-condemnation, that is, a major sense of lack of worth. External narcissistic supplies are thus very important to an intuitive character. An operational character is not as focused on external narcissistic supplies. His supplies are more internal, less dependent on the outside. Hence, his self-esteem can be expected to be relatively high; grace given by his own conscience is his good. If he measures up to his internal standards in themselves, for example, being unto himself or one of the crowd, reticent or assertive, loving or self-sufficient, he is narcissistically gratified. Such abiding, dissociated standards also imply an ability to particularize, that is, classify, and an ability to swing back and forth between concrete instance and the general trait, the kinds of operations available in the thing sphere to a concrete operational child.

An operational character appears to have tolerance for painful affect, e.g., anxiety, guilt, and depression. Apart from any tolerance for pain, the affects he experiences are not as intense and all pervasive as those experienced by an intuitive character, since his superego structure coordinates and particularizes his investments—those things he regards as taboo or meritorious. Also, these investments often center on his function and control of his function; hence, are more likely within his control than if his investments were in terms of external supplies as are the intuitive character's. Since an operational character generally has high self-esteem, as noted above, and is not dependent on externals for enhancement, he could be expected not to experience narcissistic injury as readily and be able to tolerate it better when it occurs. His disappointment is particularized, classified and graded, not global. While feeling bad about his defect, he does not feel totally defective.

An operational character is a more self-contained unit, has a more structured system. An intuitive character looks to external supplies: being loved, admired, taken care of. While also needing such things, an operational character is not as centered on them, does not find them as essential. In fact, some operational characters vigorously resist any efforts of others to take care of them. Invested in their own function and control of their own function, they are concerned that they take care of themselves, that is, that they be autonomous. In the extreme, they may resist help when they are in need of it. Others may seek dependent gratification, ask to be told what to do, and state their helplessness. However, these particular operational characters use their bid for dependence to defend against their more genuine wish to be autonomous or assertive, about which they feel conflicted, guilty, or anxious. It is much like those operational characters who present a defensive facade of self-effacing verbalizations.

In keeping with his need for external supplies, the intuitive character is subject to shame and humiliation, while the operational character, more of a self-contained unit, is more subject to guilt. Shame and humiliation imply a witness. Guilt is an internal matter. Caught or not, an operational character will feel guilt. An intuitive character, if not caught, may not feel any self-condemnation, like the intuitive-stage child who equates punishment with guilt. If his transgression is known or could be known it is more serious to an intuitive character. To some, the pain of shame and humiliation preempts any other pain or dysfunction. An intuitive character is likely to think or talk about the pressures of the situation, his needs of the moment, his not usually lying, or the lack of injury to the other party, in order to escape all blame. An operational character is likely to try to balance off all these factors, tempering his self-condemnation to some extent, but not escaping guilt. His rules, while modulated, are encapsulated, dissociated from the circumstances of the event. He feels guilty whether he has injured someone or not, and whether he was under considerable internal or external pressure, although these factors may temper his guilt, these factors being coordinated into his guilt. Basically, his judgment of guilt parallels the concrete-operational child's coordination of dimensions into operational understandings of physical attributes.

An operational character's concept of a virtue is abstract in its not being dealt with as if it were a tangible commodity in short supply. An operational character may envy a person who has the approbation of another, but he does not automatically feel deprived as an intuitive character may.

This type of response in an intuitive also betrays a blurred boundary between self and object in terms of attribute. An operational character's judgment of himself is less respondent to the environment than is the intuitive character's; his self-esteem is not as likely to rise when he is in association with an exalted group or fall when with a depreciated one. He is not invulnerable to such influence, but the setting's impact on him is generally not as intense or influential from moment to moment or situation to situation. His self-esteem is more respondent to his own internal set of values, closely tied to his own function. Unlike the intuitive, an operational has a separation of value of self-representation from value of object-representation. Similarly, an operational does not subscribe to the concept of immanent justice; that one gets what one deserves and deserves what one gets. Primarily, he employs an autonomous system of values (e.g., generous or parsimonious, kindly or hard-headed, etc.) to judge himself or another as relatively good or bad.

Whether consciously acknowledged by the operational or not, it is usually clear that his parents were interested in his best interests. This is usually evident in spite of any of his complaints against his parents. He experienced protection, sometimes overprotection. We fail to elicit the relative neglect that we elicit in the history of the intuitive character. The operational accordingly learns to trust the social world he has known. He may be distrustful and concerned that others, especially authority figures, will control him as his parents did when they overstepped their bounds, held him back or pushed him forward unnecessarily in their efforts to serve what they saw as his best interests.

The operational character is generally trustworthy and trusting. Trust or distrust is not the global, abiding issue for him that it is for the intuitive character. Distrust, however, when it is an issue, is limited to specific types of situations involving specific functions. Suspiciousness is not for the operational character an abiding stance toward the world of people, as it is for the intuitive character. An operational character may be overtrusting, expecting that others are like himself or the family he has known. He may assume that all others are out for his own good. If this is his usual stance, it can readily be corrected by an experience with an untrustworthy person. An operational character who is prone to overtrust, however, will likely repeat his overtrust with the next person he encounters.

To the extent that he overtrusts he may be subject to being duped and display a limitation in his reality testing, much as when he is overly suspicious that authorities are attempting to control him. However, these problems with reality testing and trust-distrust are circumscribed, compared to the reality testing problems and trust-distrust focus of either the intuitive or the symbolic character.

Excluding specific relationships as in the above, an operational character is generally aware of the other person's point of view, takes into account intent, something that is not characteristic of an intuitive character, and something an intuitive-stage child cannot do. An intuitive character usually assumes the other person is out for himself as he himself is, just as the intuitive-stage child thinks his view of a set of mountains is the same as someone else's who is on the other side of the mountains (Piaget, 1937). Intellectually, an intuitive may take into account the intent of the other to gain an end, for example, in closing a sale, but generally in his automatic social function intent is not given much weight. For example, Mrs. R. understood that Mr. L., because of his victorian attitude, may have been intending to please her when he offered to just take her home after dinner. However, his intention did not count; what he did mattered. One intuitive had asked his girlfriend to get a calculator for him at the wholesale price, which she was able to do. She then offered to give him the calculator as a Christmas present. He assured her it was too expensive and unnecessary. She withdrew her offer, and he was extremely disappointed. He recognized that she felt generous toward him when she made the offer, but then recognizing the high cost of the calculator she changed her mind. Understanding his girlfriend's intentions did not matter to him. The deed, not the intent counted. To an operational, intent may outweigh the deed.

Someone who is untrustworthy or impulsive is not an operational character. Conscious or unconscious, stubborn, defiant behavior should not be confused with untrustworthy behavior. Similarly, counterphobic behavior should not be mistaken for untrustworthy or impulsive behavior.

The operational character is often genuinely concerned about ethical matters, which generally do not interest the intuitive character. An intuitive character may agree that it is good to tell the truth and bad to tell a lie or cheat, but he is not particularly invested in such matters. When discussing such concepts, a vein of defending himself (or, perhaps, condemning another) may be observed running through his discussion. That discussion is not separate from his self-valuation. He is able to take into account degrees of justification for a given lie as well as the range of possible effects and assert that failing to meet one's contracts is bad. However, his behavior will override such codes when it is to his advantage, sometimes with little concern about the degree of justification for the override and, in some cases, with little consideration of any possible consequences. So it is not that an intuitive character as a rule cannot talk about or understand ethical matters just as an operational character does, it is rather that the intuitive character's automatic thinking and behavior may be inconsistent with such talk or understanding and such understanding generally is not of special interest to him.

Let us return to the example of a psychotherapist who is called upon to tell a half-truth to a patient for the patient's welfare. An intuitive character could be expected to have trouble balancing off what might be the greater good for the patient since he has trouble seeing an issue which is not in front of him at the moment, coordinating past with present, and he generally does not operate with a hierarchy of abstract goodnesses separate from current self-interest. He might be unable to see the needs of his patient or be unable to see the patient as having needs different than his. In contrast, an operational character usually can see the other person's needs or points of view, and see them as separate from his, and, as mentioned, take into account these dimensions when acting (including evaluating) in the situation. An intuitive character would be inclined to make his decision on the basis of what was best for himself at the moment.

Just as the pathologic prototypes of the intuitive character are the behavior disorder and narcissist, the obsessive-compulsive/anal personality is the pathological prototype of the operational character. Although some obsessive-compulsive/anal personalities are symbolic, none are intuitive. Conversely, behavior disorders and most narcissistic personalities are not operational.

On entering treatment, an operational character's chief complaints generally involve some aspects of his function. His complaints are particulate (classified or set apart) not global. He states that he is not doing well at something. "I'm having trouble completing or starting my assignments." "I'm too crabby." "I have trouble making decisions." "I'm not doing a good enough job with my children." An operational character's complaint is presented as a difficulty he is having with part of himself rather than trouble stemming from external forces. He tends to see his conflicts primarily as internal. (Sometimes this may occur even when the problem is largely an external one, for example, his having an infantile spouse or his having to deal with a treacherous superior at work.) The operational character's "I can't make decisions" is a complaint about a particular function, not a general lack of direction. Such a complaint is more often due to an inhibition rather than his not knowing where he wants to go or due to his not having an investment in where he goes. Sometimes he may feel he knows what he wishes to do, but has difficulty in initiating action, finds he is unable to do or complete the activity, regardless of his making an intense effort. In such instances, it turns out that he is unconsciously ambivalent, anxious, or guilty about these goals. Sometimes he is more concerned about disruption in his function than about the pain from his symptoms.

Although sometimes an operational character is inhibited in starting, continuing, or finishing (as we just noted as possible chief complaints) which will show in his therapeutic work, he is usually problem-oriented. He may take off on his own, his associations deliberately or automatically centering on certain issues of his function. Some operational character's focus on a problem may take place to the extent that each session begins where the last left off and no "seeming" extraneous ideas can creep in. The result of this overly controlled approach can, of course, be to exclude some of the most relevant intrusions. (When this characteristic is as extreme as we are now describing, one should be alert to the possibility that one is treating a symbolic character, not an operational character.) Effectively or not, the operational character is involved in the therapeutic enterprise itself, sometimes more focused on process, or who is running it, sometimes on outcome, like the concrete-operational child who is invested in the game, winning it, and how to play it.

The operational character tends to use the defenses we associate with obsessive-compulsive/anal personalities: undoing, isolation or compartmentalization, and intellectualization. He may use rationalization, externalization, or denial on occasion. However, such use is not typical as it is for the intuitive character. The intuitive character tends not to use any of the obsessive defenses. The consistency of an operational character's use of obsessive defenses will be clear when we discuss superego formation in Chapter 8. Simply stated, autonomous superego formation appears to rest upon good caretaking, while obsessive-compulsive/anal personalities (with an operational character structure) have experienced caretaking overdone. We seldom see reaction formation in *active* use during an operational character's interviews. Reaction formation, as frozen into traits of neatness or promptness, is often present. Active use of reaction formation may be more indicative of a symbolic character.

In contrast to the intuitive character, the operational character tends to use thinking as opposed to action as a coping mechanism. An operational character is not necessarily hamstrung when it comes to action, although some operational characters are and some are inhibited in specific situations. Rather, the operational character often opts for thinking. In treatment or in his outside life, he is less inclined to act than is the intuitive character. As previously stated, thoughts and intentions—his own or another's—are meaningful to him when considering the parameters of a human situation.

Although there is very little overlap between the operational and the intuitive, on occasions, an operational character makes use of cognitive mechanisms that are more integral to the intuitive character and vice versa. When an operational character has a full stomach he may think that all is right with the world. Thereby, he may show a diffusion of ego boundaries in the sphere of valuation, something we expect from an intuitive. The day was not any worse or better before he had a full belly and felt good. An operational character may at times use typical intuitive defenses such as denial, just as intuitives may on occasion use typical operational defenses such as undoing.

Nevertheless, we expect the typical defenses, investments or behavior characteristics of either an intuitive or an operational to be evidenced by him most of the time and in the majority of circumstances. In keeping with this frequency (and in consonance with an individual's coherent organization of social cognition), we expect that in any unstructured interview* we will encounter a predominance of these part-functions that belong to either one or the other syndrome. Deviations will be infrequent. As a consequence, in any single hour we usually can decide whether the person is intuitive or operational. Aside from frequency, intensity of investment in any deviations from the basic features of the syndrome is not generally great. If the operational character's attention is drawn to his intuitive reasoning, that is, his feeling that the world is affected by his mood or vice versa, he can drop it or correct it readily. Also, syndrome-dystonic features are not as automatic. The intensity of investment will not be like Mrs. R's (Chap. 5) when she judged her lover to be untrustworthy then became temporarily bewildered by a contradiction only to return to her original stance. Likewise, if one listens closely to an intuitive character who is stressing the morality of an issue, one may be able to detect the gain he expects from such a posture or one may find that his principled position dissolves in the face of discomfort or when a new opportunity arises.

In the less invested, less automatic, less integrated way, we find signs of "regression" (or "progression") in a person or a given character structure. However, we think that under stress a person does not change character structure, but rather

---

*Unstructured interview is a very important constraint. In structured interviews and in ordinary social encounters, it may be very difficult to detect the cognitive style or basic investment of an individual.

becomes more symptomatic, generally choosing from the array of behaviors available to him as a function of his personality and character structure.

AN EXAMPLE OF AN OPERATIONAL CHARACTER AND THE COGNITION OF AN OPERATIONAL-PERIOD CHILD

Perhaps it is gilding the lily to present a case study of an operational character, since most clinicians are able to differentiate him as the optimal psychoanalytic case who has an autonomous superego, has no major ego defects, and is able to benefit from nonintellectualized, genetic insight. The operational character configuration is evident in a few papers (Freud's 1953b) as well as implicit throughout most of the psychoanalytic literature. Nevertheless, if for no other reason than to lend balance to the organization of this book, we will present an example of an operational character.

Mr. S., a conscientious, considerate, conservative, bright junior partner in a large corporate law firm, proposed that his fears were caused by increased workload when he became a partner and was elected president of his local professional organization. Added to increased obligations inherent in being a partner, Mr. S. reluctantly accepted additional work pressed upon him by a senior partner. Mr. S.'s new positions of prominence, his knuckling under to his boss as well as the old guard of his professional group and his long-standing sexual conflict with his wife, not the amount of work, were most significant in his development of symptoms.

He dated the onset of his phobias to one afternoon when he was ready to return from consulting with a client in Queens, N.Y. He became fearful that he would be incontinent of urine on the train. Although embarrassed, he asked to be driven to his office in Manhattan. When crossing the bridge he panicked and insisted they get off on Randall Island to find a bathroom.

Thereafter he ceased crossing the bridge, fearing that he would scream, become a "maniac."

In classic fashion, his phobia spread. He became progressively incapacitated by fear that he would vomit or lose control of his bowels or bladder in public. He no longer ate out with friends, family, or business associates. He was unable to attend church. He did not take public transportation nor ride in someone else's car. He avoided meeting in client's offices. In one social setting after another he was nauseated or had the urge to defecate or urinate.

As his phobia spread, he became increasingly distraught. Anticipating his being unable to work and support his family, he feared he would lose them. Interestingly enough, he observed that while he evaded anxiety-laden situations when his presence was not critical, when any activity was essential in order to hold onto his job or his family, he participated regardless of his anxiety.

Mr. S. remembered that prior to the onset of his phobias he had had a transient episode of anxiety when he attended a business meeting during which he and the other new partners were expected to lead discussion groups. As he waited his turn to be a discussion leader, he became increasingly anxious, then nauseated, and felt the urge to have a bowel movement. Mentioning that he felt ill, he asked one of the other new partners to lead the discussion. As soon as the other partner agreed, Mr. S.'s symptoms disappeared. Although surprised and relieved, he felt bad that he had not braved it through and led the discussion, especially when he saw his replacement trembling as he led the group. Mr. S. had broken his code. He felt guilty.

After this episode Mr. S. was asymtomatic for several months. In fact, he noted he did not have his usual difficulty in starting urination when in a public facility. Although he was pleased with this improvement, at times he wondered if he might have prostatitis. So he improved with his promotion to partner, felt like a big man, then undid it by his fear he was getting an old man's disease.

Prostatism had multiple meanings for Mr. S. On the one hand, it signified he was old and ineffectual. On the other hand, it identified him with his father and father-in-law who gained the attention of the significant women in Mr. S's life. When his symptom of urinary urgency was in full flower, he had to chart his course from bathroom to bathroom in order to get to any destination. He classified himself as just like the old men he stood beside as he urinated in Macy's basement. He had significant exposure to knowledge of prostate diseases in elderly males. His father had prostatism, necessitating frequent stops on the highway. Also, for several years Mr. S.'s father-in-law lived in Mr. S.'s home because of a heart attack following prostate surgery. Mr. S.'s wife devoted considerable attention to caring for her father. About a year and a half before the onset of Mr. S.'s symptoms, he and his wife were near divorce over her involvement in the care of her father. Partly, they argued because Mr. S. resented her father's presence in their home limiting their sexual activity.

For some months prior to Mr. S.'s becoming a partner, Mrs. S. urged that he practice coitus interruptus rather than that she use a diaphragm. He threatened to become impotent and abstained from sexual intercourse. Following this he had premature ejaculations. Also, prior to the onset of his phobia, flushed with his status as a partner, he found himself tempted to have an affair with several women who indicated their interest in him. It is also worth noting that the day of the onset of his urinary urgency on the bridge, his client had insisted that Mr. S. go out to lunch at a topless restaurant and while at lunch to have a few drinks, something Mr. S. avoided during working hours. Mr. S. thought it was vulgar, but gave in. He noted that he had always been titillated by such things, though he hid such feelings.

His urge to defecate, urinate, and vomit were classic conversion symptoms; in body language they spoke his resentment toward his bosses, certain clients, and his wife. The symbolization allowed him to identify with his father, gaining and disguising his oedipal sexual and competitive expressions as well as exacting secondary gains. His identification with his father/father-in-law, in order to get the attention of his mother/wife was clearly part of his symptoms. At the same time his symptoms denied his wish to better his father. His escape from obligations at work and in general was the secondary gain of his symptoms. During treatment he mentioned that in the first law firm where he had worked, he became nauseated when he had to practice general law, which he considered beneath him. He also noticed that he became nauseated when he was about to see a client who expected a perfect legal solution to an unresolvable legal dilemma that the client had knowingly developed for himself.

Mr. S.'s symptoms were multidetermined and their meaning obscured by much of the data being unconscious, revealed only piecemeal over the course of months. Mr. S. was involved with whether he was brave enough, virile enough, sufficiently proper. He was concerned with the honorable, the principled, and the conventional. At first in treatment, central issues were control and embarrassment, with anal referents. Later, as his symptoms abated, sexual function, control, and social roles were his primary concerns. Chiefly worried whether he would succeed in his profession or not, whether he would be found wanting as a parent, husband, or man, Mr. S. felt like a little man sexually and not brave enough in competition with other men. Of course, while his manifest anxiety was that he might not succeed, his more basic anxiety centered on the opposite, the possibility of fulfilling his wish to do well, to feel too big or too successful, equalling or besting his father and siblings.

He felt cowardly that he was a pushover at work, that he gave in to overly demanding clients or senior partners, that he failed to insist upon appropriate compensation, that he accepted assignments that required more hours than could be managed or that should go to a junior member of the firm, and that he failed to insist upon being made a partner long before it was offered to him. Central was his wish to be a super-partner who would suit his controlled and controlling mother/wife, yet anxious and guilty over such an achievment. His automatic, unconscious, and stable identity with his feisty father, including temper outbursts, bragging, and having to be right, showed through.

Although prior to marriage he had very little sexual experience, he thought of himself as oversexed, because he had "thought of women as merely sex objects." By this he meant that when working with a woman or meeting her socially, he would wonder what she would be like in bed. He feared the day that he might have sexual thoughts about his own daughter. In this type of concern he revealed his somewhat exaggerated but clear investment in sexual/social principles and codes, but also his investment in thought. This contrasts with Mrs. R., to whom thoughts did not count, especially if she did not speak them out loud. He struggled to shelve his sexual urges, was tempted to have extramarital sexual affairs, resented his wife's tepid interest in sex, and felt less a man in his inability to gratify her sexually.

His codes, while somewhat rigid, could be bent. Although guilty when he yielded to temptation, guilt did not overwhelm him. His moral precepts were in form the same as the concrete-operational child who can modify a code and no longer sees the code as divine in origin. Being a Catholic, initially he refused to use sexual contraceptives. Finally, his wife prevailed. During this early period of contraceptive use, he noticed that the next morning he would find some excuse to be angry with his wife. He diagnosed the cause of his angry outbursts as his guilt over use of contraceptives. Whether or not he was then able to accept contraceptive use as he claimed, it was clear he could bend his codes to some extent and that understanding the origin of a problem benefitted him.

Mr. S. was very concerned about nonproductive meetings which wasted a client's money, even if the client was wealthy and if the client seemed unconcerned that small talk added to the legal fee to be charged. Not only could he see another's view, but also he was invested in their best interests. His juggling his investment in their well-being with their lack of concern about their consuming money with small talk with him attests to a graded ability to role take in the Piagetian sense, to see the other person's view of "the mountains." While Mr. S. assumed his clients should be invested in saving money and being efficient, he also corrected for this to some extent by recognizing the difference between him and them in frame of reference, that is, their being very wealthy, they were apparently not as concerned as he in saving on his fee. His conflict parallels our mythical operational psychotherapist's. Mrs. R. would have recognized a client's lack of interest in saving fees (which might have been transitory if indeed someone squandered his money) and might have thought, "Well, if that is what he wants, what is the conflict?" However, if she were caught wasting the client's money or if she heard of someone else doing so, she would think it was unforgivable.

Wrecking things somehow for someone else was one of Mr. S.'s genuine, though exaggerated concerns with the other person's viewpoint. He feared he might embarrass or traumatize his daughter if he were to vomit in a restaurant in her presence. He feared if he vomited on the street, others would become sick along with him. He refrained from going to the bathroom while his daughter's friend was in the house, because he worried that if he passed gas she might hear it and his daughter would be embarrassed. He quit bowling because he worried that he might let his team down, since if he were unable to complete a game because of his symptoms, they would be left with his partial score. Mr. S. was concerned and interested in what was good for his friends, his wife, his children, his clients (although the reaction formation is evident).

He felt bad if he lied or misled anyone. Early in his therapy, after most of his symptoms had abated, he stated even if his nausea were to disappear, he would continue treatment indefinitely since he would always need to talk to someone. A few sessions later, feeling guilty, he referred back to his remark, saying he was trying to get on the therapist's good side. It is very unlikely that Mrs. R., having attempted to mislead the therapist, would have found it necessary to set the ledger straight. Aside from evidencing his investment in his moral codes yet showing some flexibility, this attempt to bribe the therapist betrayed his distrust and untrustworthiness in certain situations. Nevertheless, trust/distrust was not a sweeping issue for him as it was for Mrs. R. Mr. S's distrust focused around specific concerns. Would the therapist want to control or to keep him in the child's role? Would the therapist not treat him appropriately, if Mr. S. did not pledge to be a patient forever?

He had abiding, not readily alterable rules, rules for himself in which he was truly invested, but which could be bent at times. He felt guilt when he broke his own codes, which tended to be rather stringent, moral, and conventional ones. When he breached his codes at times, sometimes under pressure from another, sometimes when it was reasonable to do so, sometimes in response to his own impulses, he did not fully accept his rationalizations or externalizations for his behavior. While he experienced guilt, he also did not condemn himself totally as Mrs. R. did when she (rarely) accepted the blame for her behavior. In fact, Mr. S., while basically disapproving of his transgressions, could recognize positive aspects, use multiplicative, graded operations in assessing certain transgressions. He could see his wish for sexual conquest as an achievement or a step forward, while he disapproved of himself for having such thoughts. He could see his father's and his own displays of anger as indices of concern, although he disapproved of such behavior. He had a multiplicative, graded appraisal system for evaluating his social function.

Mr. S. thought he had a good childhood and a happy one, growing up in a big family whose activities centered around church, school, and amateur athletics. We found no evidence to contradict this. His parents had his interests at heart. Mr. S. remembered having injured himself while exploring a deserted house. He was careful not to reveal to his father the circumstances of his injury, knowing he would have been severely chastized. On the way to the hospital, father treated him with concern and tenderness. Because the family was poor, Mr. S. and his brothers and sisters were expected to contribute their earnings to the household coffers. Mr. S.'s father agreed to Mr. S.'s earnings being used to finance his going to college, although the family needed additional income. Mr. S.'s parents were very proud of their son's academic and professional achievements.

Mr. S.'s early memories of his mother centered around a restraining and protective influence that she had. Mother would say he could not be a Marine, something he always wanted to be, because he did not brush his teeth. Marines had to have good teeth. He took her assertion literally that he could not become a Marine, and yet he also commented that she might merely have wanted him to brush his teeth. He also remembered his mother entering his room to interrupt a fight between him and his brother. Mr. S. complained that she never hugged the children.

None of Mr. S.'s relationships with others had the erratic, volatile, intense, disruptive qualities that Mrs. R.'s had. Although he was embarrassed by his father's storming and bragging and although he felt his mother had not been affectionate enough, Mr. S. cared deeply about his parents. He did not discard his siblings although he was hurt by their not including him in some of their activities and although none of them had acquired the tastes or managed the social achievements he and his wife had. His relationships with each sibling was different, like a complex series with multiple dimensions, ranging from one with whom he exchanged confidences to another whom he seldom saw and did not miss. After Mr. S. began treatment, in a fairly intimate and open manner he and his brother exchanged ideas regarding their early life. His brother pointed out that Mr. S. was just like his father, that he had to be right, that he had the same uncontrolled outbursts of anger. He did not like his brother's interpretation, but was able to recognize it as correct and not project it or deny it as Mrs. R. likely would have. At the same time, the negative aspects of it did not have an overwhelming effect on him as attribution of a negative quality to Mrs. R. might have. Mr. S.'s responses were more particulate, less global.

When he became a partner in his firm, he felt he and the partners must be perfect, that is, "in control" and free of biologic urges. In this specific type of interrelationship, in his concept of the authority role (though intellectually he knew better) he manifested a global, ungraded kind of thinking, a kind of undifferentiation or failure in classification. He dreaded that he might have to excuse himself to go the bathroom during a business meeting. If he stayed more than a minute or two, then it would be evident that he had had a bowel movement. He was aware that this was a foolish concern, yet it worried him. As a partner, he felt he must make no off-color remarks, nor reveal any sexual interests. He had always looked up to one of his senior partners, who came from a socially prominent family, had attended the best schools, and so forth. Mr. S. was astonished when this man made a sexual reference about a woman.

Mr. S. felt he did not belong in the rarefied professional atmosphere in which he found himself. He felt guilty and anxious about socioeconomically equalling or besting his father and siblings. Mr. S. interpreted his fear of going crazy as not that he would become psychotic, but that, trapped on the bridge, he would start screaming, have a tantrum like his father did. Similarly, his sour stomach was a way of identifying with his father, who suffered from ulcers. As noted his urinary symptoms symbolized his fear of being like his father and his father-in-law as well as his wish to be like them, both of whom received women's (his mother's and his wife's) attention and catering.

He was devoted to his wife and their children. He complained about his wife's overspending and yet felt satisfaction in providing luxuries for her and the children. She, like his mother, exercised a restraining influence over him. She postulated that his father's rages at the dinner table caused Mr. S.'s nausea. She squelched him when he was angry. For example, if someone crowded him on the freeway, he would let fly a string of expletives. She would squeeze his hand indicating he was behaving improperly in the presence of his daughter. He might then become angry and retaliate by speeding up and cutting in on the offending driver. He never approved of these losses in control, especially if they were directed at his wife or children, although he recognized his tantrums were like his father's, not entirely bad, that is, they represented a kind of investment in things.

Generally, however, he did not respond in black or white terms. His responses were graded or multiplicative. He might complain about a friend or loved one but not be tempted to discard him. He did not have the extreme mood or valuation shifts we encounter in the intuitives. His obsessive features and evidence of operational thinking went hand in hand. He would make an assertion, support it, then undo it with a doubt or qualification. He might displace responsibility for an insight, saying his wife pointed out something to him and his brother something else. He did not recognize that he had selected from what they said. At the same time, occasionally his brother's or his wife's interpretations were not correct. Correct or incorrect, Mr. S. was able, through citing his source to stay uncommitted, to distance himself from the information and attendant affect. He might complain at length about his wife concerning a particular issue and then counter with, "but you have not heard her version." At the same time, as he undid his complaint, he took into account an alternate view of a situation.

His compartmentalization (particularization or multiplication), while overdone and hence obscuring, also approached a graded, operational classificatory response, like the 8-year-old's. It took into account fully (maybe overly so) the outside source of his knowledge, his wife's, his brother's point of view. In contrast, such views were of no particular consequence to Mrs. R., except as they served her feeling better or worse. Taking another's point of view is not done by a preoperational child (whether in viewing a set of mountains or in judging a moral transgression). Overdone or underdone, done for defensive purposes, shifting from one view to another was an integral part of Mr. S.'s social cognitive style. This style allowed a modulated comprehension of a situation which was typical for him and was almost never employed by Mrs. R.

His stock in trade was the obsessive defenses: undoing, intellectualization, isolation. His symptomatology employed conversion and displacement. Reaction formation was frozen into the structure of his personality traits, for example, promptness and neatness, and sometimes invoked to deal with a current conflict. On occasion he used rationalization, that is, reasoning from the end stage, or denial.

He was neatly and conservatively groomed and dressed. His demeanor was friendly, open, and appropriate. He rarely swore. He was proper, but not prissy, effeminate, or stilted. He was pleasant and likeable, rarely a bit obsequious and occasionally helpful, picking up the therapist's mail or turning on a light. He came for his appointments on time, cancelled only with advance notice, paid his bills promptly, would talk for most of the hour, occasionally stopping as if expecting a response and after a bit resuming. All these suggest compulsivity, if you will, but also indicate a general control and an investment in the rules of the culture.

Generally his interviews were a complex mixture of his unconscious stubborn defiance, his partial compliance, his guilt, his concern for precision and his use of precision to distance himself from his feelings and ideas. Through all this he worked actively. Much of the time he offered up the material not trying to make connections. It was clear that after he left he worked on the data that he had revealed during an interview. At times, he reported that in a previous session he had spent the interview avoiding talking about certain thoughts. He gave precise pictures of any events he spoke about. He had near total recall for the interviews. His affect was appropriate, but not intense during his therapeutic sessions. He tended to compartmentalize as he discussed in a confused way that he feared his mind would be controlled by the therapist. He asserted he did not want to quit being obsessive, that he was distinct from his mind and that right now his mind (presumably his symptoms) was controlling him.

Unlike Mrs. R., Mr. S.'s self-esteem was fundamentally sound and not heavily reliant on outside sources for support. For instance, while he gave lip service to being unqualified because he had not attended a prestigious school, had not gotten all A's in law school, and did not socialize with socially prominent people, apparently he was confident enough not to bother with these accoutrements. He was content to get A's in his major areas of interest. Following his army service, he returned to college, because he resolved not to take orders from people who knew less than he. Fears of losing his job or his wife or (earlier in life) a girlfriend, in each instance followed his lapse in interest in each. His surface uncertainties covered basic confidence.

Like his self-esteem, his sense of right and wrong (codes) was not greatly affected by external factors. In fact, he could not readily shift his codes in the face of changed times, for example, his views on use of contraceptives. Only rarely did he go along with group pressure when it violated his codes, for instance, his going out to topless bars or drinking during business hours. On the other hand, he gave in to his wife, his friends, and business associates when he did not want to, not generally in order to be liked, as much as out of fear of his own anger or that of another, or out of fear and guilt over his wish for autonomy. Unlike an intuitive, he readily comprehended another person's point of view or investment, such as his wife's, his brother's, his clients'.

In contrast to Mrs. R., he quickly took responsibility for secondary gains, for example, how his symptoms excused him from difficult assignments. He took responsibility for his symptoms, his failure to stand up to his senior partners or clients, his allowing himself to be intimidated by his symptoms. In specific instances, his sense of responsibility was exaggerated, for example, his blaming himself for his wife's frigidity.

Mr. S.'s response to insight varied. His recognition of his expectation from the therapist for a miraculous cure, that after a few visits all of his symptoms would disappear, enabled him to realize that certain of his clients expected miracle solutions from him. He adapted by setting limits on these clients and on his own expectations of himself. When he recognized that he felt guilty that he had excelled his father and siblings socioeconomically, he tested this recognition against other supporting data before he accepted it. Although he found this insight of interest, and, although having accepted it may have felt less guilt, he manifest no clearcut shift in his behavior following this. He remained conscious of the understanding and continued to puzzle about it. Other insights that he was not ready to accept were handled by repression as when he forgot the subject of the hour during which he told of his identification with his father through having stomach trouble. He responded to other insights with symptom relief. Following his learning that if he allowed himself to make his own interpretations he would feel too big, he absented himself from therapy for a few weeks, worked out a number of answers for himself, including the fact that he tended to cling when he felt guilty over wanting to behave on his own.

It is clear that Mr. S. was an operational character. He showed almost no intuitive qualities nor did he have any major identity-reality problems or involvement with attachment.

Chapter 7

SYMBOLIC CHARACTER

The symbolic character's involvement with *attachment, identity, and reality-testing, and his use of particle-to-particle thinking* distinguish him from either operational or intuitive characters. As we have emphasized, the dividing line between intuitive and operational characters is distinct while the boundary separating symbolics and either operationals or intuitives is not always discrete. Like operational characters, some symbolic characters have autonomous superegos, have particularized affects, and are concerned with function and control of function. Other symbolics are like intuitive characters, have heteronomous superegos, process affects globally, and are focused on narcissistic supplies. Still other symbolics have a mixture of intuitive and operational characteristics. Such an aggregate of operational and intuitive characteristics helps us recognize a symbolic. Manifest operational or intuitive qualities alone may mislead us, however, causing us to believe someone is an operational or an intuitive, although at root he is a symbolic.

A symbolic character has identity concerns, uncertainty about *who he is and what he wants.* In keeping with any identity problems, he may also have significant difficulty with reality testing, sometimes tending to develop a thought disorder. In severest form, his identity problem may show in his uncertainty whether he exists or whether a characteristic, a part object, belongs to him or to an associate. Some symbolic characters have relatively distinct, but warded-off identities. Their identities are bad identities, as if their essence were evil. If a symbolic character's goals are evident, that is, if he seems to know his direction, his goals tend to be narcissistic ones. Although he may be involved heavily with roles, codes, and function, often one finds these interests serve narcissistic needs. Nevertheless, more basic than any need he has for narcissistic supplies, and integral to his focus on roles, codes, or function (if present) is his need for or struggle against attachment and/or his struggle for or against confusion, that is, issues involving identity and reality.

When unattached, a symbolic character may experience a sense of no identity, no center, a sense of being lost and empty, a feeling of being "cut off" or of being "in between," of being incomplete. He may have an inclination to circle around some other person in an attempt to feel whole and centered. A symbolic character may depend on external clues, e.g., ascribed roles, expectations of others, and in some cases "signs" to define himself and his world. One man, who was a clerk in a large university, felt big as a part of this large and socially significant organization. When he quit to go to school, he did not know who he was and became preoccupied with what words were and whether he knew how to speak.

A symbolic character may wish strongly for attachment or merging and at the same time be afraid of it, on some level realizing that merging may result in further identity confusion or that his attachment and dependency on another makes him vulnerable to separation and loss. One symbolic character handled her conflict by attachment to three men so that if she lost one she still had two-thirds of the attachment. Another, Mr. B., whom we will mention several times, avoided close relationships to prevent being engulfed and taken over by the partner, that is, having to do all the partner's bidding. At work, he essentially defined his responsibility and goals as any need presented by any situation. He failed to differentiate his goals from the implied demands of a situation, a part failure of separation of self-representation from object-representation. When not pressed by employers, friends, or their obvious needs, he could not find an interest of his own.

Attachment may also be to "causes," religions, movements (often the attachment to a movement may be an attachment through a particular person to the movement), or to alcohol or drugs. A partial identity or attachment solution may be through a somatic illness or through countless medical appointments.

Attachment may be a coping device providing an identity solution for some while it is a threat of the opposite—a dissolution of identity and major break with reality—for others. Whether sought or avoided, attachment is of special significance to the symbolic character.

Essentially in a symbolic character, identity, dependency, narcissistic gratification, and self-esteem are intertwined, not differentiated from each other. Often a loss of self-esteem, depression, causes him to lose his identity, that is, become psychotic. "If I am not special" or "if I am bad" [in some way], "I am nobody." He goes from a part valuation or part identity to the whole self; his worth and identity are set from moment to moment by the part that is in focus.

Along with identity and reality undifferentiation, another kind of undifferentiation is manifested by some symbolic characters. As we have mentioned, certain symbolics, in contrast to intuitives and operationals, evidence a mixture of intuitive and operational characteristics. Intuitive and operational characters have an internal consistency that distinguishes them from each other. Their defenses and goals differ as do their general approaches in the fundamental areas of trust, control, dependency/autonomy, need for narcissistic supplies and reality testing. In terms of any of these functions, an internal consistency may not prevail in certain symbolic characters. In these symbolics, we find use of projection alongside undoing, or we may find obsessive defenses serving narcissistic goals. Trust/distrust is always an issue for the symbolic just as it is for the intuitive. Nevertheless, some symbolics may be focused on function, which is not of concern to an intuitive, and/or on narcissistic supplies, which is not very important to an operational. As previously noted, a mix of these factors helps us recognize a symbolic character.

The extremity of a defense or of a characteristic, rather than the type, is another aid to recognition of a symbolic character. As is evident, a symbolic character is not defined on the basis of whether he is trustworthy or trusting, whether his goals are narcissistic or not, or whether he is dependent or not. He may be suspicious or trusting, dishonest or reliable, self-centered or self-sacrificing, dependent or independent, function-oriented or not. He may present as an extreme narcissist, as a criminal, as a saint, or as none of these. When a person presents in an exaggerated form, that is, super-moral, entirely selfish, gruesomely criminal, consumingly narcissistic or dependent, brooking little or no compromise in his approach it is likely he has a symbolic character structure. Many a symbolic character is an extremist and/or perfectionist. He may expect to be perfect or to perform perfectly, one not necessarily differentiated from the other. The symbolic character's defenses may be strong or weak, sweeping or absent. Psychotic decompensation should not come as a surprise. The extremity of, the unyielding quality and/or brittleness or weakness (that is, transparency) of his defense mechanisms or presentation (narcissism, not usually a defense, is like one in these cases), is often diagnostic.

A psychotherapist who was a symbolic character gave his psychopathic patient the key to the psychiatric hospital in order to show the patient that he was trusted. While this therapy had a theoretical rationale, it was uncompromising in its failure to take into account the risk to other patients in the hospital or to consider the approach might not work. Furthermore, in his act, the therapist placed his own well-being as a professional in jeopardy. The therapist could not begin with a less extreme, more tentative expression of trust. Even when the situation was past, the therapist could not consider, even in discussion, a more tempered approach.

With little or no stimulus barrier, that is, weak defenses, some symbolic characters are particularly vulnerable to pressures and feedback, both from within and without. Mr. G. whom we will discuss shortly identified with little lost animals. He could not pass a stray animal in the street. Since he saw the vulnerability of the animal, he was responsible for doing something about it; to do otherwise would have been negligent. He had to find a home for each stray or keep it himself. To an extent the situation, the presented-needy-cat, defined Mr. G.'s direction. At the same time, Mr. G. confused his identity as an abandoned child with the cat. He had a major diffusion of ego boundaries.

Related to a symbolic character's lack of defensive structure, his affect may be diffuse and overwhelming (often out of proportion to the stimulus); may be experienced physically (psychosomatically); or may be disorganizing to his thinking. When depression is present, it may be severe. Similarly, rage, terror, or humiliation may be unbounded; or the opposite may prevail. Defensive operations may be so stringent that he may have nearly absolute control of his feelings or experience delay of a week before he can reconstruct what he would be expected to feel in a situation.

His defenses may be transparent. In contrast to an intuitive's use of action or acting out, if a symbolic character uses flight, its defensive function may be obvious. An intuitive character's denial of fear of being alone may not be obvious at all. His complaint of how unsatisfactory a resource his roommate is and his threats to throw him out may successfully hide his fear of having no one to depend upon. A symbolic character's denial of his lack of worth as he is about to decompensate may be transparent as in one woman who for an entire hour told one way and another how wonderful, unselfish, generous, attractive, and intelligent she was. She attempted to define herself by good parts, some of which were wishes, not facts. Likewise, another symbolic character repeated carefully each little thing he had done for his friend, volunteering that he was sorry if he might have put away the glasses in the wrong place in the cupboard, or calling attention to his clearing the table of someone else's dishes after dinner. Thus, he denied what was obvious to anyone else, his feeling of lack of worth and selfishness. An intuitive character's denial is more likely to fool the observer as well as himself.

A symbolic character's defense mechanisms, in addition to being weak or absent or exaggerated and likely brittle, often are the same ones an intuitive character uses: denial, projection, externalization, rationalization, and acting out. As stated earlier, however, some symbolic characters may employ undoing, isolation, and intellectualization, along with denial, projection, etc.

Mr. B., whom we mentioned, was driven to do things absolutely right in all situations. He was a great asset to any organization. He had the other marks of obsessiveness: stubbornness, retentiveness, and concern about autonomy and control. He was inclined to procrastinate and was a perfectionist. His drive to do everything perfectly was motivated not by reaction formation against aggressive impulses, as is classic for the obsessive, but rather by an expectation that at some point security and being loved would follow; his goals were dependent, narcissistic ones. Once this constellation was clear to him, he relaxed in his efforts at work, but then for a prolonged period found nothing that interested him for its own sake.

A preschizophrenic, anorexia nervosa patient became engrossed in house cleaning to take her mind off eating, because of her fear of growing obese. Her house cleaning then turned into a full-fledged, highly scheduled compulsion. While her house cleaning was a reaction-formation to (or way of denying) the dirt she had been raised in, the major driving force in this woman was her need for attachment and her dependent narcissistic needs. She was childlike and yet she was expected to function as a mother and wife. Minimal responsibility was too much for her. Escape from responsibility dissolved her compulsive rituals. The point we want to stress is that her obsessive-compulsive system served oral narcissistic goals.

A symbolic character may act up or act out, but not necessarily be running from discomfort or toward that which looks promising at the moment, the kind of motivation we expect in the intuitive. In a symbolic character simple, involved activity such as hobbies to take his mind away from the risk of confusion, is often a valuable coping mechanism. Impulsivity in itself does not help us differentiate a symbolic character from an intuitive character. However, unbridled, primitive impulse in fantasy or activity or extremely stringent control of impulse or transparency of an activity's defensive function is more diagnostic of a symbolic character. So we come back to the quality of defenses rather than the type as a distinguishing feature of symbolics.

Control, an important issue for the operational character, may be critical for a symbolic character. If not pulling the strings, he risks the other person's getting to know his weak side and enslaving him. A tightly contolled symbolic character who is not likely to be irresponsible at all may dread the slightest deviation from his absolute moral behavior. If he lets down his guard, he fears impulses will break forth and chaos will reign, whether this is a possibility or not.

Each character structure type has its own sphere of undifferentiation. *The symbolic character does not separate his identity from that of the object while the intuitive character does not separate the judgment of value of the self from the judgment of the value of the object. The operational may have difficulty knowing if his function belongs to him or to an authority, whether he is functioning for his own sake or for another.*

As already suggested, holding a position in a prestigious organization, such as in a governmental agency or university, may serve a double purpose for a symbolic character. It may provide him with a sense of significance, his being part of this special organization. Also it may provide structure and identity. "I am part of this big thing which does these things." In the center of such a structure he can feel good and may define himself and his directions. Such role definition, where he understands his identity in terms of external criteria may be a very important coping mechanism, helping him to avoid confusion. However, it should be noted that he is defining himself on the basis of a part function, not on the basis of his whole function, that is, his history. At the same time there is a fusion of self with outside world, not different from Jacqueline's assertion that it is not afternoon, because she has had no nap or Millar's (1968) child's thinking of herself as a writer as she scribbles.

Closely related to a symbolic's relying on roles or social structures to define himself is his depending on the environment for a sense of self-esteem, just as an intuitive character does. Mr. G. (to be presented shortly) felt himself to be a very important person because he was recognized on the street by someone from the film studios. Later the same day, he felt worthless because a salesperson waited on someone else who had come into the store after he did. On other occasions, when he was already in distress, if a salesperson did not wait on him when his turn came, he considered whether he was visible. He would worry whether he existed in the living world. Any cut off from desired feedback could result in loss of self-esteem and a loss of identity.

Mr. B. commented, "If I try to do something and can look back and see that I could have done better then I can feel guilty. That's not so bad. If I look back and see I did my best and still there was no pay off then it is much worse. It means I must be defective." In this instance, he was defining himself. It is similar to the intuitive character's belief in immanent justice—if something bad happens to me, I must be bad—but it is more sweeping. He is both defining himself and valuing himself.

Mr. B. felt that admitting to himself, let alone someone else, that he was desirous of something or someone was equivalent to saying he was a defective person. Such an admission had to be carefully avoided. He was confused between part and whole, part and part. A single want or desire was equivalent to not being complete and to being totally inadequate. The presence of wish was equated with having an actual defect. Although a wish signifies there is absence of something, a wish is often a desirable attribute. For example, wanting to be helpful or wanting to love are hardly defects in our culture. However, to him, wishes were defects. His use of "wish" involved a kind of undifferentiation as found in Jacqueline's use of illness when referring to the humpback. Mr. B., shaped to be self-sufficient at all costs, had an understanding of "defect" as total and absolute. Mr. B. reported that if he "verbalized any weakness, his mother became panicky and would counter with a flurry of denials and exhortations."

An intelligent professional woman had virtually no motivation except in terms of the needs of others. On occasion, she desired time to herself, perhaps to read or just to be alone, but even those desires were not legitimate to her until she had been sapped by her family and sometimes not even then. Otherwise, nothing really interested her in itself: cooking, art, her body, food, advancement in her profession, etc. She felt that the goals of others were more important since they were more invested in their goals. She was in awe of persons who had intense motivation, was glad for them, was puzzled by it all. Her goals were the goals of the outside, her children's, her husband's, her clients'. A brilliant and beautiful woman, who could do advanced work in her field or could rise within the administrative structure or make money or decorate herself, etc., did none of these things and was interested in none. Her directions were defined by others and her goal was attachment or sometimes withdrawal and isolation.

The mothers* of symbolic characters are not necessarily neglectful, but basically confused or confusing. They may be overwhelming, panicky, or overprotective, but are not usually indifferent or absent. While not absent or negligent, the mother of a symbolic character usually is a symbolic character herself and uses the child to meet her own needs which include identity and attachment. We think the child often learns early to get his needs met by meeting mother's needs (symbiotic). Or, unable to learn this, because of his own characteristics or because mother's needs are so erratic or idiosyncratic, he becomes hopeless or confused. He fails to form a sense of self and learns to look to the environment for clues to know how to behave, to know who he is, and in extreme cases to assure himself of his existence. Either in order to appear to be a better mother or because of her own fear of social interaction, a mother of a symbolic character may be overprotective of her child thus creating great fears of the outside world or, on the contrary, she may thrust him forward to deal with the world she fears.

The mothering experienced may be overwhelming or somewhat neglectful, but the protection from the mother has a kind of unpredictability for the child and involves role reversal, to an extent. By role reversal we do not mean simply that the child takes care of the parent. A child who generally is expected to take care of a parent instead of her taking care of him, we would expect to develop into an intuitive character. We use role reversal in a very specific way, referring to the interpreting or

*When we use the term *mother* we mean the parenting function; our comments could apply to father as well.

guiding function of caretaking or protection. The child during the symbolic stage is apparently subject to tremendous flux as his identity and reality shifts from moment to moment, now he is in the looking glass, now out here; the cat is a dog when it is grey, and a cat when not; the child is or is not an author provided he has the same writing materials as mother and makes similar marks and movements. Along with these shifts are momentous affectual and social shifts. Hence, the mothering during this stage is a particularly powerful social instrument as she interacts with him, but basically shapes him in terms of her interpretation via labels for and responses to his needs and interests, as well as via her demonstration and labels for her own, the child usually being the less skilled communicator of the two. Included in this interaction is mother's idiosyncratic interpretation of her culture. The interaction of the mother and the future symbolic is marked by the child's having significantly to protect her, first by having to read her and know what makes her more comfortable and stable, before she is whole enough to be a reliable support for him. This is what we mean by role reversal.

Once a mother is made whole, in contrast to the typical mother of an intuitive characters, she is somewhat giving and understanding or protective. When this symbiosis is established, the situation is fairly predictable for the child, although it may require great loss of self or self-interest by him.

The mother's proof to herself that she is a good mother or a good and whole person may rest on somewhat incomplete or hollow evidence, that is, part objects or events. For instance, she may feel that if you are a good mother, your child does not become ill and therefore does not see a psychiatrist nor take pills nor manifest fright. As a consequence, she may go to extremes to prevent her child's being treated or his exhibiting his own difficulties. As long as he is not seeing a psychiatrist or taking medication or showing anxiety in front of her, to her he is not emotionally disturbed and therefore she is not a bad mother or a bad person. It may be the opposite. Mother may feel whole and worthwhile as long as her child is the ill member of the family. Hence, he must be in treatment. Such a mother may run roughshod over her child as if he were nonhuman as she pursues her desired (and necessary) image of herself. Oblivious to aspects that do not fit a formula, she may raise her child to the letter in accord with her pediatrician's prescription.

This type of mother,* a type of symbolic character in her own right, merits comment. Her behavior, often necessarily directed through people as she pursues a desired image of herself, may be leveled at a spouse or at a nonfamily member, not just at her child, as she strives for a sense of worth and identity with little concern as to who may be in the way. For instance, a psychiatric program leader with this approach toward (through) people may discharge patients prematurely in order to make his program look good. Or, if the yardstick of his program is reemployment, this type of program leader may see that his patients have jobs, come what may. He is not able to respond to the individual differences of his patients. It is the same as Jacqueline at about age 4 including Lucienne into her game as if she were a doll, not a person with her own interests (Piaget, 1962a). As one may imagine, this type of symbolic character, relentlessly pursuing his part goals in business or elsewhere, may be highly successful. The imperative quality of his goals defines and values him; accordingly, he may be an outstanding salesperson. We are describing a type of symbolic character who confuses part for whole, symbol for thing, current behavior for concept. Perhaps one of the best descriptions of this phenomenon is in the chapter on mothers of schizophrenics in *Psychotherapeutic Intervention in Schizophrenia* by Hill (1955).

While our understanding of the symbolic character has been illuminated by our encounter with the more pathologic mothering found in the history of schizophrenics (as well as when we have interviewed mothers of schizophrenics), it may

*Here we are talking about the mother as a real person, not just the child's construction of his mothering experience.

be possible that mothers of some symbolic characters may not have directly elicited role reversal as mothers of schizophrenics usually have. For example, one (manic depressive) symbolic character who suffered a profound depression when his wife divorced him described the extremity of his attachment. It was comparable to an addiction which could only be assuaged by reattachment to another woman. He suggested that it derived from the extreme poverty he experienced during childhood. His father died when he was six. He saw his mother "take food out of her own mouth to feed" him. He felt that kind of setting made for intense closeness and sharing. Although we do not have sufficient history to be certain his mother did not actively parentalize him, we think it possible that his strong attachment needs and role reversal could have developed from his being aware of his mother's sacrifices for him and the profound need they had for sharing in such a poverty-striken setting.

Mr. B. was parentalized to some extent. He learned early to betray no anxiety or unsureness; otherwise, his mother became panic stricken, telling him that he was not frightened and that he was as good as anyone and not to be intimidated. Somehow his mother's safety depended on her child's appearing strong. Once this requirement was met, Mr. B.'s mother was a very reliable resource for him.

A child, subject to more stringent control by his parents, may surrender any chance to live as a separate being. The child may be torn, feeling drawn by the closeness and specialness of the union and at the same time struggling against the union and its requiring him to sacrifice having a life of his own. This child, in some ways, does not know who is mother and who is child, what parts of him belong to him and what parts do not. He finds he must be a certain way whether it fits his internal condition or not. He may have to learn to eat when his mother needs to feed him in order for her to appear to be a good mother. It is not surprising if he becomes confused as to whose needs are whose, what is outside and what is inside, what is real outside and what just facade or fragment.

All along we have suggested a close relationship between schizophrenia and the symbolic character. We think that the type of parenting just described is a significant factor in the development of the symbolic character including those who have schizophrenic episodes.*

The type of social cognition pathognomonic for the symbolic character is obvious in the symptomatology of the schizophrenic. One schizoaffective patient, who had just recovered from a psychotic episode during which she accused her therapist of having had sexual intercourse with her, justified (and explained to her therapist) her accusation by saying that the therapist had smiled at her. The patient equated the therapist's smiling at her with his having sexual intercourse with her. She went from part to part, the smile to the sexual act. The fantasy of an affair, the wish or the word was equivalent to the deed, no different than Jacqueline declaring the room was not cold when she wished it not to be or that oranges were not green when she observed camomile tea to be yellow (Piaget, 1962a).

It is much like Deutsch's patient who believed she could become an analyst by associating with Deutsch (1942), or one of the patients of A. Reich (1953) who thought he was a movie star because his smile resembled the movie star's. It differs little

---

*It must be clear that we are only discussing environmental etiologic factors in such syndromes. We in no way discount a genetic component as as etiologic factor in psychosis or in character formation. There is no inherent incompatibility between a combined psychogenic and hereditary cause of schizophrenia. One of us proposed a theory of schizophrenia which suggested that damaged, less sensitive pleasure centers would blur distinctions in social cognition (Malerstein, 1969). Lidz's psychogenic theory (1973), while different from ours, also easily accommodates a hereditary component. This book is not the place to explore these. However, a point not to be ignored is that the symbolic character may have organic givens. Just as an intuitive character may be born with such intense or erratic needs that no parent could meet his demands, so a symbolic character could be so constructed that he cannot differentiate when certain needs are involved. Of course, an organic factor may be paramount in the formation of one person's character style and insignificant in the formation of another's.

from Jacqueline, when she was almost 2, pretending to play hide and seek with her cousin whom she had not seen for several months, then becoming "Clive running, Clive jumping, Clive laughing" (Piaget, 1962a, p. 125), while strutting.

A middle-aged woman had had a schizoaffective, depressed episode six years previously. Since that time she had not been psychotic. She was a large, pretty, pleasant, religious woman who appeared to be and who generally was conscientious, competent, and sensible. For some time she had been having an affair with a quiet, shy loner, a gambler who had no friends and was rarely seen. She had hopes they would marry. He was devoted to her; however, he was not about to marry anyone. One day the patient became exhilarated, thought her marriage to her boyfriend was made by God and that she would have a special child. Inside and outside, wish and reality were confused. For many months thereafter she would turn over a card to see what she would do that day. When she encountered a design on a floor she noted which way the design pointed. She read the pattern as being a message from God indicating which direction she should take in an activity of the day. Part of her self, her goal, was dictated by external objects. This is much as it was for Mr. B., although his being directed was not part of a psychosis (nor was it at all likely he would become psychotic).

A similar woman, tall, pleasant, religious, kindly, sensible, and self-contained, was always pushed forward to take more responsible positions by employers and other associates who assumed that she was as strong as she appeared. She had a series of schizoaffective, depressed episodes, the first largely triggered by a loss of her fiance. She could not believe he was no longer interested although he had been explicit about this. At the same time she had some sexual fantasies that made her feel like an "animal, a terrible person". Thereafter, any increase in responsibility or the slightest criticism resulted in a psychotic regression with depression and withdrawal. Prominent in her symptomatology was her reading the passing of an automobile as referring to her. When a blue car passed by she thought it meant she was cool; when she saw a red car, she was hot.

For both these patients, the external world was not differentiated from the internal world. In the first instance, the confusion was largely in directions, goals to be taken. In the second, the quality or type of self was being judged by external objects or events. An attribute, part of the self, was seen as part of an external object. Abstract symbol, e.g., coolness, and concrete object were confused. Self- and object-representations were poorly differentiated in either case.

Confusion of part and whole, self and object, object and other objects is basic in the symptomatology of schizophrenia. Misidentifications usually are based on, or triggered by, resemblance of an aspect (part) of one object to an aspect of another object. Paranoid ideation and ideas of reference always have a nucleus that is valid. When the patient asserts that someone is torturing him, one finds evidence that the "persecutor" did something against this patient albeit small or one finds the patient sensed in the persecutor's expression a negative attitude directed toward him. Sometimes the negative attitude is not even directed at the patient but merely expressed in his presence.

The most flamboyant example we have encountered of someone confusing the word, a representation of an object, in a sense a part of an object, with the object or event, that is, concrete thinking, was revealed in a letter from a schizophrenic 22-year-old to his friend. In the letter he explained why he stabbed a stranger. He was seated on a bus next to a young lady. A man from another seat engaged her in conversation. Our correspondent "decided to cut in." The structure of such thinking is no different than Jacqueline's equating yellow with ripe.

A young woman, who as far as we know never had any psychotic symptoms, explained her professional dilemma. After having worked with impoverished Mexicans in Mexico, she returned to the United States to study nursing in order to work with impoverished people. She was offered a job working with poor Italians, but found no interest in working with these people at all. It is possible that she was involved in some abstractions related to Mexicans rather than impoverished people as a whole, but clearly her interest in working with underprivileged people was not an abstract goal in itself.

In treatment, a symbolic character's complaint may reflect a sense that something is missing and may be global. He may say, "I don't know who I am," or "I have no goals or direction." Sometimes he will say, "I want to be average. I want to be normal." His concerns may center on a severe depression or a sense of emptiness or panic. He may seek treatment because of pending, past, or current schizophrenic symptoms. On the other hand, his presenting problems may not distinguish him from either of the other two character syndromes.

In treatment, as otherwise, the symbolic character wishes for or struggles against attachment to the theraptist and is concerned about his vulnerability to loss of identity or to separation. If tempted by the urge to attach, he may vascillate between being overly trusting, putting his care completely into the hands of the therapist, and paranoid mistrust of the therapist. He may push the limits because of the intensity of his needs and not knewing where the limits are, or else may be overabiding of limits in order to defend against attachment or in order to insure that he will continue in the therapist's good favor and therefore avoid separation. Often he wants and needs feedback for reality testing or to assure himself he is in union with the therapist.

In keeping with his particular defensive structure (stringent or almost absent) a symbolic character may present as constricted or flamboyant, lacking in insight or may, without having been exposed to prior treatment or psychological teachings, demonstrate rich insight into himself and others.

A phenomenon, perhaps not unusual generally, but of particular importance in symbolic characters, may be encountered: When present, anxiety breeds anxiety; depression, depression;

and confidence, confidence. His awareness of his own anxiety or his anticipation of being confronted with an anxiety-stimulating circumstance may escalate into panic. Those symbolic characters given to depression sometimes appear to be sucked into depression. This may occur by merely referring to a past depression. In the opposite direction some success tends to feed upon itself. Even when only a small step is taken by the person, it may be helpful in bolstering his confidence and ability to take the next step. Like Jacqueline as Clive or in the glass or on the mountain side, in large measure the symbolic defines himself at each step in the process. If he has a success he *is* a successful person; if he has a failure, he *is* a failure.

AN EXAMPLE OF A SYMBOLIC CHARACTER AND THE COGNITION OF A SYMBOLIC-STAGE CHILD

Mr. G., like Mrs. R. and Mr. S., came for treatment of a phobia. Mrs. R.'s anxiety centered around being trapped by a situation in which she had more to lose than she had ever had before as well as trapped by aging. Mr. S.'s anxiety and guilt centered around his success in a masculine competitive endeavor. Mr. G. became anxious when he was in jeopardy of being unattached and ill-defined. While each patient's presenting complaint was the same type symptom, the basic issues for each differed greatly and were issues typical of each one's particular character structure.

Symbiosis, attachment, being cut off and lack of a separate identity were major issues in Mr. G.'s life: his life with mother, with his girlfriend, with his therapist, with cab drivers, and with his pets. His narcissistic involvements were in terms of identity and connectedness, not primarily in terms of narcissistic supplies, as were Mrs. R.'s, although these were important too.

Mr. G., a freelance filmmaker, had recovered from a similar phobic episode three years before. He regarded his intervening asymptomatic period as a mask, three years of good acting.

His previous panic was precipitated by his sense that he could not be the Don Juan his father was. He equated his having a job, his working and his driving, that is, his function, with being a man. He referred to his panic as being "caught by the balls." While much of Mr. G.'s focus was on sexual issues, the more basic issue was one of identity, translated into sexual-role terms. Both Mr. S. and Mr. G. were concerned about being virile young men. Mr. S. was concerned with whether he measured up to his standards. Mr. G. needed his roles to define himself. He described his phobia thus: "It's almost—It's not like everyone's out to get me—It's that kind of fear. It's real terror, like a child afraid of the dark. You'd avoid it no matter the humiliation or anything."

His phobia recurred during a year when he had little routine and did much introspecting. If he had been going to a job he thought he would not have been as vulnerable. His phobia spread from fear of driving to fear of walking alone or of standing in lines. He was afraid of being caught "in between" or "cut off." He had certain safe bases, the studio, his therapist's office, places where there were people he could count on to rescue him if he panicked. He feared having a panic so severe that he would go to pieces and be locked up in a mental institution. He was not sleeping well; noises seemed louder; automobile exhaust fumes bothered him; cars, people, and he himself seemed like automatons.

Although he was never frankly psychotic, he had major identity and reality testing problems as well as a major focus on being attached or connected. A particularly articulate young man, he detailed vividly his early close relationship to his mother including his sensitivity to her needs and what he felt he must do to maintain their relationship; he described their role reversal very well. When he was 2-years-old his father deserted him and his mother. After that he spent long days in a nursery school while his mother worked. He felt abandoned in the nursery school, feared his mother would not return. He was all alone. One pretty nursery staff member talked to him while he waited for his mother. He remembered that her talking helped him. Evenings with his mother were precious, close hours. He listened as she prepared toast or whatever they could afford. His mother has referred to this same period as her happiest, with her working in the house and listening to him play. Those evenings he felt the world was he and his mother alone having to depend on each other to survive. He remembered each night lying awake reluctant to fall asleep. He felt ill knowing he would have to go to nursery school in the morning. Morning was "harsh and brutal."

He had his first panic attack at age 3 when his mother pushed him out of the car after she threatened to do so if he did not quit misbehaving. She drove slowly beside him; however, he did not know that she would not leave him. He never forgot that. He said thereafter he toed the mark, was absolutely obedient. From age 5 to 8 he came home from school, sat in an empty house, usually in the same place in the same room, listening to the radio, frightened and waiting for his mother to come home. He felt as if he must not go out, that he might get lost. He said the feeling he had then was like his phobia.

At age 9, he became intensely anxious after his mother's remarriage. He "shadowed" his mother and stepfather everywhere. He was terrified to let his mother out of his sight. He was frightened of going out. Strangers horrified him. Two factors helped him gradually overcome his anxiety. His stepfather, who was accepting and sympathetic, bought him a bicycle. Second, a teacher took special interest in him and provided him with photographic material and equipment. The reparative effects of these two factors will be clear a bit later. He continued to have high regard for both this teacher and his stepfather who remained a part of his life even though his stepfather deserted his mother and him when he was in high school. When his stepfather left, his mother became very disturbed. Mr. G. became the man of the house. After a year his mother returned to work, but she cried on weekends. Mr. G. felt it was as if it were all a cruel joke. He would wake to her screaming. She would say she had had a dream in which she was being held by his stepfather. She said she needed to be touched. Mr. G. would hold her and look the other way. He felt disgusted. In retrospect, he was uncertain whether his disgust disguised his sexual attraction toward her. He noted she was a very attractive woman, scantily clad. His mother alternated between turning to him and casting him aside for other men. (Aside from the sexual aspect, he was expected to be grown up and to meet his mother's emotional needs.)

The things he could not forgive her for were not tangible. He asserted that her giving him her hangups and her insecurities were nothing she could have avoided. He saw her as a woman left alone with a child, not knowing what she was doing, plugging along. He wondered if he resented her for telling him to stay where he was until she got home or for placing him in the position of head of the household. He noted that parents of other teenagers were something to be against. The teenagers were having a good time. They knew where they stood. His mother, on the other hand, he decribed as erratic. He could tell her something that would please her one day. A similar thing the next day would make her angry. He would say to himself, "What did I say?" He observed he could not be against his parents as other teenagers could which he saw as a form of security. "I happen to love my mother very much and I have seen her in a very sympathetic light, which made it worse. On the other hand, I would get angry with her for not pulling herself up by her boot straps and for letting herself be walked over by men. On the other hand, I saw her so sympathetically, that's what caught me." That is what caught him; consider how thoughtful he was of her plight; not only did he have to read his mother, not she him, but also it was difficult to read her.

At one point his mother encouraged him to move out of the house to make it easier for her to take a lover, one who was Mr. G.'s age. During this period, on one occasion Mr. G. was out of town visiting an older woman whom he had been attracted to for years. On the verge of having sexual intercourse with her, he thought of his mother, became disgusted and terrified. He fled for home, realizing he was afraid to live up to his fantasies of being a sexual man of the world. This experience triggered a phobic episode. He gradually improved with treatment, but felt he never made a full recovery. He felt he had made a full recovery when he was 9 or 10, when his stepfather bought him a bicycle and his teacher provided him with photographic material. With the bicycle, "It was me going somewhere, my feet; and that was a tremendous sense of power. So that's how I got over that, I guess. And then, also, I got this identity in school. I was known as a good student, a photographer. I forgot it for ten years, just pushed it out of my mind." That he forgot completely about his past fears is what he regarded as a complete recovery.

When he had no role to play, was not the bicycler, photographer or student, he had no mental picture of himself, that is, he lost his sense of identity. He said he wished he was 20 years older, in the sense that "I will have come twenty years in some kind of work to where I am, to think, to know who I am, to not feel so flighty." His reliance on roles or symbols to define himself is like the 3-year-old's wearing a badge making him a sheriff or Piaget's daughter thinking of her sister as someone else when she was wearing her bathing suit, taking of a symbol or part object for the whole. "Whereas, this last time I've never forgotten it since I was always aware of the fact that I was doing things I hadn't done. Almost like you're unsure of your footing." As much as he got around, thereafter, he was always conscious of a period in which he had not. "It was like someone had a leash on me." He was the little, helpless, attached child or animal. He defined himself, identified himself from moment to moment, and from particle to particle, just as a 2- to 4-year-old does. The fact that as he does something and remembers he had not done it, to himself, in a significant way, he is that person who did not cope. He is unable to think of himself as a person who is doing well now although he is inclined to be phobic (a whole with parts). He is one or the other, a phobic or a person whose mind is wiped clean of any fears.

Aside from the lack of structure to his day, two other factors were significant in precipitating the phobia which caused him to see us. First, he felt inferior to his lover, since she was supporting him while he felt trapped by his emotional dependence on her. At the beginning of their relationship he had been able to walk out on her. Later he could not. Second, when he first met his girlfriend, his mother was emotionally ill and he "took charge" of mother. Just before his phobia recurred, however, his mother had found a man and was recovering. He theorized that when his mother was well and had a man, he felt insignificant and abandoned and became ill. Likewise, when he got well and found a woman, she felt abandoned, felt insignificant, and became ill. It was as though there were only two possible roles for them, the caretaker or the cared-for. All of Mr. G.'s episodes have followed a crashing of his grandiose fantasies of himself as a "big man" or a "big time operator" and "in charge." Whenever his fantasy crashed he saw himself in a passive position, a helpless child or little animal, dependent on the uncertain mercies of adults or authorities for care.

His identification with little animals and abandoned children was undisguised. (This identity while automatic was undesired and unstable.) If he saw a cat running between cars, sometimes he felt himself to be in the body of the cat or to be the cat, seeing himself in trouble and needing rescue. He had incomplete differentiation of self-representation from object-representation. Describing how he felt when his father left on vacation while Mr. G. stayed with relatives, he said he had much the same feeling he gets from people on the trolley. He is all alone. No one explains anything. "He's a little kid, like a little animal. They [children] don't understand. So don't tell them anything." When describing himself confined to the house by his phobia and hating it, he said it was like an animal in a cage. The animal hates it, but if one opens the door he may be too scared to go out. Mr. G. associated his periods of happiness with pets he had known. It was not surprising that his favorite charity was an orphanage.

His defenses were gross, at times weak. His recall was very early and vivid, suggesting a lack of repression. He was remarkably insightful into himself and into others. He had inordinate access to his motives and to his mother's.

He denied his sense of nothingness, being dead or disconnected, being an abandoned child or a small, stray animal, by becoming a triumphant hero or the essence of power itself, having power over the whole world. In his film for children there was only one person, the master puppeteer, who "pulls all the strings." If one is not pulling all the strings, one is a puppet being pulled by the strings. Once during the making of this film, Mr. G. had the feeling that he had lost control of the master puppeteer. Then he felt that he had become one of the puppets.

On the other hand, after sexual relations it was as if he had had a "narcotic." "It was not that I am Cary Grant or Erroll Flynn, but that it was a nice side of me, a strong side of me." For the moment, he identified with the supersexual movie stars. His defenses, goals, and traits were mixed. He used compulsive traits to handle narcissistic goals. For example, he took special pains in caring for abandoned animals with which he identified. However, he handled his hostile, aggressive feelings toward the animals he rescued as well as guilt over these feelings by such rituals as checking the gas jets a magic number of times (the sum of the letters in his animals' names multiplied by the number of letters in his own name). In other instances, he used compulsive rituals to assist himself in consciously constructing an identity. In spite of being a very conscientious person with certain obsessive traits and using obsessive-compulsive defenses such as undoing, he also used denial and was a very competent manipulator at times.

He was, if anything, "anti-oral." He, too easily, lost weight because he had no appetite. He did not drink or smoke. He was neat and tidy, but did not dress well or stylishly. He was frugal and saved. He saved to be sure he could buy a connection. How his buying connections worked will be clarified shortly when we discuss his dealings with cab drivers and store owners, his symbiotic connections. Suffice it to say that an obsessive trait, parsimony, served a narcissistic need. However, his narcissistic needs were primarily in terms of being connected, in terms of not being abandoned or nonexistent, rather than just in terms of narcissistic supplies as in the intuitive character.

On one occasion, Mr. G.'s thinking was concrete. He failed to differentiate a symbol from the thing it represented. When a woman suggested he study abroad, he said, "These are things I felt intuitively about myself. To be an artist, you have to get out. You can't be locked up within yourself. You have to go out and see the world. This is what I was doing earlier this year. I picked up my camera and did studies in different spots. But then I couldn't drive, and after a bit I couldn't even go out the door." He responded concretely to the suggestion as if being worldly required taking pictures in different locations. This is similar to Jacqueline's saying that camomile tea is yellow; therefore ripe, and the oranges must be yellow or ripe. She had no abstract concept of ripeness; yellow equalled ripe.

Like Piaget's daughter in the example above, Mr. G. did not fully differentiate fantasy and/or word from thing or event. One of his fears was of being on the street where there were no shops and therefore no people, only automobiles going by with mechanical men in them. "It's not like they're real people in the car. It's like they are machines—robots." He went into considerable detail about drivers who were like robots, not looking to the right or left, completely impersonal. "A man in a machine becomes a machine or part of a machine. He is like a robot, rigid. His arms are stiff and connected to the wheel. His eyes are straight ahead and connected to the road. It looks like a picture going by. The driver, having lost his humanity, does not have the power to help me if I have an attack." Mr. G. lost his ability to distinguish the boundaries between one object and another or between a symbol and its object when he saw a man in a machine becoming a part of the machine, that is, he was making a symbol into an object. In his feeling that the robots could not help him he had essentially reified his fantasy regarding robots much like a 3-year-old who thinks he is the sheriff when he wears the sheriff's badge or that he is writing a letter when he imitates daddy's doing so (Maier, 1965).

When Mr. G. telephoned someone, sometimes he was surprised that another person could be "present" on the telephone. He did not have object constancy (perhaps permanence). He had to see or hear the other person to be sure he was there. There must be a tangible connection. This kind of thinking (although it is the inverse) is similar to Jacqueline's thinking, when she checked the house to see whether her uncle had truly gone even though she had seen him drive off (Piaget, 1962a).

Mr. G., to a significant extent, defined himself by externals and defined externals on the basis of internals; that is, the boundaries between self- and object-representation were blurred. Depending on his affect state he saw his wife as a selfish, greedy, unresponsive person, or a fat, repulsive "blob" or a desirable, unattainable sex object or a small, whining animal that needed rescue. Thus, he had multiple images of his wife, rather than a fused image, plus a failure in self-object differentiation; that is, the whining animal that needed rescue is his own picture of himself. His multiple images of his wife are no different than Mahler's description of lack of object constancy prior to the age of 3. It is the same as Jacqueline in the symbolic stage having separate images of her little sister. During the symbolic stage the self and object are made up of multiple images: Jacqueline in the photo, Jacqueline in the mirror, etc., and Lucienne in a bathing suit, Lucienne in her street clothes. During the same stage two similar objects, e.g., slugs on the path, are the same.

Similar to his identity diffusion when he felt like the cat who was in danger, he displayed an undifferentiation between self and objects in terms of goals and needs. As mentioned, when he encountered a stray animal he had to take it home, if he could find no one else to do so. In one instance when on his way to work, he saw a dog skitter away under a warehouse. He went on to work, but could not help worrying about the dog. In the middle of his work day he returned to look for the dog. Able to see him, but unable to coax him out, Mr. G. then purchased some hamburger and left it for the dog. He reasoned that it was Friday, that over the weekend the area was deserted and that there would be no garbage for the dog to eat. Also, when hiring extras he had to interview all the applicants immediately, in spite of his time limitations. He was concerned that the applicants might go hungry. He projected his fears of abandonment and starvation onto them. At the same time, their goals, their wanting to be hired, essentially defined his function without his having any concern for pacing himself.

From the above example, it is clear that in the usual sense he had an autonomous superego, a stringent one. That is, he did not require the presence of an external reinforcement in order for him to adhere to a moral code. Neither did he project guilt or blame. In another sense, however, in the sense of failure of self-object differentiation, his superego codes were not autonomous at all, since the situation defined his obligation and since quite clearly he was caring for himself when he cared for the abandoned strays and starving job-seekers.

Prominent and presumably primary for his identity was the undifferentiation between his mother and himself. The recurrence of his mother's illness, and especially the fact that her symptoms were the same as he had had before, made him feel he would not get well, that underneath he would still be ill. His proof that he was subject to recurrent illness resting on his mother's having the same symptoms as his was an example of transductive reasoning. He reasoned from particle to particle, that is, symptom to symptom and symptom to illness, no different from Piaget's daughter's reasoning about the hunchback's illness or about the ripeness of oranges.

He was told by a previous therapist that he was not his mother. He said, "I know I'm not my mother. I can't separate it." He felt that if it could happen to her again, it could happen to him, that one does not get well. "When you're well it's a mask. It is like you're a good actor. Underneath is this sickness."

When he had a "truimph" in his work, such as selling an idea to the producer, Mr. G. had the feeling that he was one power pulling the strings. If he could not sell the idea he felt passive, helpless, and panic-stricken. A single event defined him including his value as a person.

Not having attained self-constancy, Mr. G. tried to integrate his experience, force his perception into memory to fix in his mind that he had had an experience. He practiced the memory so he could call on it and not be dependent on perception alone. When, on occasion, he had overcome his fear of walking down a certain street, at the end of the walk he looked at the heels of his shoes and repeatedly told himself, "These shoes have walked down Sunset Boulevard." Then he counted up to 10, the number of letters of his first and last names combined, equating the number to the number of toes on his feet that walked down Sunset Boulevard. His intent was to impress upon himself that he really had accomplished the feat. He believed that if he could retain the sense of the experience he might be able to repeat it and walk down Sunset Boulevard again. The issue was one of identity. He was trying to define himself as a person who walks down Sunset Boulevard. He is defining himself at each step by parts. To the extent he defined himself in terms of part functions, his walking down Sunset Boulevard or his riding a bicycle, he exhibited a failure in differentiation of part self from whole self.

He did not distinguish an event from his action upon it or a part of the event. For example, if he saw a building that he had filmed at a previous time now being destroyed, depending on whether he was feeling negatively or positively about himself, he believed that his previous filming of it had either caused its destruction or that in fact it was not being destroyed since he had already preserved it on film. His response was much like

Jacqueline's being frightened at seeing herself on the mountain-side in a photograph, or her talking about herself as if she were a different person in the mirror than she was otherwise. Mr. G., like Piaget's daughter, was seeing a representation of an object as an object itself. Mr. G. was also failing to differentiate his own action on an object from the object. One fact of interest is that whether Mr. G. was feeling good or feeling bad, his cognition, that is, his reality testing, was not any better. He still was inclined to think his photograph influenced the existence of the building. When he was feeling good about himself, however, his general function in life was improved greatly. He could do things. He felt like a man, etc.

When seeking to make sense of the world, the symbolic-stage child looks for design or pattern, if asked to group discs and squares, he makes a house or a train. When trying to understand correspondences, for example, which strength chain will lift which size box, he will choose on the basis of pattern rather than attribute. Wagner (1975), an associate of Piaget's, provided children with a series of different size boxes, A through E, and a series of color-coded chains, 1 to 5, in order of strength; that is, E, the heaviest house, could be lifted only by chain 5, any other chain would break. At one stage of understanding a child who learns that chain 1 will hold box A, may predict that chain 1 will break with B, C, and D, but not E. Similarly, he may predict a neighboring box will be lifted by the chain in question. He is looking to pattern for under-standing. Essentially, Mr. G. uses the same kind of reasoning. At a time of success, for instance, walking alone down Sunset Boulevard, if someone opened a drape so he could see the lighted window or if he saw a falling star, etc., he took this event as a sign that he would be able to retain and repeat the experience.

He saw the world as a design or picture where all things fit together much as the child believes in design as explanation or believes in parental order. Neither Mr. G. nor a child makes provision for chance. If Mr. G. had filmed a building and it was being destroyed, he must somehow connect these events. That is, of course, how the child learns and without his greed and facility to connect events (to assimilate), he could not learn. It is the essence of transductive, egocentric reasoning—intake. Mr. G. was arrested at this stage in a significant part of his thought process.

Mr. G. saw the therapist as a caretaker whom he paid for the service. In the beginning, whenever he panicked at being alone and needed to feel "connected" to someone, he phoned the therapist. At other times he did not call but connected to the therapist by chanting to himself something the therapist had said. Often what had been said had not been particularly helpful. There was usually something about the form of the sentence or some kind of symbolism in the sentence that struck Mr. G. as a revealed truth. Even if there were no particular sense to the statement out of context, it comforted Mr. G. and reconfirmed his connection with the therapist. Prior to consulting us for psychotherapy he tried to treat himself by repeating to himself the words of his previous therapist, "What do I get out of this?" This chant eased his sense of helplessness and sense of passivity. He felt in charge over the panic, not it over him. These sing song chants, out of context and idiosyncratic, often helped. Sometimes they symbolized the connection to the powerful one, sometimes they symbolized being powerful. In addition to their being a semitangible connection, they exemplified part-whole undifferentiation. The symbol was taken for the thing.

The theme of paid connections, the re-creation of the symbiotic position, ran through Mr. G.'s history. In order to get a response from others to deny his aloneness he was willing to pay. Paying was a part of it, just as good behavior and listening to mother and father were. When he was seven he could offer to share baseball cards with his friends; later he became a practiced and charming story teller, a concerned and attentive listener. He always had money in his pocket so that at any time, if he started to panic, he could legitimize his going into a store and conversing with the shopkeeper. If necessary, he was prepared to buy something to keep the contact going.

He rode in taxis. [On a bus] "I'm in-between, terrified, no one to talk to, except a bunch of hostile faces that are looking at me, and it drives me nuts." If he took a cab, he could exchange a few words with the cab driver, "just ask him how he is, not a running conversation." He felt he would not panic, or if he did panic, the cab driver would get him to his appointment or any other destination. "The cab driver isn't impersonal, contrary to what people think, and he'll talk to me. . . .We don't have to talk about profound things. I can just ask him if he lives in the Valley. He'll talk back to me. There's an exchange of communication. That's someone who told me I'm alive, because he heard my question and answered it." It is apparent that he was uncertain whether he existed as a live object. He went on to discuss his fear of death, being in the ground, people walking over him, and being cut off from everyone. Being cut off from everyone was also what he feared in being hospitalized.

In his film of the master puppeteer at one point he felt the master puppeteer was free when the strings were cut. At another time as mentioned he felt he had lost control of the master puppeteer and had become a puppet. Again, the symbiosis is re-created—the powerful and the powerless, the caretaker and the cared-for—all connected by cords, with a constant vascillation or confusion as to who is "in charge," just as in his relationship with his mother.

Symbiosis, the connectedness, the role swapping—now the child is the mother, now the mother is the child—the failure to have separate identities is no different in Mr. G. than in the 2- to 4-year-old, who, at times, has object and self fused together, that is, not separate one from the other and, at times, has multiple separate images of the self or of an object.

Although examples of concrete operational and intuitive social cognition were manifest by Mr. G., the basic organization of his social cognition paralleled that of the cognition of the 2- to 4-year-old. The basic organization of Mrs. R.'s social cognition, on the other hand, paralleled the cognition of the 5- to 7-year-old. Finally, Mr. S.'s social cognition paralleled the cognition of the 8- to 11-year-old. The isomorphism between the thinking of the symbolic character and that of the symbolic-stage child, between the intuitive character and the intuitive-stage child, and between the thinking of the operational character and the concrete-operational-stage child are striking and abiding as well as coherent and relatively exclusive.

Chapter 8

SUPEREGO FORMATION

Inherent in our concept of the three character structures is the idea that the child's superego, his system of goods or bads, is constructed from his understandings of his relationships with his caretakers. Once into the Concrete Operational Period, a child has the maturational option that enables him to have an understanding of a value or attribute that is separate from any number of appearances of the attribute and yet coordinates these appearances. The cognitive ability that allows for construction of attributes of physical or social objects is the same. However, the variation in social interrelationships results in major variations in children's understandings of the attributes of the social world.

We differ from Piaget (1965a) in that we postulate that protective parenting, not interaction with peers, leads to development of an autonomous superego. We think the objects that a child encounters again and again in his social world are his parents, his caretakers. It is the dimensions of these encounters, not the encounters with his peers, that he integrates into his superego. He encounters his caretakers especially around issues which involve his needs and hence his affects. In their interaction with their child, the caretakers show him that they are safe, protective, hostile, indifferent, needful, undifferentiated, confusing, etc. They provide him with the data and models which he must coordinate to understand his social world. In keeping with interactions between himself and his parents, a child constructs certain attributes concerning persons and himself, that persons do what they say or not, that they are fair or not to him, that they are available when needed or not, that he needs a great deal or not, that they protect him in accordance with what he needs or not, etc. This type of construction of attributes of persons, the child's social world, then forms the basic attitudes the child takes toward others and himself as social beings.*

Piaget's concept of development of moral judgment, that is, development of an autonomous superego, was much like his concept of how a child learns conservation tasks: A child encounters different people, principally peers, and their values until he is forced by their discrepant viewpoints (when he has achieved an appropriate developmental stage enabling him to entertain more than one viewpoint at a time) to construct a superordinate system of values. In his system are coordinated these different people's values in the same manner as different views or perceptions of things are coordinated in a concept of quantity or length.

Piaget saw the autonomous superego as a natural outgrowth of development, a product of a child's interacting with

*We distinguish between the person or self as a social being and the person or self as a thing. Some person cognition studies have focused on the child's developing knowledge of persons as things. For example, these studies investigated when a child recognizes that a person or the self is made up of a trunk as well as limbs and a head (Lemke, 1973). This type of study of person cognition is not the kind of study of person or self cognition that interests us here.

the environment, provided his parents did not impede this process. We see the autonomous superego as one possible outcome, a function of a child's understanding of protective caretakers.

Piaget (1965a, p. 373) wrote that P. Bovet's work "was the true begetter of our results." Bovet proposed two prerequisites for the formation of a moral code: One, the individual must receive commands from another person; two, the individual receiving the commands must respect that other person and therefore accept the command. A third factor is provided by the child's use of reason to unify contradictory or conflicting commands from his parents and between his parents and other respected individuals. According to Bovet, the child initially sees his parents as perfect. When the child is disappointed at discovery of a fault in his parents, the child transfers these demands for perfection to ideal beings of the culture. The good comes to free itself from custom and the subject's ideal goes beyond that of those who inspire it as he must coordinate and establish hierarchies of the various influences. ". . . If the child accepts the morality of the group, he does so as it is embodied in respected beings" (Piaget, 1965a, p. 378). That is, parents in their commands are, on-balance, transmitters of the rules of society.

Piaget felt Bovet's theory had a defect, failure to distinguish respect toward a superior, that is heteronomous respect, from respect toward an equal, that is mutual respect. Piaget did not believe an autonomous conscience might be formed from relationships involving only respect for a superior. He argued that the child's contact with his peers, who are not as solicitous as his parents and who confront him with their codes and intents, stimulate him to use his reason to integrate these conflicting codes. Piaget contended that, once the child is out of the Preoperational Period, in relationship with peers there is a new ingredient, mutual respect, the ability to see another's point of view. Piaget asserted that out of unilateral respect there can only be morals based on constraint. (This in a sense is true. However, the appropriately protective parent respects his child's integrity and limitations.) With the cognitive achievement of being able to see from another view, including another's intent or wish, it becomes possible to assimilate the multiple points of view of peers* and then to coordinate them into autonomous codes, that is, conscience (Piaget goes into a complicated formulation of this process in *The Moral Judgment of the Child,* p. 383).

An additional support employed in arguing that an autonomous superego is based on interaction between equals was Piaget's contention that over the course of history social structures have evolved from authoritarian structures toward democratic ones. His implication was that social evolution and individual development reflect one another.

Whether Piaget still adhered to the concept that interaction among equals is a *sine qua non* in the child's passing from morality of the Preoperational Period to morality of the Concrete Operational Period is unclear. In his more recent book, co-authored with Inhelder, *The Psychology of the Child* (1969), although he detailed some of P. Bovet's constructs he made no mention of parents being absent while peers take over, the mechanism he proposed in *The Moral Judgment of the Child* (1965a), originally published in 1932. In *Play, Dreams, and Imitation in Childhood* (1962a), he did not address the function of peers. He put forward his basic concept that development of moral codes is one function within a system of values that develops out of the preoperational structure into an operational structure.

Piaget's study of development of morality focused heavily on the development of rules for the game of marbles. Piaget pointed out that alongside the actual rules of a game, "consti-

---

*Twice in *The Moral Judgment of the Child* (pp. 137 and 319), Piaget addressed the possibility of parents, rather than just peers, playing a role in the child's progress toward coordination of differing points of view into an autonomous conscience. He indicated that only to the extent that the parent functioned like an equal, that is, like a peer, would the parent facilitate such progress.

tuted rules," is evident another kind of rules, that is "constitutive rules," for example, the belief that an innovation which demands less skill or less cleverness is not a suitable way to play. Such an innovation is thought of by the child as unfair because it depends on luck. When a child by mistake put down a valuable marble instead of one with lesser value, all children agreed it would be unscrupulous for one of the other players to knock this marble out of the square and keep it unless the shooter stated a special word. So it was regarded as unfair to just sneak a shot at it. Here, sneaking was forbidden. To be a good constituted rule, the rule must embrace the constitutive rules.

We wish to emphasize that the child's concept that skill, taking risks, and fair play are considered to be moral while doing things the easy way, in accordance with chance or by sneaking are considered to be immoral or bad. These qualities or values, the constitutive rules, are all inherent in playing any game of rules or in being interested in rules at all. Piaget proposed that constitutive rules are to constituted rules as an organ is to its function; a circular relationship. He implied thereby that there is very little difference between constituted and constitutive rules. We like Piaget's analogy of the difference between an organ and its function. It seems to us, however, that one has to grow, that is develop, an organ and that function derives from the organ, not necessarily an organ from function (unless one is willing to wait out an evolutionary epoch). We think it is likely that Piaget in his study of marble players was studying a group of children who had a well-developed sense of constitutive rules. We think he was studying how moral children learn to play marbles.

Piaget went on to say the rational rule (constituted and constitutive) is due to mutual respect. He asserted that a child, if freed of adult or older generation constraint and allowed to play with his equals, will develop such a system. He stressed the fact that older children lose interest in marbles and thus leave the younger ones free to interact with each other. Thus, there is no longer an older group of marble players repressing the younger ones. Because of this the younger children are now free to interact, because of this they may cooperate and develop rational rules. He saw the Intuitive Stage of the Preoperational Period as one of imbalance while the 11-year-old's smooth performance in the game demonstrated the child had found a state of equilibrium as a social being. He had "re-discovered the schema [sic] of experimental legality and rational regularity practiced by the baby. . . ." The eleven-year-old submits "to the norms of reciprocity. The motor being and the social being are one. Harmony is achieved by the union of reason and nature" (Piaget, 1965a, p. 100). Piaget saw the organism, if unimpeded, tending toward higher order equilibrations as it interacted with the environment. We do not see equilibration as if it were a driving force, however, but rather that the organism always organizes or equilibrates, given its state and its experiencing of input.

Our understanding of superego construction assumes that the underlying developing cognitive structure provides options that are exercised or not, depending on the social aliment available. Our view is consonant with Lickona's (1976, p. 239). Acknowledging Piaget's broad developmental outline for conscience, Lickona wrote, "children's moral judgments do not exist in a social or cultural vacuum . . . they are very much subject to direct and indirect social influence both in their rate of development and, at least for some judgmental dimensions, in the shape they take in adulthood."

Following Piaget, we see superego development as one product of the cognitive structure, a structure which processes both social and physical data. Superego formation rests upon the child's ability to embrace an abiding value or attribute of goodness and badness much as he embraces the concept of quantity or length. We see morality as a construct of the ultimate (long-term) good for the self, good on-balance, bad on-balance, taking into account different views. The differing views which must be taken into account in a superego are the attitudes, acts, and verbalizations of the parents, in interaction with their child and those shown by example.

The 7- or 8-year-old is cognitively ready to construct concepts that take into account different views. Having constructed relatively stable person (as a thing) and thing object representations as he leaves the Symbolic Stage, a child is confronted with apparent discrepancies in the appearance or presentation of those objects. Pouring a quantity of liquid from one container to another, the height of the liquid increases while its width decreases; the liquid object, once transformed, may be transformed into its original appearance if placed in its original container. In the Concrete Operational Period, these transformations are included in a child's construct of the concept of quantity. He reorganizes his thinking so that his momentary perception becomes only one parameter in his integrated understanding of objects of the physical world.

Likewise, in the moral sphere, he is cognitively able to do the same thing. His parents* also offer discrepant appearing dimensions to the child. They provide him with food, clothing, cuddle him, show him approval and respect, and otherwise offer him nice things, all very pleasant. At the same time, they may send him to bed without dinner, spank him, disapprove of him, and violate his autonomy. An Intuitive-Stage child could be expected to see the caretaker's behavior as discrepant, for instance, punishing him sometimes, sometimes not; praising him sometimes, sometimes not. The question is, do they do this generally based on their concern for the welfare of the child? If they spank him when he plays with matches and wait for him and even praise him when he ties his shoes slowly, yet punish him when he dawdles in the street, then the concrete-operational child is at a stage of development such that he is able to construct an operational concept of goodness-for-him, socially,

---

*By parents—as noted previously—we mean those person-objects who provide the caretaking function for the child; it could be a Kibbutz.

as presented by the social world he knows. It is the same as when he is able to construct an operational concept of quantity that coordinates surface discrepant appearances, e.g., high in one container and low in another. Included with his system of ultimate goods and evils for him that he constructs are the things or events his caretakers claim or indicate are good or evil. During this period of cognitive development, it is possible for him to construct operational systems of codes, an autonomous superego.

Obviously, this construction in the social sphere is more difficult to make than it is in the physical sphere. A ball of clay is still the same amount no matter how its shape is changed. With the behavior of human beings, this kind of predictability is not possible. A parent, when he is ill or harassed, may not be concerned with what is good or bad for his child. A parent's behavior may vary depending on whether he is out in public or at home and whether he is tired or rested. Similarly, a child's interpretation may vary, depending on his state or situation. It is very likely that in this dimension, the formation of a concept of social values, person cognition lags behind thing cognition in contrast to other cognitive function. However, if on-balance the parent punishes the child when he does something bad for himself, permits or rewards him when he does something good for himself, the child should be able to develop an operational system of goodnesses and badnesses (for his social world) just as he develops an operational system of length or quantity.

The cognitive mechanism involved in autonomous superego formation likely parallels that required in construction of an understanding that quantity is conserved. An autonomous operational system of codes, a mature superego, embraces coordinated, but different points of view, different perceptions. It coordinates history and compensating dimensions. The child is able to judge ultimate good for himself, a balanced understanding of his fittings into the world and his fittings into his family.

The mechanism is available to all three (future) character types regardless of the type of parenting they have experienced. However, what is integrated within or by a code is dependent on the type of experience that is available to be integrated. As we have described, a child who has a history of stable, interested parenting has the task of integrating surface discrepancies (that is, being punished when he does something bad for himself and rewarded when he does something good for himself) into a coherent organization. He becomes the operational character who has an autonomous superego. He is function-oriented and capable of considerable (seemingly) selfless function in the service of his codes.

On the other hand, the child who experiences absent, erratic unreliable, nonprotective parenting has essentially nothing discrepant to integrate into abiding principles of what is good (for him) in his social world. What he sees is what he gets. Hence, he keeps the heteronomous superego of the Intuitive Stage. A child who on-balance experiences neglect or deprivation, one who will likely grow up to be an intuitive character, is not learning ultimate, long-term goods and bads (for himself) from his caretakers. His parents may promise to get him something later if he does something now that they wish, for example, be quiet, not be a nuisance. Later, when his parents are not feeling any pinch, the reward may not come. He has surface discrepant perceptions to coordinate into an abiding principle, but they do not deal with long-term good. The discrepancies he must embrace are between promise (now) and payoff (later), the words and deeds of his caretakers. He must construct his abstract good for himself coordinating his observation that the words and deeds of his caretakers may not agree, that promises will not be kept, that he had better take what is available now, that his caretaker, his social world, responds in accord with the caretaker's own needs at a given time. The future intuitive knows that when something that appears good comes along, he had better take it. It is not likely to come along later when he needs it more. When something comes along that is bad, he had better try to avoid it. He cannot count on balancing out if he delays. He experiences that his caretakers do not watch out for him, keep him from getting into trouble. He is not spanked or punished for his own good. He recognizes that it is when he causes trouble that he is punished, that he is punished for the parent's good, when the parent feels like it.* Since he senses that when he is punished it is usually not for his own good, there is nothing to coordinate. It just hurts. Taking the bad his parents dish out to him will not provide him with an eventual, more satisfactory payoff. His 5- to 7-year-old intuitive position with regard to social cognition fits his social world. He has no delusion that the outside world (as exemplified by his "caretaker") has his interests at heart. The outside world takes what it wants. He takes what he wants, but he has to keep an eye on the outside world, the other takers.

The future symbolic character, subject to a mother who is protective, but protective in terms of her own fears and needs, protective provided certain of her own needs are met, will have a much more difficult job in integrating the complex disparities he confronts. Generally, the caretakers of symbolics are not neglectful once their emotional needs are taken care of. A given mother such as Mr. B.'s mother had to feel her child was not frightened (as she had been). As long as Mr. B. showed no fright his mother was a good caretaker. He developed a stringent, abiding, autonomous (in the usual sense) conscience. To the extent that, in her pursuit of her "ideal child," the mother is focused on herself, her child will experience a kind of neglect and hence may be expected to manifest qualities more like an intuitive character.

Strictly speaking, we are not proposing a lag-explanation of differential superego development. We propose that the child merely organizes his constructs of his social world as he experi-

*The matrix out of which the child constructs his understandings is described in its extreme form. Obviously a parent must consider a child's welfare to a considerable degree for the child to survive.

ences it, given his stage of development. He draws on his symbolic, intuitive, or operational organizing system because one of the three best organizes his understanding of his social world. Protective parenting is aliment that is coordinated into the autonomous superego found in an operational character, while neglectful parenting is "coordinated" into the heteronomous superego of the intuitive character. The symbolic superego may have either an autonomous or heteronomous style, but will also show an undifferentiation between part self and whole self or self and object.

Our proposals imply that physical and social cognition are separate subfunctions of basic cognitive maturation. Both may vary from each other, but are expected to co-vary with age. This is precisely what Sullivan and Hunt (1967), as well as Rubin (1973), reported. If age is parcelled out there is no clear unitary factor between personal and impersonal role taking, the ability to understand another's perspective in a social or physical context. Wolfson (1972) asked subjects ranging in age from 4 to 30 whether when they were older if they would be the same or different. She found that development of their understanding of identity of self paralleled their understanding of identity of a quasi-plant (a chemical that appeared to grow like a plant when placed in water) and of identity of a piece of clay (transformed from a ball into a cylinder). At the same time, she found that reasoning about identity of the self tended to lag behind reasoning about the identity of the plant which in turn lagged behind reasoning about the identity of the clay. Our position, supported by these findings, is that conscience and social cognition may not keep pace with physical cognition although they are both subject to the same developmental organizing phases.

Turiel (1977) viewed physical and social cognition as completely separate. He subdivided social cognition into three distinct domains, one processing moral data, another, data involving the psychology of individuals, and the third, data related to social conventions. He contended that the different domains merely exchanged information, were not structurally interdependent. Like Turiel, we think that the social domain is separate from the physical domain and we subscribe to his argument that the available aliment significantly affects the final forms constructed in the different domains. We think convention and moral domains have the same origin, however, and would expect them to start to differentiate from each other during the Intuitive Stage. Often enough, in the automatic function of adults, convention is not clearly differentiated from morality as when adults feel virtuous in mistreating a member of an outgroup. Damon (1977), studied younger children than those studied by Turiel and, in contrast to Turiel, found that morality and convention did not begin as separate domains, but were distinguished by the likelihood of punishment for the former as opposed to the latter. Damon's subjects reasoned that a child in a story was not as likely to be punished if he wore a dress or played with a doll or for eating with his hands (all breaches of convention) as he would be if he stole (a moral transgression).

We are particularly interested in Damon's observation that a child's voluntary obedience around 7 or 8 ". . . is based on the belief that the authority figures' power and superiority . . . [will] . . . work to the advantage of the self. Obedience is the price one pays for this advantage" (p. 113). This finding supports our formulation that the Concrete-Operational child constructs his superego based on his perception of his long-term (if any) interests as demonstrated by his parents. Damon reported that one child chose his team captain on the basis of who was the best hitter, another on the basis of who was the hardest worker. Damon pointed out that the logic is the same. This is true certainly; however, the question remains, where do these criteria come from and why are they different? These criteria are constitutive rules, which we propose, in their primordial form, derive from the interaction between child and caretaker.

In construction of a mature superego a child need not test every dimension. He would merely have to believe that what Daddy and Mommy say is good is generally good for him and what they say is bad is generally bad for him. Thus, there is allowance for many defects or idiosyncrasies in such integrations.

One 7-year-old's mother, a modern non-Jew, wanted her child to learn about the manner in which Jews celebrated Hanukkah. She brought her youngster over to their neighbors, the Millsteins, a family of red-headed Jews. After witnessing the celebration of the holiday, the 7-year-old's mother said, "Now that you've seen how the Millsteins celebrate the Jewish holiday, we will go over to the Goldbergs and see how they celebrate the Jewish holiday." Her youngster responded, "The Goldbergs aren't Jewish. They don't have red hair."

We have no idea how many "red heads" are in our concepts of Jewishness or goodness or badness, or other concepts. We think it is likely that, raised in an appropriate setting, an operational character is capable of holding immoral views or performing very immoral acts. We think that he might be more resistant to group pressure provided his codes and the group's codes did not match. If his codes and the group's codes did match or if one of the codes of the particular operational character was to abide by social mores, however, then we would expect him to be capable of participating in group atrocities. Here we differ from Piaget who saw a democratic orientation as a sign of a mature superego. We think a person may have a mature, that is, an autonomous, principled system of codes and be fascist or royalist, theist or atheist.

An example of the blind spot or idiosyncrasy in an adult operational character's conceptualization was evidenced by an otherwise sophisticated psychiatric resident who burst out in a seminar that a mother would not behave toward her child as the seminar leader described. The seminar leader had described a mother who directed her hate verbally and physically toward her child. Even though this resident "knew better" then, and subsequently corrected that part of his system of codes to some extent, his concepts continued to show such irrational tendencies, which had to be corrected consciously from time to time. He continued to think all mothers were basically devoted to their children just as he thought his mother had been.

As we have pointed out, there is room for blind spots and idiosyncrasies within the autonomous superego, so there is room for inclusion of various cultural and subcultural goodnesses and badnesses (conventions). Further, our proposal that protective parenting is a prerequisite for autonomous superego formation fits with the fact that, as noted earlier, operational characters generally are invested in the codes of their culture. This could be expected to follow since for autonomous superego formation to take place, the basic role of the parent is to protect the child. The process of appropriate protection would include inculcating certain cultural codes. The rules and roles provided by an appropriately protective family generally would not be too much different from those of their culture or subculture (including the neighborhood children's) or else it is likely that the parents would not be concerned with their child's overall welfare.* Hence, the content included in the codes of a youngster who has a mature superego may be expected to correspond to those held valuable by his subculture.

In describing conscience formation, including how certain errors as well as cultural conventions may be incorporated into an autonomous conscience, we do not imply that our description is a complete explanation of the course of development of moral codes or cultural conventions. Obviously, final organizations for ideational, verbal and behavioral expression of morality or convention in the adult is very complex, the product of current and past interactions.

Three factors in our concept of superego development differ from Piaget's. The first is that the dimensions that are

---

*This could be an unconscious process along the lines described by Erikson (1950).

coordinated in the child's set of moral codes, his conscience, come from his relationship to his caretakers rather than from his relationship to his peers. The second is that if the parents are on-balance understood by the child to be appropriately protective of him, he will be able to differentiate, that is, construct, a superordinate system of codes of goodnesses and badnesses which coordinate surface discrepant dimensions. Finally, we suggest that a critical mechanism for autonomous superego formation is identification with the example set by these trustworthy parents. This last factor will be addressed at the end of this chapter.

Supporting Literature

Since we are introducing a new typology, it is not strange that we cannot draw upon existing literature that directly corroborates or explains our syndromes. Rather, we must extrapolate from studies of established clinical syndromes. For example, from studies of delinquency we may infer the genesis of the heteronomous superego function, hence intuitive character formation (even though we know that any group of delinquents will include symbolic characters along with intuitive characters, and that many intuitives are not delinquent.) Such studies offer some support to our concepts.

As Hogan (1973) has pointed out, clearly Piaget was mistaken when he contended that instrumental to autonomous superego function is interaction with peers. In order to realize that peers raise adults who have sorely defective superegos, one need merely consider the studies of the "Bezprizorniye" (Garbarino and Bronfenbrenner, 1976), the nine million child victims of the chaos and neglect of World War I in Russia, who left to their own devices became a public menace. Similarly, case histories of San Quentin prisoners confirm the correlation between uncaring, erratic, disrupted caretaking and impaired moral function. Glueck and Glueck's (1950) and Bowlby's (1944) studies of delinquents also support the position that neglect spawns heteronomous superego function. Gould (1972) found that good parenting correlated with moral behavior while poor parenting correlated with delinquent behavior.

Gould's theoretical position differed from ours. She saw the concept of a superego precursor as specious, while we think an important distinction is made in the concept of superego precursor since it is the type of superego that intuitive characters have, a heteronomous superego. As we have pointed out, intuitive characters (and many symbolic characters) tend to project their guilt outside (perhaps fail to internalize guilt is the more accurate way of describing their style of function), and do not have an abiding, demarcated system of codes, separate from self or setting. Much influenced by Melanie Klein, Gould was inclined to see the superego as developed very early in childhood. She took the fact that a very young child may feel badly about things that he does as evidence of his having a fully developed superego. We have no argument that little children can feel bad or that intuitive characters can feel bad. In fact, although intuitive characters are usually successful in externalizing blame, when they fail to do so they are vulnerable to more intense self-condemnation than is an operational character. Our argument is to the contrary that the self-condemnation of the operational character is modulated in intensity and demarcated, in the part of the self that is condemned as well as the kinds of transgressions which will call self-condemnation into play at all. Like Piaget, we think that the ability to dissociate a value system is unavailable to the child until about 7 or 8, and it is this dissociation of a coherent, coordinated system of values that is a hallmark of the autonomous superego as opposed to mere presence or absence of self-condemnation.

Becker (1964) distilled the findings of a very large number of studies of consequences of parental discipline. His system for analysis integrated complex and, on the surface, conflicting results by dividing parental behavior along two axes, one extending from warmth to hostility and the other from permissiveness to restrictiveness. Generally, measures on these two axes were independent of each other; that is, a parent who was warm toward his children might be permissive or restrictive, and the same was true for a hostile parent. This division of the data netted consistent findings. Lax-hostile, that is neglectful parents tended to have delinquent, noncompliant and maximally aggressive offspring. Parents who used love-oriented techniques for shaping, for example, praise or reasoning, had children who showed signs of internalized reactions to transgressions (feelings of guilt, self responsibility, and confusion*) and used nonaggressive cooperative measures in social relations; while parents who used power-assertive techniques had children who manifested externalized reactions (that is, heteronomous superego function) to transgressions, e.g., fear of punishment, projected hostility and noncooperative, aggressive behavior. A mother's withdrawal of love as punishment for transgressions correlated with signs of conscience in her child only if that mother had a warm relationship with her child (only if the child had something to lose). Erratic or inconsistent discipline, both within and between parents, correlated with antisocial behavior or, among nondelinquent boys, correlated with aggressiveness. Finally, in one study, maximum adult role taking in doll play occurred in children who had warm, permissive parents while in another study children who had warm, restrictive mothers were maximum rule enforcers at age 12.

The major thrust of Becker's analysis of studies of consequences of discipline in child-rearing supports our findings and reconstruction—that operational characters who have demarcated, abiding superegos, have had concerned, interested par-

---

*It is interesting that confusion was one of the dimensions in view of the fact that as we noted many symbolic characters have overly stringent superegos. The reader perhaps should be reminded that inconsistency of the behavior of parents of symbolic characters is an inconsistency in terms of the innards of the child, hence the confusion. The parents' behavior may be very consistent with some particular external matter, e.g., making mother look like a good mother to herself or proper etiquette, hence may provide particularly consistent aliment for superego formation.

ents, while intuitive characters who have poorly encapsulated, easily externalized systems of moral judgment and one of whose pathologic prototypes is the impulsive personality, have been subject to erratic or neglectful caretaking. These studies suggest that in children identification with adults including incorporation of their rules is facilitated by parents' caring about their children, regardless of whether the parents are permissive or restrictive. Depending on whether the parents are permissive or restrictive, a child then has a different quality with which to identify or different behavior to coordinate.

Some additional findings cited by Becker pointed to the complexity of sex and age variables. For instance, girls raised by severely punitive mothers were inhibited in aggressive behavior in school, but did not inhibit their aggressiveness in doll play or when they were at home. They engaged in symbolic aggression, just as the intuitive character may engage in symbolic impulsivity or stealing. None of the findings analyzed by Becker contradict our thesis.

Both peer interaction and a shift toward a democratic ethic are parts of Piaget's thesis expressed in *The Moral Judgment of the Child.* As we have said, we do not think that peer interaction is a necessary or standard route toward development of an autonomous superego. Neither do we think that the human organism has some overall inherent tendency to develop toward embracing democratic precepts. Kohlberg (1964) reported that children do not become more democratic as they develop nor is there a shift in children from unilateral respect for adults to mutual respect for peers. Children raised in a Kibbutz, where emphasis was on peer group morality were no more other-intention oriented than children raised in ordinary families (Kugelmass and Breznitz, 1967). Chinese-American children who were more closely tied to their families were ahead of white American children in their moral development as measured by development of a subjective concept of responsibility (ability to take into account intent rather than the amount of damage caused) (Liu, 1976).

These findings and the others on delinquency are difficult to explain in terms of interactions with peers being a primary building block in construction of a mature superego or by parents being required to step aside to allow for the normal course of moral development to take place. We do not dismiss interaction with peers as an important factor in socialization. However, we do not think it is usually a primary factor in autonomous superego formation. It may be a primary factor in superego formation in a given family or circumstance (Freud & Dann, 1951) in which caretaker function is given over to peers. We also know of persons who have used peer interaction as a corrective device when child-parent interaction was somewhat faulty. When interaction with peers (not older siblings) is primary in superego formation, we do not expect development of an operational character to result.

Chandler (1977) reviewed the growing social cognition literature which bears on Piaget's work. Most of the research is directed at developing more precise measures, testing performance across tasks to see if development is stagelike and replicating Piaget's findings regarding the timing of certain cognitive achievements. Very few publications deal with individual differences or pathology, areas that might relate more directly to our interests.

Nevertheless, a few social cognitive investigations of individual differences or psychopathology clearly allow for our position. For instance, Sarbin, (1954), Cameron (1947), and Sullivan (1953) each reported that schizophrenics and delinquents had difficulty in role taking. Since delinquents and many schizophrenics* have nonautonomous superegos, we would expect them to have difficulty understanding another's point of view. Also, ability to role take correlated with prosocial behavior (Chandler, 1973; Gough, 1948; Gough & Peterson, 1952;

---

*It was noted earlier that some symbolics, aside from sharing heteronomous superego function with intuitives, lack separation of superego from object or self.

Neale, 1966), supporting the contention that an operational superego is a coherent structure that includes the rules of the culture. Inability to role take appears often to last into adulthood (Flavell, 1968). This last finding fits our position that intuitives and many symbolics would have great difficulty in perspective taking in their social life.

An unusual type of study is Brock and Del Guidice's (1963) which supports a psychodynamic clustering of the sort we describe, an integrated, intrapsychic structuring of social-moral systems. They found that second through eighth graders who resisted temptation to take money were better oriented to concepts of time: yesterday, last month, and next week. Stealers were now-oriented and did not use time as much in their stories. Their stories also did not cover as great a time span.

Some confusing but interesting findings suggest a type of peaking occurs at 6 or 7. Rosenhan, Moore, and Underwood (1976) found heightened altruism at 6 to 7 years of age. Ugurel-Semin (1952) found the tendency to share to be greater at 6 or 7 than before or later. Curdin (Lickona, 1976) found that children who came from fundamentalist families and were older or younger than 8, demonstrated belief in immanent justice more frequently than 8-year-olds.

These findings might prove especially important in any phase-specific consideration of development. Our position has been that the form of superego is a product of an abiding experience over the first 5 to 7 years. However, obviously at some stages certain types of interaction are more significant than at other stages. Certainly, a child at a particular time is ready for certain types of aliment and is not as ready before or later. Longitudinal studies such as Wynne, Singer, and Toohey's 1976-7 of children (and their families) who are at risk for schizophrenia will undoubtedly help us understand how influential the phases are as opposed to steady-state interactions. It is likely that the general quality of the child-parent atmosphere, e.g., protective, would be abiding from birth to 8 years and beyond. This likelihood would obscure phase-specific impact. It is an open, empirical question whether children who experience protection (or neglect) before, but not after, age 6 to 8 or 10 (when superego construction becomes possible) become operational or intuitive characters.

Imitation-Identification in Superego Formation

While we have discussed the ingredients and cognitive form taken in autonomous superego formation, we have not discussed the means of construction. Identification, the taking in of the characteristics of another as an integral part of the self-representation, has long been held to be the basic mechanism for superego formation (Freud, 1957). Imitation, as used in psychoanalytic literature, denotes a more conscious (Fenichel, 1945), a less internalized (Blanck and Blanck, 1974) as well as a more fragmentary process than identification does. However, in keeping with Fenichel ["The concept of primary identification denotes that actually 'putting into the mouth' and 'imitation for perception's sake' are one and the same and represent the first relation to objects" (p. 37)], imitation as used by Piaget is equivalent to identification.

In the Piagetian system, imitation is a primary method for learning about or accommodating to the social and physical world. During the Sensorimotor Period, in a child's imitation of the motion of an object with his hand or in his imitation of an experimenter's opening and closing his eyes by opening and closing a fist (Piaget, 1962a), the child is learning about (assimilating-accommodating to) objects and events. Sensitive to the global patterns, the overall spaciotemporal configuration change, the child's behavior is automatic, more contagious than it is motivated consciously. Further, it is holistic and consonant with the undifferentiation of the self, the self-object continuum, of the Sensorimotor Period. It is difficult to tell whether Piaget's child was imitating or whether he was making an interesting spectacle last, or both, when he moved his head back and forth as Piaget ceased moving a bicycle back and forth (Piaget, 1962a). In this case, the two are undifferentiated. The child's moving his head back and forth essentially made the bicycle move back and forth as far as he was able to "preperceive" it. However, his head going back and forth was also an imitation of the movement of the bicycle. Imitation as a phenomenon and as a system for building of the self and object world is evident throughout Piaget's observations.

He accorded imitation a special role in construction of mental images. In *Play, Dreams, and Imitation in Childhood*, he traced the development of the ability to imitate both things and persons, until in Stage 6, using imitation the child constructs a symbol. Lucienne, while trying to get a chain out of a partially open match box, gazed fixedly at the box and imitated the box by opening and closing her mouth, wider and wider, after which she opened the box wide enough to obtain the object. Later in Stage 6, presumably the imitation, the symbolization, is interiorized, done intrapsychically since the imitations are not manifest. It is then a mental symbol, no longer an overt-action, body symbol.

In the stage following the Sensorimotor Period, the Symbolic Stage, we find the child in his play imitating-identifying [with] others. For example (as mentioned earlier), Millar (1968, p. 13) writes, "As I write—my 3-year-old sits at a small table, her head earnestly bent over sheaves of paper. She, too, is writing a book. Her pen had to be the same color as mine, her sheets of paper the same shape, and every now and then she looks up to make sure her scribbles resemble mine." There is no distinction between this kind of imitation and identification. If the identification seems fragmentary and incomplete in this instance, it is only because the cognitive embrace of a 3-year-old is limited. However, the big idea, in parts, is grasped by the child as best she can in her effort to appear to be like Mommy —all of which looks so big and powerful and nice. Such play may be corrective or may rest on identification with the aggressor as in the instance of the child who, following his visit to the doctor, forcefully examines his sibling's throat. To an undetermined degree, the cognitive processing and motivation involved may be unconscious. Also, this kind of play at being Mother or doctor exists for the child anywhere on a continuum between make-believe and reality.

So at least well into (and beyond) the 5- to 7-year stage there can be imitation-identification. There is a taking on of roles all along: playing Mommy, playing Daddy, playing the sheriff, playing teacher. However, with poor differentiation of self, object, and symbols, make-believe and reality are not distinct and the quality of introjects or identifications is necessarily defective or incomplete.

As development proceeds the child's embrace of self and external objects modifies. The advanced level of cognitive development provides new kinds of organizations of what is perceived that can be identified with. Prior to the Concrete Operational Period, a child has no holistic world, just his momentary views of mountains and people. His view is not differentiated or abiding. After 4 years of age, during the Intuitive Stage, his notion of self and objects is reasonably stable. So one may expect when he imitates his mother by caring for a doll that he will not usually confuse his play with the real thing; that is, he will not think he is a mother or that his doll is a baby or that his playing is true caretaking—all of which he was not clear about when he was 3. However, recognition and coordination of another's point of view, for example, the appearance of an object when it is observed from a different vantage point or the past appearance of an object once it is transformed, as well as operational understanding of attributes and interrelationships of objects is unavailable to a child until after he is 7 or so. Accordingly, he cannot be expected to see himself or another in terms of roles or attributes prior to the Concrete Operational Period. According to Flavell (1968) not until 8 is a child able to take the role of another to solve a problem. Before then he has no true comprehensive embrace of such things. Hence, he could not be expected to incorporate or identify with fully differentiated attributes, rules, or roles. He can only take in part-attributes, part-rules, or part-roles prior to 7.

Piaget (1965a) does not accord imitation-identification a role in superego formation. At one point he notes a child need not learn rules by example since a parent may successfully forbid his youngster from touching his desk while the parent freely does so. At the age at which a child may learn this, the touching is part of the desk and part of Daddy. The child is unable to incorporate rules as yet. In this instance Piaget was being concrete when he put forward his argument. He failed to recognize that in his prohibition he was laying the groundwork for much more profound kinds of rules. There are probably some things he allowed himself to do or prohibited himself from doing as well, and this is the kind of example he was providing his child to be taken eventually into a more mature cognitive system when the child is ready to assimilate surface-discrepant dimensions into holistic, coordinated rules.

In any case, identification as used by Freud and imitation as used by Piaget differ only in Piaget's conceptualization's being more inclusive, since it includes imitation of things and events as well as persons. As long as one eliminates instances of mimicry, then imitation is a ubiquitous process applied to inanimate and animate objects, a major way of learning about and constructing the world. It is a help in righting the aggressions of the world against the child and a way of carrying the protection and niceties of a loved one with him. It occurs all along in development and is an extremely important developmental device.

Mussen (1977) asserted that in both experimental and naturalistic studies, identification-modeling is the critical factor in moral behavior. He emphasized that prosocial behavior is complex and necessarily affected by multiple factors, including intellectual ones and that when it comes to behavior, mere knowledge of the more socially-oriented act is a weak predictor of behavior. Also, if no moral model is provided, nurturant experiences in themselves, while important, are not a strong force in stimulating moral behavior.

Mussen views Yarrow, Scott, and Waxler's (1973) work as definitive. In their investigation, children were provided a nurturant model and a nonnurturant model during several weeks' contact in a school setting. Using appropriate crossover design, the model displayed prosocial behavior, such as being helpful and sympathetic toward a colleague who bumped his head. Subsequently, the children were tested in parallel situations that could be expected to elicit prosocial behavior, for example, a kitten caught in string. Having a nurturant, prosocial model was strongly correlated with the child's prosocial behavior. This work supports both our position (of a caring model effecting internalized controls) and that identification-imitation is a vital mechanism for learning social roles and codes.

We are not proposing that learning in the social field is simply through identification. At times we learn not to identify with a model, one whom we can observe to suffer as a result of his behavior (Bandura, 1963; Liebert & Poulos, 1976). Certainly, timing, affect, and cognition play roles in the development of moral thought and behavior (Aronfreed, 1976). It is even clear that we also learn social function through didactic interventions.

Lickona (1976) pitted four training techniques against each other to see which was most effective in helping children to take into account the intentions of the transgressor. Using cartoons to assist the children in maintaining motivation and consequences in mind produced 32 percent subjective judgments. Debating with a subjective peer improved objective subjects 60 percent. Witnessing two adults argue netted a loss in 5 out of 16 subjects. Authoritative, didactive training yielded a 76 percent gain, plus the only significant generalization of intentionality to a story about children who lied. The exact mechanism instrumental in this last example is uncertain, but didactics clearly play a role.

At the stage of superego formation, identification probably is the paramount mechanism, although as pointed out by E. Duckworth (personal communication 1978), one can only identify or imitate at the level of one's understanding. Put another way, the quality of one's identifications varies greatly in accord with one's understanding. Development of the cognitive apparatus makes possible identification with holistic, coordinated roles which prior to the Concrete Operational Period could not be perceived. Identification on a sophisticated level, that is, including within the identification some understanding of the operational rules of the person with whom the child identifies, is not likely before 7 or 8. He then has the structures for identification of this higher order, while identification-imitation is a device that he has used all along. It is understandable that in the Concrete Operational Period he can begin to assimilate a superego, an abiding, organized system of codes, and as a subfunction of such codes, sexual identifications, in the sense of some understanding of being masculine or feminine and values placed thereon.

Even if avoidance of threatened castration may be a prime motive for identification with one's oedipal rival as postulated by Freud (1933), identifications with both parents take place all along. It may be that some identifications will have to be rejected and others accepted and integrated as the child defends against aggressors or goes off to school carrying pieces of his protectors with him, those things that serve him best and cause him the least amount of emotional pain. The oedipal triangle may provide a force for superego formation, especially with regard to sexual identity, while cognitive development provides the opportunity. We do not think it is possible to have an abiding, encapsulated, abstract system of values, an autonomous superego, without having experienced protective caretaking.

Another quality of the superego must be dealt with. The superego is a subsystem that is separated off or dissociated within the ego. This separation is also consonant with concrete operational function. Not until the child becomes aware of his intent and others' intents, as separate from the moment, can he be expected to have awareness of his own intent as separate from his function. Gardner (1973, p. 63) put it, "The young child is ... totally egocentric—meaning not that he thinks selfishly only about himself, but to the contrary, that he is incapable of thinking about himself." A split or dissociation of his wishes from his self, construction of abiding attributes separate from self [much like length, quantity, or other attributes are split from external objects or the concept of sidedness (that is, the right or left side of objects) (Laurendeau & Pinard, 1970) is split from the object or the self] becomes possible after the Intuitive Stage. He then has the possibility of observing himself, observing abiding aspects of himself as they change—on an anatomic or behavioral level, or a social or moral level.

Cognitive development allows for both the split and the quality of whole-role identification that is necessary for superego formation (and eventual observing ego function). In the social or affective sphere, the style of parenting appears to determine whether a system somewhat independent of momentary external or internal circumstances can be formed.

We think of the Intuitive Stage or the oedipal period as a major way station; that when the child's organization goes on in the Concrete Operational Period, to the extent that it is possible for him, certain incorporations and rejections of data into various systems just may happen or become necessary. Who knows how many "red heads" are in our concepts? (See p. 168).

Inherent relationships as between the child's dependency on his mother and his incessantly repetitive, relatively imperative need to eat, etc., will to an extent determine the kinds of inclusions. We are inclined to think the end of the assembly line for character structure is age 7 or a little later, perhaps as late as 11, and that before this time major internal organizations or reorganizations may take place and be included in total coordinated function. Supporting the contention that psychic plasticity is not permanent is Inhelder, Sinclair's, and Bovet (1974) report of regressions in understanding of conservation in Intuitive-Stage children and nonregression in a child once he is Concrete Operational in several tasks. Also, Bovet (1976) has suggested that if a child fails to reach concrete operational function in physical cognition, he may arrest at this level. So, even in the physical sphere, cognition may become set. Our proposal of such fixity for social cognition is clearly tenable.

Evident is the primacy of the 5- to 7-year period as a formative stage, out of which reorganization and new equilibrium may take place in all spheres, whether one refers to this period as the oedipal phase, which we feel is not general enough, or the Intuitive Stage. The 5- to 7-year period is an especially crucial one in many ways, perhaps based on a major biologic shift.*

We assume a biologic base to Piaget's periods and some of his stage shifts including the transition from Preoperational to the Concrete Operational Period. Furthermore, we are inclined to think that social and physical cognitive development is played out on an organically based maturational time schedule and that Piaget has documented the milestones of the system as it affects thought processes. In taking such a position we

*There is a revolution in cognition, the passage from the egocentric position and resolution of the oedipal conflict with massive repression. Other changes also suggest a major shift takes place at this time. Visual images disappear from the dreams and the thinking of children blind before 7, yet persist if blindness occurs later (Blank, 1958). Children who suffer injury to the Broca speech area of the brain prior to age eight have excellent recoveries (Geschwind, 1979). Kagan (1969) drew our attention to the importance of distinguishing "genotypic" disturbed behavior evidenced in a 5-year-old which may be quiescent during latency and which may gain full penetrance as a thought disorder in late adolescence. Kagan thereby documented a phenomenon that has been implicit in psychoanalytic understandings since the beginnings of psychoanalysis.

differ from Piaget in emphasis. His position rests less heavily on biologic shifts. We would stress that biologic shifts open (and close) the door for the major reorganizations of periods and perhaps the reorganization of certain stages, e.g., Stage 4 of the Sensorimotor Period, or the shift from proximal to distal receptor systems in Stage 3. At the same time we recognize that the psychological preparations, that take place as a result of the child's interaction with the environment and that Piaget has so beautifully documented, almost force the biologic door open as all works hand in glove.

Chapter 9

THE RELATIONSHIP OF CHARACTER STRUCTURE TO PERSONALITY AND FORMAL OPERATIONS

Although character structure type is likely set in the period from 8 to 11, other major structural changes take place during adolescence. Social cognition is reorganized in accord with formal operations. Personality which tends to serve character structure is impacted in a significant way during adolescence with part of personality often becoming a subfunction of formal operations.

The following is not meant to be a comprehensive elucidation of personality. Rather, it is only understandings that were pressed on us by our model. We conceive of character structure as an ever-present, not always observable underlying organizing influence in social thought and behavior. In contrast, we think of personality as more obvious to the observer and in many individuals more state- or situation-specific, i.e., may operate under some internal and external circumstances and not under others.*

There are inherent relationships and thus affinities between certain personality types and certain character structures. As noted in Chapter 7, the pathologic prototype of the symbolic is one of the schizophreniform syndromes. Included in the schizophreniform syndromes are both the schizoid and paranoid personalities as well as preschizophrenics and schizophrenics, none of which do we expect to encounter in operational or intuitive characters, although the symbolic may present as a behavior disorder, narcissist or obsessive-compulsive personality, configurations that are generally part of the intuitive or operational character. An intuitive rarely has obsessive traits and an operational never is a behavior disorder or narcissist.

Personality often provides an organized, automatic solution to a major concern or dilemma of the person's character structure. For instance, a schizoid personality handles conflicts concerning merging and expresses and handles distrust at the same time that it defends against attachment. Both paranoid and schizoid personalities use different traits to deal with attachment needs, part of their symbolic character structure.

Other personality types are more loosely associated with a particular character structure. For instance, while a hysterical personality is most frequently and readily a solution to the

*Differentiating personality from character is particularly important for treatment since the overall treatment approach taken toward a patient should be geared to his character structure, not usually to his personality. To know a person's character structure is to know his language. The therapist is not interested in changing a person's language, but to treat him one must speak his language, one must know where he lives. If the therapist mistakes personality for character structure, he may be misled in his treatment approach. For instance, analyzing hysterical qualities in an intuitive character may be irrelevant, in a symbolic character, harmful, and in an operational character, essential. Theory of treatment using this model has been addressed elsewhere (Ahern, 1978). Suffice it to say that the context of treatment, that is, the overall approach to the patient is paramount.

concerns of an intuitive character, with seduction and drama serving narcissistic needs, a person who has a hysterical personality may be symbolic or operational. In these latter instances, hysterical personality may not be as fully integrated into or subservient to the character structure as a whole. Impulsive and narcissistic personalities readily fit with an intuitive's end-stage reasoning and are a solution to his interest in narcissistic supplies, but may almost as readily serve a symbolic's need for attachment and identity.

An obsessive-compulsive personality is easily integrated into an operational character, serving operational foci. On the other hand, an obsessive-compulsive personality may be an important, integral solution for a symbolic character. Thus far, we have not found an obsessive-compulsive personality who has an intuitive character structure.

A few persons, encountered outside of treatment, appear to be intuitive characters and yet have some obsessive traits. Some of these are intuitive characters who have quasi-obsessive mechanisms, e.g., a cautiousness or a concern for precision. Sometimes in their work they acquire expertness in certain fields which automatically embrace certain principles, for example, the study of moral behavior. Hence, they have a certain obsessive cast to their function. It is likely most persons who have mixed intuitive and obsessive traits would prove to be symbolic characters if examined in the psychotherapeutic setting.

Obsessive-compulsive personality in the operational serves his interest in control of function and fits his focus on rules. Additionally, we think the genesis of the obsessive and the operational explains their close bond. If the operational character is the product of protective parenting and obsessive-compulsive/anal traits are products of protection overdone, then both have a common origin in the experience of protecting parenting. Obsessive-compulsive/anal personalities generally give a history of parents who minded their child's business too well. To the extent that a child is overprotected, he is overcontrolled.

He is safe enough, but his chance to be autonomous is suppressed. The encapsulation of his superego may be excessive since there may be considerable distance from code to self or confusion as to what is self and what is code; what is his parents' (his social world's) code and what is his own code; what is his business and what is theirs; what are his parents' codes and what are society's. He may think everyone wants him to succeed or wants him to be a certain way. He incorporates the "ultimate good" put forward by his parents but may be expected to resent it and struggle against it.

Freud's (1953a) finding of a relationship between obsessive traits and bowel training is undeniable. As noted in Chapter 6, if one allows an obsessive-compulsive personality to free associate, invariably anal and sadomasochistic, homosexual referents will make their appearance, allowing one to replicate Freud's findings. However, Erikson (1950) has drawn our attention to the child's increased ability not only to control his bowel function during the anal phase but to control other motor functions as well, especially locomotion, and that in the anal phase control and autonomy are major foci in the interaction between the child and his parents. It is likely, though not without exception, that a parent who overprotects or overcontrols will do so around all of these motor functions (and before and after any phase).

One can also see that overprotection done to a turn is not true protection. Extreme overprotection will foster obsessive-compulsive or anal traits, but will militate against formation of an operational character structure. Extreme overprotection is consistent with symbolic character formation. Thus, it should not surprise us to find the stern superego that we do in some symbolic characters. This type of superego is literal, fixed, and perfectionistic, that is, partakes of the symbolic style of cognition. It is overencapsulated, not modulated nor coordinated, and may be brittle. Occasionally such persons who are remarkably constricted may have outbursts of flamboyant, impulsive, uncontrolled behavior. Those symbolic characters who have a rigid superego describe having experienced protection to the point of being stifled (superoverprotected), being molded to the parents' precepts with little chance for selfishness or autonomy. Yet, such a symbolic character generally has experienced considerable parental love and concern. In large measure, it was concern for part of his self or a certain style of self that may have reflected well on mother, suited her need or concept, sometimes a hollow one, but one which completed her in her own eyes. Unlike the future intuitive character, the future symbolic character could usually expect a return for fitting the mold. The mold might be moral or even perfectly, precisely moral.

One must consider that there are all degrees of protection-neglect and all degrees of arbitrary shaping that may be visited by a parent on a child. What may be protection, neglect, or excessive molding for one child may not be so for another (Escalona, 1963). His genetics, his sensitivity to scolding or cuddling, or his having sensory modality change, e.g., deafness, are all significant factors.

However, we would like to point out another factor by raising a qualifying question. How much role reversal is role reversal? How much neglect is neglect? How much overprotection is overprotection? Was everyone who has a symbolic character structure called upon to subject himself primarily to making his caretaker feel whole and worthwhile? Was the major tone to an intuitive's or operational's interactions with his caretaker neglect or protection, respectively? Aside from the tremendous variation that children's needs may have and that to one child minimal neglect may be major, we must consider the intensity and imperative quality of children's needs, generally. From the child's point of view, in order to qualify as satisfactory, caretaking may require careful tailoring. The style of caretaking as understood, remembered, or revealed in the formed adult may rest on relatively small variations that took place when he was a child. The abnormal variants give us clearcut prototypes, guidelines, but we cannot expect to find actual neglect in normal intuitives or actual role reversal in normal symbolics. Knowledge of delinquency or obsessiveness and their structures and their fairly distinct developmental history allows us to extrapolate backward to explain behaviors of the milder form. However, given the same kind of structure in a normal intuitive and constructs of the caretaking style made by him when he was a child, if we consider the child's frame of reference and any variances in child-caretaking match, it is doubtful that retrospective reconstruction will yield much. Even prospective longitudinal studies may demand open-ended clinical methods to confirm or deny our constructs in nonpathologic character types. Traits themselves, while often an expression of the person's character structure or personality may not be a part function of either. Hence, in a given instance, a trait may be no measure of either. For example, the sociopathic therapist may perform very well during training, i.e., serve his patients' interests, but become end-stage, self-serving when not under supervision. All in all, this limits hopes to trace these phenomena back to their origin in nonpathologic syndromes.

We do not see personality configurations as of the same order as character structures. Personality may either be side-by-side with character structure or be a solution to a given character type. Personality is complex in its drawing on understandings of different periods and may in certain persons be evident throughout their life and in almost all their living, e.g., some children are neat and clean from age 2 or 3 on. In other persons, their personality type and traits may be almost purely situation-specific, appearing only under special circumstances or may even switch to its opposite pole (e.g., neatness to sloppiness in certain situations) and at times be under full, voluntary control.

This flux and quality of voluntary control parallels the conceptualizations of the formal-operational child who can theorize, carry concepts and ideals to a limit, and yet be separate from his theory, not have to act upon or be part of the actual situation. It seems likely that the cognitive development of the Formal Operational Period provides the option for personality to be fully dissociated, autonomous, free to be invoked or not, as a unit or part.

Before we discuss our proposal of how character structure and formal operational cognition relate to each other, we will address two additional questions. One, are there subcategories of the three character structures? Two, is there a character structure that corresponds to the Sensorimotor Period?

As noted in Chapter 7, there is one variant of the symbolic character who has a fairly clear, nonfragmented identity but whose identity as an evil person would be painful, hence his identity is usually warded off. This subtype of character structure may correspond to a phase between the Symbolic and the Intuitive Stage. Other substructures may be found; however, thus far we have not found them.

The Sensorimotor Period appears to make its contribution during adult life in symptoms, e.g., hallucinations. One may draw parallels between certain stages of the Sensorimotor Period and the cognition of the three character types. However, there is no need to invoke these as direct anlagen since the parallels can be found much later, e.g., ages 2 to 11. Further, in the Sensorimotor Period, there is only minimal division between the social and physical worlds for the child. Constructs of distrust, attachment, dependency, roles, or rules have little meaning to an 18-month-old. Finally, we have no reasonable theory of superego formation that would help bridge the gap from the Sensorimotor Period to adulthood.

FORMAL OPERATIONAL PERIOD

Clearly people change over time and at different stages of life. If we do not think that character structure changes once it is set during the Concrete Operational Period, how may we place character structure into the later developmental period, the Formal Operational Period?

Characteristic of formal operations, beginning to appear at age 12 is thinking raised to the second power, the ability to think about thinking. The adolescent as he becomes the thinker about thinking may become principled about principles, may moralize about morals. His philosophizing about ideals and an ideal society parallels his hypotheticodeductive thought usually tested for by Piaget by posing various physical and chemical laboratory problems (Inhelder & Piaget, 1958). For example, the adolescent is asked to determine which parameters, length, weight, size of arc, or initial thrust, govern the oscillation frequency of a pendulum or if weight, length, material, and other factors govern bending of rods. In the laboratory, a formal operational child varies such parameters systematically including combinations of parameters to discover the relevant ones. The concrete-operational child does not have a comprehensive plan based on having conceived of the possibilities. Hence his experimental approach is unsystematic and his interpretation fails to consider all the possibilities and therefore may be faulty. However, his observations will be accurate (no longer biased by his expectations). The formal-operational child considers the possible combinations and subordinates reality to the possible.

In its simplest form, formal operational function in the social sphere for an operational character is no problem for our system. An operational character in adolescence begins to consider the possible parameters involved in his social concepts. For example, he may wonder if it is truly good to tell the whole truth all the time or are there circumstances in which truth may be harmful, like the operational therapist (see Chap. 6) who was conflicted over whether to tell his patient all about himself when it was best for the patient not to know certain things. A first approximation of his thinking could be formulated as

$$O(O),$$

Where O is operational cognition. Likewise, the first approximation of the intuitive character's social cognition may be formulated as

$$I(I),$$

where I is intuitive cognition, as he rationalizes his pursuit of what looks good to him at the moment.

On the other hand, all along we have been uneasy about our position regarding the intuitive character when we thought about two of his qualities. One was his ability to function in terms of enlightened self interest and, two, his ability to see another's point of view and make use of it to gain an end, for example, to make a sale. In the case of enlightened self-interest, he deliberately abides by a principle for a postponed, but greater or more sustained payoff. He uses operational thinking to net his personal gain. In the same way he may role-take, use operational thinking in recognizing someone else's investment, even an operational investment, in order to make a sale. In both behaviors operational cognition is an instrument used in the service of intuitive, egocentric cognition and motivation. The important point, however, is that in making a sale and in enlightened self-interest, thinking in accord with principles and role-taking both, while they are manifestations of (concrete) operational cognition, are bent to an intuitive stance. Social cognition in the intuitive character, then, may be formulated as

$$I(a_1I + a_2O)$$

Where a_1 and a_2 are individual variables.

Of particular interest and the major reason for troubling the reader with this formula is that it implies that the I, that is, character structure, becomes the I outside the parenthesis of $I(a_1I + a_2O)$. In the Formal Operational Period the social cognitive style set during the Concrete Operational Period, that is, the character structure, is that which is raised to the level of *thinker* (about thinking). The I of the earlier stage is the actor, not that which is acted upon. In the Formal Operational Period, the newly acquired portion of cognitive structure, then, is that which is acted upon, plus its relationship to the actor.

This formula derived in the social domain likely has relevance in understanding formal operations in the physical domain. It may help us to explain inconsistencies in achieving formal operational level of cognition in different cultures or in certain domains.

The formula has epistemological and educational implications. While demonstrating that adolescents may use a more highly developed cognitive organization (that is, formal operations) than they used in latency, Piaget, nevertheless, remained obscure about the origin of the components of this organization. Our studies of social cognition appear to shed light on the origins of these components. If a preoperational style of social cognition may be set during preadolescence, as occurs in character structure formation; then we might assume that, given certain types of aliment, preoperational style of thing-cognition may also become set early. The result would be that in a certain sphere, for example, mathematics, the thinker would retain a basic preoperational suborganization that would limit his intellectual achievement. It also follows that if an educator is to reach such children when they are older, the educator (like a therapist [Ahern, 1978]) must take into account who his thinker is.

Let us return to the operational character. It must be recognized that operational characters may cut a few corners, cheat a bit on occasion, that is, break their own rules. Yet, generally they are guilty about or aware of the conflict of their abiding codes with their yielding to any short-term temptation. A more general formula for social cognition in the operational character, then, becomes:

$$O(a_1O + a_2I)$$

Thus far in intuitive and operational characters, a_1 appears always to be greater than a_2.

By the same token, the general formula for social cognition in the symbolic character becomes:

$$S(a_1S + a_2I + a_3O)$$

where S is symbolic cognition. In the case of the symbolic character, the relative values of a_1, a_2, and a_3 are unspecified.

In ordinary enterprises, including the unstructured psychotherapeutic hour, symbolic thinking in intuitive or operational characters is not common. However, it is not quite correct that intuitives and operationals never have access to symbolic thinking. The exceptions are in their dreams, free associations, jokes, and so on. Coming full circle, the general formula for the operational now becomes:

$$O(a_1O + a_2I + a_3S)$$

and for the intuitive becomes:

$$I(a_1I + a_2O + a_3S)$$

where a_3 is not only quite small, but where a_3 demands a type of qualitative shift in psychological state.*

The values of a_1, a_2, and a_3 would necessarily have a close relationship to personality traits. The factors within the parentheses may always have a degree of flexibility, being subject to change and fairly responsive to situational influence.

This completes our understanding of development of adult character structure and how it fits into the economy of the individual. Let us appraise our constructs and their interrela-

---

*One unmodified variable, a_4, should be included in each general formula to account for social cognition unaffected by formal (i.e. adolescent) cognition, e.g., a symbolic formula may read $S(a_1S + a_2I + a_3O + a_4)$ to represent times when unmodified symbolic thought is used, e.g. when the word is taken for the thing. One final complexity must be considered. Is this the limit of nestings that may occur? At least in one instance it is not. For example, when a symbolic character, such as Mr. B., does his duty, in the hopes of narcissistic return, ultimately to serve his investment in attachment and identity, then one has a 3 level nesting, $S(I(O))$.

tionships. First of all, we have little question about the existence of the three character structures. We confirm this every day in our practice. We can only ask that the reader keep in mind the basic interest and social cognition as we described them, and he will confirm our observations. Second, there is essentially no basic question about Piaget's stages of cognitive development, especially the first three periods, the ones with which this book is most concerned. Third, we have demonstrated a parallel between the social cognition of certain adults and the general (based primarily on tests in the physical domain) cognition found in children during specific stages. Fourth, we think Piaget is certainly wrong in his concept of moral development when he contends that interaction with peers is the usual basic moralizing force. Generally, developing children, who have looked to peer influence to offer basic shape to their consciences, construct sorely defective superegos. Certainly we also know that stable, secure experiences are settings which spawn fully developed consciences. Fifth, if Piaget's concept that moral do's and don'ts, that is, concepts of goodness and badness in the social sphere, are merely attributes of social beings much like bigness and littleness are attributes of physical objects and if such attributes, constructed by the child in the Concrete Operational Period, may take into account or coordinate various momentary past and present dimensions, then, as a sixth proposition, we contend that the child must take into account primarily his interaction with his parents or their substitutes. Finally, we propose a general formula for the social cognition of each of the character structures which takes into account both concrete and formal operational cognition.

Chapter 10

THE INDIVIDUAL VIEW OF PERSONALITY, NORMALITY AND CULTURE

In postulating an equilibrated, abiding, intrapsychic organization, not a statistical aggregate of rewarded situations, and in our stress of the intrapsychic essence of character and personality, we are emphasizing the individual as opposed to the social view of personality. That is, we hold to the common sense notion that a person has certain abiding constructs and that he will be recognizable internally and externally in varied social situations as well as over time. To some degree the individual position is assumed in any of the psychodynamic approaches to psychotherapy. This stance, however, lost favor for some time in academic circles. The individual view of personality was assaulted by situationists, largely behaviorists, who held that the specifics of situations govern behavior, that any evidence for an internally-organized personality structure that is abiding across situations is exceedingly weak, that correlational statistics (the usual yardstick of proponents of the individual view) do not prove a relationship, and that concepts of internal dynamics are unmeasurable, hence, pointless. More recently, however, the fallacies of the extreme situationist position have been brought to light by Bowers (1973).

Bavelas (1978) has charted the struggle between adherents of the individual and social positions as well as Bower's interactionist position, including the statistical problems of all three positions as pointed out by Golding (1975). The methodology of earlier pro-situationist personality studies has been questioned. The correlations of traits across situations have been found to be higher than originally thought (Burton, 1976), thus supporting the individual view. It has been noted that duplication of behavior by experimentation, stock in trade of the situationists, is not proof of how a given behavior is ordinarily formed. Finally, Bowers argued the importance of theory, an irrelevancy to many situationists. He pointed out that without a theory of gravity we would be limited to measuring how and where things fall on this earth.

Suffice it to say it appears that none of us are too firmly in the saddle at this point, and there is yet a good argument for an individual view of personality as significant in explaining human social function. To us it seems likely that each discipline's views are heavily influenced by its methodology.

As clinicians we are particularly interested in the approach taken by Bem and Allan (1974), who, aware of the limitations of trait measures and the heavy influence of situations on behavior, still argued the individual position. They asserted that it is not possible to do better than predict some of the people some of the time and that some persons are best measured on traits and others on situations. They pointed out that one must content oneself with smaller slices for study, the slices being selected for their meaningfulness to the subjects studied.

In large measure, this is what the clinical method of treatment and investigation has been about, the essence of the psychoanalytic or uncovering psychotherapeutic and the Piagetian clinical approach. It follows the old social work principle, "meeting the client where he is." A classic investigation in this vein was Deutsch's (1942) study of the "as if" personality. Although few clinical inquiries have the scope of Deutsch's, the clinical literature abounds with similar painstaking investigations. Some are observations which focus on content, such as Freud's (1953a) study of the obsessive-compulsive. Some, like Deutsch's, focus on context or structure. All draw on very small parts of the tremendously rich material provided by each patient seen.

Investigators, outside of clinical practice, find such reports difficult to evaluate at best and may view the findings of psychotherapists as invalid, because these outsiders themselves cannot readily verify the findings or because some findings are not easily measured. Deutsch's or Freud's findings, however, may be replicated if one takes the time to learn the technique, that is, to develop the skill necessary for use of the instrument. One difficulty is that the technical instrument one must use is oneself. It takes time to learn to use oneself as an instrument and some human instruments have greater resolving power than others. In this regard, it is interesting that Deutsch, who listened to the same output of patients that other analysts listened to, was able to hear her patients better. We propose that many people are not able to depart from the professional frame of reference within which they operate. Deutsch was not one of these. In our opinion, with all its problems of subjectivity, the clinical interview remains the most powerful method for the study of psychological function.

The Three Character Structures as Normal

Generally speaking, character structure is silent in adult life, expressed through choice of spouse, community, occupation, political party, hobbies, etc. Sometimes we get to see the character structure when there is an error in choice of setting or when the setting shifts for some reason. Urbanization of a

farm setting, shifting of the economics of a profession or indus-
try, personal physical impairment, even improved health may
disrupt the self-selected mesh between character structure and
setting.

One symbolic character who had experienced much disruption and insecurity, even hunger throughout childhood and
adolescence chose to teach in a homelike junior college in a
small, friendly community. The pressures of political action
plus the erratic responses of administrators, who were in turn
pressed by a community gone activist and a legislature intent
on cost cutting, caused the entire tenor of our patient's setting
to change. He then became symptomatic and sought help. No
doubt his particle-to-particle reasoning and his need for a stable, secure, rule-abiding setting to define him and to make him
feel worthwhile would have been evident in an unstructured,
nondefensive interview before he was symptomatic just as it was
after he lost his symptoms. However, his cognitive style and
approach toward life was no problem to him or his community
until a change occurred in the balance he had found between
his character structure and his setting.

An ambitious operational, eager for fame and fortune, was
extruded from a large organization because of his difficulty in
"playing ball," in trading favors, and in proving that his need
to be part of the organization was more important to him than
his serving under an incompetent superior or his heading a
nonfunctional unit. In this instance, the operational selected
poorly in terms of any long-term equilibrium between himself
and the organizational setting. Later, in his own small business
he was more comfortable and reasonably satisfied.

We feel the character structures we describe should not be
relegated to the pathologic just because the people who consult
us are in turmoil or someone else says they are, or if they are
not that they should be.

Although primarily our constructs were derived from
study of the "pathologic", that is, our own studies and other
clinician's studies of patients in the psychotherapeutic setting,

we doubt if the three character structures are pathologic per se. One character type is not "sicker" or less adaptive than another. None of the three types is confined to any walk of life, although one type may be more suited to a given setting or subculture and accordingly may be overrepresented at times. No experienced clinician need be reminded that except in extreme cases his patients are generally more normal than otherwise. It is unfortunate that the findings of psychotherapists are often dismissed automatically as pathologic by some other social scientists, their reasoning presumably being that if a person is seen for psychological problems, then any findings are necessarily abnormal.

Other aspects of our typology justify the contention that ours is not just a typology of pathology. We find that we are able to categorize all our patients into one of the three character structures. This is true regardless of the degree of dysfunction or discomfort the patients manifest or experience. Accordingly, there is a wide range in each of these groups, some of our patients having only minimal difficulty. When these patients leave treatment and (hopefully) are more comfortable and more functional, they still think about social matters basically as they did and they still have the same social investments; they have the same type of character structure. Nonpathology, wellness, is not defined by change in social cognitive style or basic life investment. Most often, the improved patient is more successful at satisfying his basic interests and finds settings that serve his interests and mesh with his cognitive style. He becomes like the person who has the same cognitive style and interest but who has no need to consult us. Although it is difficult to estimate the frequency of the three character structures in the general population, the style of thinking and basic investments are certainly not confined to persons who consult psychotherapists. Ordinary social encounters, newspaper accounts, and even biographies do not lend themselves to the kind of observations that can be made in unstructured psychotherapeutic sessions. However, instances typical of the cognitive style of each of these character types are not hard to find. For example, classifying as pathologic all findings which are made in psychotherapists' offices is itself an example of particle-to-particle reasoning. Certainly, an important part of much creative thought is particle to particle. Sales and business, politics and parts of the law are necessarily end-stage oriented, while investments in codes of crafts, of social or political creeds, and of cultural institutions are inherently operational. At the same time, the kind of indications most significant in categorizing someone's character structure are in-context revelations. These are matters that our patients are not necessarily aware of and accordingly not what they consult us about. Their cognitive style and investment are revealed as they tell their story, that is, as they offer us content. The kinds of context processes which define character structure are very much like the processes Piaget focused on, not content-bound. Tied to structure, not content, the mechanics we describe, while not necessarily general, are neither normal or abnormal as such. Let us return to the range of discomfort and dysfunction. Starting with the criminal, we can document that when he was a child he was subject to neglect, that is, absent, disrupted, and/or uncaring caretaking. With the preschizophrenic or schizophrenic, we elicit in our interviews that when he was a child major segments of his individual understandings and interests he experienced as preempted by his caretaker's pursuit of his own sense of wholeness and worth. In parallel fashion from a severe obsessive-compulsive, we elicit that as a child he could not tell whether his function, including his bowel movements, belonged to him or his caretaker. In each of the three pathologic states we find a gradation of pathology which roughly corresponds to the degree of style of caretaking they experienced, extending from extreme to subtle—neglect, role reversal, or protection. The degree of pathology and style of caretaking grades off into more and more subtle forms. Yet, these "milder" cases still are separable in terms of style of ideation and history of caretaking though neither is as obvious. As noted in Chapter 9, the pathologic viewed in the clinical setting provides the opportunity to see certain interactions in relief, interactions which are obscured in the two-dimensional view usually afforded investigators.

Even if the three character structures prove not to be universal as we propose, character structure is not something wrong with the person. Patients generally do not come to see us requesting a change in their character structure, nor do we see such change as our task. Character structure does not necessarily cause a patient or society more pain nor make him less adaptive. In fact, the three character structures appear to insure greater probability for species and culture survival, each character type being more adaptive to one environment than to another.

Pathology Relative to Culture

Pathology-normality is relative to both the culture and intrapsychic function and cannot be defined in terms of one or the other exclusively. Man does not live uninfluenced by social forces; neither is he only what his culture makes of him. While in extreme forms character structure is generally pathologic either from the individual's point of view or from the culture's, even though these extreme forms of character type may fit into or serve certain cultures particularly well. Someone who almost constantly uses particle-to-particle thinking may be a priest or seer in certain cultures, or in other cultures just tolerated as are the "quare fellows," paranoid schizophrenics, in rural Ireland. At the same time, such a person may suffer internal difficulties aside from whether he is tolerated or even lauded by his group. Subject to extreme shifts, he may be confused and may feel as if he were always entering into the middle of a play. He may experience abrupt, violent, and sometimes painful shifts in his affects. Similarly, in other character types, extremes in investments or reliance on a cognitive style with little defensive modulation guarantees confusion, emotional pain and dysfunction in terms of rules of the culture or in terms of intrapsychic measures.

Our conceptualization of normality, defined as minimal pain and dysfunction, is necessarily partially tied to one's social role. Certain societal structures embrace one type of character structure and tend to extrude others. An operational character will have trouble functioning as a manipulative administrator and be unhappy in the bargain; while an intuitive character may often be competent in such a position and be gratified. A symbolic character may be especially effective and comfortable in a corporate or family structure. Certain occupations lend themselves to the qualities of a given character structure. Sales and politics befit an intuitive; accountant and shoemaker, an operational; poet and artist, a symbolic. Nevertheless, no occupation or any particular standing in the community is bound to either of the three character structures although the different character structures are adaptive, personally and societally, in certain situations and less so in others.

Certain social pursuits, e.g., power, prestige, wealth may suit one character type more than another, but on that basis alone, one cannot distinguish a character type. Rather, it is the character's interests, his motivations, that a given social pursuit serves, which typify his character structure. For instance, wealth for an operational character may be an end in itself. For an intuitive, wealth, if sought is not generally an end in itself, but rather a means to self-esteem through the money itself or what it can buy. In addition to these intuitive or operational possibilities, wealth to a symbolic may help him define himself or enable him to buy attachments.

Some cultures or subcultures may be expected to allow for a different proportion of one character than another. The free enterprise, big business, growth-oriented setting should have considerable room for intuitives, while certain tribal cultures would be particularly attuned to symbolics and craft societies should suit operationals. It seems to us that all stable cultures would suit some proportion of each of the three character structures, the operationals' guarding the rules, the intuitives' being lubrication for the system, and symbolics' being the glue (as well as some of symbolics' performing the function of the other two). All three would provide their own styles of disruptions as a function of their interests, when exaggerated. Since cultures are inherently conservative, they serve survival of the group, hence the species. To the extent that an individual's characteristics serve his group, he is tolerated. To the extent that he conflicts with his group, he may feel pain or be dysfunctional; to some extent then, character pathology in this system is relativistic, that is, a part-function of the culture.

Late Life Changes

We see late life changes as external to the structure of character and that in adults the product of existing structure interacting with life change does not yield major internal reorganization as may result in earlier periods. Obviously considerable change in behavior occurs long after young adulthood; however, we think of these as more quantitative than qualitative, such as Vaillant's (1979) finding that with age the use of primitive defenses declines in frequency.

We also realize that great gain may accumulate, leading to profound achievements or realizations in middle life with attendant rewards and consolidations. Nevertheless, in schematic terms the developmental tasks of middle life are to address intrinsic and extrinsic declines, whether they are one's diminishing intellectual or physical facileness, one's accumulating of wrinkles and gray hair, the losing of ability to procreate, the maturing and leaving of offspring, the increasing loss of associates to death, or the lessening of work opportunities. In old age, what was pending and statistical becomes actual with retirement, physical as well as intellectual incapacity and loss of friends and spouse. We anticipate responses by a person of a given character structure will depend on his particular investments whether they lie in function, beauty, attachment, or identity and to the extent to which his personally significant areas are affected. So as opportunities for service of these needs falter, adjustments are demanded. It is not, of course, predetermined that decline of function and beauty and breaks of attachment plus losses of self-defining roles will necessarily take place, although they are the statistical likelihood of aging whether caused by organic atrophy or by cultural definition. An individual may increase his ability to function, surround himself with beauty, diversify attachments or find less age-vulnerable roles depending on which of these are paramount to his sense of safety and worth.

In short, we see the later life stages, like any happening in adult life, will be dealt with for good or for ill on the basis of who the person is, that is, his basic cognitive style and his major life investment, given the opportunities he has available. In this system, we do not anticipate any new basic structure reorganization as takes place during the earlier periods. Once adult equilibrium is established response is not a true reorganization of structure but the equilibrated structure interacting with change whether it is to a later life stage or to illness or to coming into wealth. This is as far as character structure and its function are concerned. We do not minimize exploitation of individual traits including level of intellect or training in handling or capitalizing on life's shifts.

Chapter 11

OTHER CHARACTEROLOGIES

Having presented our concept of character structure, we will compare our position with that of several other contemporary authors.

Our characterology and Kernberg's (1970) differ in a major way although both draw upon current psychoanalytic findings. Kernberg's characterology is a linear continuum. He divided character into higher, intermediate, and lower levels of organization of character pathology. Above his "continuum" is normal character, and below it, psychosis. His lower level corresponds to borderline personality organization. In categorizing a patient at one of his levels, Kernberg took into account: (1) instinctual level especially expressions of pregenital aggressions, (2) superego integration and predominance of sadistic superego precursors, (3) defensive operations whether splitting and defenses (e.g., "denial, primitive forms of projection and omnipotence" [p. 804]) associated with splitting predominate or whether repression and less primitive defenses (e.g., "intellectualization, rationalization, undoing, and higher levels of

207

projection" [p. 804]) associated with repression predominate, and (4) finally, object relations—part and whole objects (object constancy) and integration of self or not.

He stated that certain personality types (descriptive characterological diagnosis in his terms) correspond to his levels of organization of character pathology more than overall function does. For example, hysterical personalities tend to have a higher level organization while infantile personalities have a lower level organization. On the other hand, people who are very successful and function quite well may be borderline, that is, have a lower level organization. He wrote that there are small groups of patients who have a repressive level of organization overlapping a more primitive organization. These patients are subject to major shifts in organization. In most other patients, the levels of organization are stable.

Except in certain of our symbolic characters, we see the syndromes as more discrete than Kernberg did. We group our defenses a bit differently. We include rationalization with denial and see splitting as a condition more than a defense. Also, we see psychic structure or ego development, definition of one character style, as more a matter of coherence of attributes than a matter of summation of deficiencies which he seemed to imply. However, descriptively our construct of the syndromes and his could possibly be reconciled. It is our use of a different model that differentiates our view from Kernberg's.

Our system is more complex in that we conceive of three norms of development each of which has inherent alliances with certain personality types and symptoms, but each of which on the whole is specially adaptive to its own family experience as well as certain settings, subcultures, or cultures. Kernberg explained adult configurations by calling upon a concept of regression to, or fixation at, early levels of development. Although our understanding does not employ fixation in a strict sense, a more obvious difference between Kernberg and ourselves is the timetable of development. We see symbolic social cognition in the adult, even in psychotics, drawing from age 2 to 4 while Kernberg (1972) pegged this much earlier. We see character structure as a resolution (or equilibration) by the child occurring at a period of cognitive restructuring, a resolution of his abiding experiencing of his social world, especially his experiencing of his relationship to his caretakers. This resolution becomes possible as the child is able to make concrete operational constructs, age 8 or so. Both Kernberg and we approach our study through the pathologic and while we agree there is a continuum of primitivity to maturity found in the thinking of the three character structures (although this does not quite hold for superego function in an entire group of symbolic characters), our concept differs from Kernberg's in that Kernberg conceived of the character as being a function of greater or lesser damage inflicted at stages of development. We conceptualize each of three phases following the Sensorimotor Period as providng developmental options that give the organism potential adaptational range and increased survival value.*

Our position is not dissimilar from Erickson's (1950) who saw the culture pressing on the family which in turn shapes the child to fit into the culture, although we do not date such influences to as early an age nor credit the libidinal issues with the same importance as Erickson did. Most importantly, we embrace a different mechanism of construction of character structure. The mechanism we invoke is Piaget's stage-related cognitive restructuring which differs from Erikson's,

Kohut (1977), firmly based in traditional psychoanalysis, proposed major departures in psychoanalytic metapsychology and came close to our theoretic position in a number of ways. He explained pathology of the self as a resultant of parent-child interaction. He called for a psychology of the self, separate from any drive-defense model. he emphasized the role of empathy in child rearing. His concept of empathy corresponds closely with

---

*Simpson (1976), like ourselves, saw morality as a function of "personality" and postulated that in survival cultures one will see no principled behavior. One's beliefs need not be true, only advantageous, that is, work for a time.

our conceptualization of good caretaking. He proposed that adult structures reflect basic defects in relationship between child and parent and derive from an abiding stance of the parent toward the developing child. That is, structures are not just phase-specific results as proposed by Kernberg.

We believe our view of character structure and our use of the Piagetian framework provide a more general system that can accommodate Kohut's constructs. Also, we emphasize the reorganization of structure that takes place at the close of the oedipal-intuitive stage, which he does not. Incidentally, we would categorize Kohut's narcissistic personalities as symbolic characters with narcissistic or impulsive personalities.

As noted in Chapter 2, we found Hogan's (1973) definition of character and ours matched. Nevertheless, his final understandings and ours are very different. Drawing on various personality inventory tests, he proposed that character could be described and moral behavior explained on the basis of five dimensions: (1) knowledge of social rules; (2) socialization, the degree to which one regards rules, values, and prohibitions of one's society as personally mandatory; (3) empathy, the ease with which one may put oneself in another's position; (4) autonomy, governing one's actions by a personal sense of duty; and (5) moral judgment, the degree to which one is invested either in one's personal conscience or the rules of society. He then excluded knowledge of social rules which closely correlates with intelligence, as a major factor in adult conduct. He suggested that character structure types are made up by combinations of emphases on any of the remaining four dimensions. For instance, someone who scores high on personality measures of empathy and socialization would be expected to be morally mature; someone whose score on both is low, would be expected to be delinquent. Someone high on socialization and low on empathy, would be expected to be a rigid rule follower, while someone low on socialization and high on empathy would be emancipated, mildly sociopathic.

Hogan proposed that there are points in development when one dimension is called into play or is more important and that once exploited brings about qualitative changes in the underlying structures of moral conduct. In infancy when nurturance is most important, child-parent interaction has its effect on socialization. At age 4 or 5 peer interaction impacts empathy, that is, role taking. Finally, in young adulthood, autonomy solves the conflict between internalized demands of the family and the expectations of the peer community. He emphasized that "attainment of the later 'stages' is *not* dependent on successful transition through the earlier levels. Rather, all three stages are distinct developmental challenges whose outcome defines each person's unique character structure" (p. 230). Essentially he defines character structure as the scores on each of his basic dimensions.

Hogan started with essentially the same definitions of character and personality as we, as well as a sophisticated clinical orientation. Even his embrace of Becker's (1964) and Bronfenbrenner's work (Garbarino & Bronfenbrenner, 1976) coincided with ours. Nevertheless, his observational arena, the types of data collected using personality tests, led him to postulate a markedly different characterology than ours.

Kohlberg (1963a) used Piaget's cognitive-developmental system and findings as an inspiration for his own work, and like ourselves, proposed a cognitive–developmental theory of socialization. Like us, he relegated to developing cognitive structure the primary role in the organization of thought process in any sphere. Both Kohlberg and we view the processing of social life as a subfunction of the more basic cognitive structure. However, he is inclined to see the cognitive structure as more unitary across dimensions (physical and social) and driven toward expressions at the highest level according to Kohlberg's measuring system as adulthood is reached, a linear system, while we think of the developing cognitive structure as providing options that may or may not be called into play, a branching system.

Kohlberg based his theory on his own experimental work and on his analyses of many experimental, epidemiologic, and clinical papers. His theory was exclusively cognitive developmental with an underlying drive for effectance or competence and self-esteem. In his exclusiveness, he did not accommodate psychoanalytic findings or theory and other observations that suggest parent–child relations are of special importance in socialization (Aronfreed, 1976; Becker, 1964; Bowlby, 1944; Garbarino & Bronfenbrenner, 1976; Gleuck & Gleuck, 1950) We conflict with Kohlberg in a number of ways. His moral stages appear more gradual and more quantitative than would fit our concepts (1963a). He contended (1963b) that signs of conscience develop later than suggested by either Piaget or Freud, and that identity plays no significant role in superego development.

More importantly, we question the validity of some of Kolberg's "stages." For instance, he asserted that the ultimate in moral development (Stage 6 in his system) is evidenced by one's ability to stand up against authority when authority is in opposition to one's moral code. While this is surely a highly desirable, albeit uncommon attribute, it is not necessarily the ultimate level of moral development. To us, it is just another value, no more advanced than feeling that democratic interaction is the ultimate form of social development, as Piaget apparently thought in 1932 (1965a). It is, however, probable that ability to revolt or to take distance in one direction or another tends to maximize in adolescence.

Kohlberg (1964) tested moral judgment in children and young adults by posing dilemmas such as the Heinz story. Kohlberg asked the subject to suppose Heinz's wife were dying of cancer while the pharmacist refused to dispense life-saving medication unless he were paid. After some efforts at another solution, Heinz, who did not have sufficient money, stole the medicine. The child is asked if Heinz should have stolen or not, and why. Response to such questions was judged to be at the stage six level, provided the testee was able to say one should act in accordance with a basic principle even if that principle in a given instance conflicted with authority, e.g., the law. High-level performance on these tests correlated with intelligence as well as with age. We assume that a number of our intelligent, sociopathic, intuitive characters, who can rationalize effectively could perform quite well on such test questions. Supporting our assumption is the finding that psychopaths scored higher on Kohlberg's stages than sociopathic prisoners or prison staff members (Link, Scherer, & Byrne, 1977). Psychopaths scored 36 percent more at Kohlberg's stage five than nonpsychopaths.

Kohlberg regards an answer such as the following as only at the level of his stage three: "I try to do things for my parents; they've always done things for me. I try to do everything my mother says; I try to please her, like she wants me to be a doctor, and I want to too and she's helping me to get there" (1964, p. 401). This answer seems moral enough to us although it is closely tied to the interpersonal relationship at home rather than to a general social principle. A patient of ours who was a symbolic, when she was asked to work on Christmas Day refused. She said that she had principles, that her family came first. In our judgment, based on our understanding her, she was acting on a principle. However, on the basis of her statement alone it is impossible to tell whether she was acting on principle or whether she was rationalizing. In fact, Kohlberg's approach cannot distinguish between operational investment and rationalization. Our position is similar to Saltzstein (1976) who, although recognizing differences between humanistic and conventional moral judgment, regards them as on a par, their both being internalized codes. Also, in the example drawn from Kohlberg, the boy's concept is fairly well internalized although his final remark that his mother is helping him suggests he lacks complete internalization of his code. In any case, the level of internalization would be hard to evaluate from this sample alone. If we agree that this remark indicates incomplete internalization, we would speculate that this youngster is on the edge of internalizing a system of codes in which the value is tied to his family, the code that family comes first. We could be seeing the mechanism proposed by us *statu nascendi* "Mother does for my own good. These codes must be good generally." Damon's studies, which we cited in Chapter 8, supported just such a developmental mechanism.

Selman (1976) reported stages of development of role taking that generally corresponded to Kohlberg's first four stages of moral development. Selman tested children with stories which, while they were complex, centered on issues that would concern a child. In one such story, Holly's father forbade her to climb a tree after she had almost fallen. Later she was tempted to climb a tree to rescue Shawn's kitten. To test for role-taking ability, Selman asked 4- to 10-year-olds if Holly knew how Shawn felt, how her father felt, and why, etc. In interpreting his findings, Selman proposed that attainment of a logical cognitive stage (e.g., the understanding of classes and subclasses, etc.) is necessary, but not sufficient to develop the corresponding stage of role taking; that attainment of a role-taking stage is necessary but not sufficient to develop the corresponding stage of moral judgment; and that finally attainment of a stage of moral judgment is necessary, but not sufficient to develop the corresponding stage of moral behavior. Supporting this one-way dependent series was Selman's finding that generally role-taking stages paralleled moral judgment stages or were in advance by only one stage and that a delinquent may be two or more stages ahead in his role taking compared to his moral judgment.

Selman pointed out that before a subject attains Stage 3 of role taking and moral judgment (age 10–12) he does not truly understand love, truth, or friendship. However, Selman commented, ". . . This does not mean that children cannot act in a trusting or loving way before . . ." [this stage] (p.310). If behavior is contingent on the stages of understanding that Selman and Kohlberg proposed, then this last observation appears to contradict their position. For their position to be correct, one would expect a child could not be loving and trusting before he understood the necessary, but not sufficient stages of role taking and moral judgment.

Selman proposed a cognitive-developmental concept of ego development as a way of approaching the clinical situation. He suggested that one consider that the child develops in roughly parallel stages of each of three domains: (1) the physical, the relationship of the self to physical objects along dimensions such as time, space, and movement; (2) the logical, the understanding of classes, subclasses, relations, etc.; and (3) the social, composed of self, self related to others, that is role taking, and means of resolving conflict (Selman's definition of moral judgment). To make a clinical appraisal, he suggested that one chart development in each of these domains. In Selman's system if one assumes that a normal person should be at approximately the same stage in each domain, then one may make a diagnosis of impairment or lag in a domain or one may look for different clusters of lags.

To illustrate his cognitive-developmental approach to clinical work, Selman presented a case study of a child who insisted that he get whatever he wanted and who had no comprehension of another person's expectations. This child scored zero on Selman's role taking and Kohlberg's moral stages. In contrast, the child's physical and logical stage levels were considerably more advanced. Keeping in mind the child's role-taking level, Selman successfully treated the child by having camp counselors repeatedly explain to him the reasons for their actions and carefully make clear to him the structure of the social interaction at camp. Chittenden (Lickona, 1976) accomplished the same kind of improvement in domineering, self-centered, 5-year-olds by training them to anticipate and reconcile the reaction of doll characters in imaginary social conflict situations. So this general approach would appear to have utility in certain types of cases. (Although follow-up and comparison of relative effects of strictly cognitive intervention to a pure limit setting strategy would provide us with some essential additonal parameters to allow appropriate assessment of Selman's and Chittenham's approach.) On the other hand, Selman's presenting of another child, who was depressed, friendless, and isolated, was much more complex and to us less convincing as a possible case for using Selman's classificatory and treatment approach.

In introducing his commendable foray into the clinical realm, Selman (1976) asked a very important question: Do cognitive–developmental stages (that is, his own and Kohlberg's) "really exist in the minds of children as well as the minds of cognitive-developmentalists?" (p.312). The Kohlbergian approach starts with the concerns of certain adults, adults who have recently struggled with the Nurenberg principle, something that to other adults, let alone children, holds little interest. We think that principles involved in marbles and hide and seek and playing house (provided this is an involvement of the children to be investigated) will more likely reveal children's concerns. We have little doubt that one can find stages of moral and role-taking development through use of dilemmas such as the Heinz story. However, such a story is inherently complex. Exactly what one is tracing in the development of understanding such a story is not too clear. Whether one is tracing fundamental factors in ordinary development or ordinary pathologic development is problematic. As difficult as is the clinical anamnesis method, part and parcel of the unstructured psychotherapeutic interview, we think it is superior when trying to explicate origins of adult concerns since it starts where the particular adult or type of adult is.

In struggling against the concept of structure as being unitary across conventional, moral, and physical cognitive function, Turiel (1977) appeared to have split from Kohlberg and Selman. Working in the same genre as Kohlberg and Selman, Turiel proposed that morality does not differentiate from convention as thought by Kohlberg (1976), Loevinger (1976), and Piaget (1965a). Turiel found young children distinguish conventional codes, e.g., whether to wear clothes or not, from moral codes, which he defines as codes of justice. Viewing social conventions and morality as fully autonomous developmental domains, he stated that conventional codes are arbitrary while codes of justice are not, that the child can observe for himself what is fair or not.

Turiel (1977), clearly disagreeing with Selman, contended that role taking is not a domain in itself or a precursor of moral judgment function, but rather one of the methods for learning about the world (the other methods being imitation, observation, and communication). What appears to be a development of a domain of role taking is merely changes in role taking due to advance in cognition.

Turiel's (1974) demonstration that peers, who are one moral stage above (not below, nor greatly advanced) the developmental level of a subject stimulated him to move up a stage, supported the position that disequilibrated transition states portend further development. Turiel's finding also supports the importance of meeting the child close to, but slightly above, his level of development if one is to encourage further development. This same finding also argued for an upward developmental thrust. However, the fact that peers were helpful in such an advance does not argue that peers are the natural or superior stimulus to such development.

Damon (1977) clearly allied himself with Turiel, including viewing role taking as a method, not a domain. Further, Damon argued that his own finding that the domain of logical cognition (tested by serial ordering and classification) and various social cognition domains develop in somewhat parallel fashion is not due to an underlying, unitary cognitive structure. He asserted that the parallel was due to inherent, shared qualities, which make for affiliations of one domain with another. For instance, because authority and convention domains both involve obedience, their development is expected to be closely aligned. Since both positive justice and logical cognition domains involve classification and ordering (or compensation) then both of these domains may be expected to develop in tandem. Damon proposed that parallels in development are a function of the similarity of environmental demand, not as a result of an under-lying general cognitive structure. While this is his basic posi-tion, he seems to soften this position at times.

In 4-to 9-year-olds he studied four domains of social cogni-tion: positive justice, friendship, peer (team captain) and paren-tal authority, and conventions (e.g., whether a boy should wear a dress or whether a girl should eat with her hands). His hypo-thetical dilemmas were much simpler than Selman's and not adult-centered as Kohlberg's were. In exploring positive justice and authority, retesting a year later supported a developmental trend.

To argue against an underlying cognitive structure, Da-mon pointed out that at times a child's social cognition may be in advance of his logical cognition, not just logical cognition in advance of social cognition. We suggest that the tests in use, in either the physical or social sphere, only reflect or approximate the underlying organizing structure; they are not coincident with it. In our practice, we doubt there is the delay in the physical domain that occurs in the social domain, especially late in development. But there is no reason why either may not lag behind the other and yet both require certain underlying structural shifts.

In all his measures, Damon used each subject's best consis-tent level of performance. We think his use of best consistent level (like Wolfson's, 1972) is appropriate for his interests, since it implies capacity. However, for us, at least at times, some persistence of lowest level of performance is of special interest. In classifying adult character structure, we give more weight to presence of primitive cognition or behavior than to the highest level achieved.

Generally speaking, while our theoretical position differs in major ways from Damon's (his seeing the child as construct-ing his moral precepts of fairness, etc., on the basis of peer interaction and his discounting of the importance of an underly-ing cognitive structure), his findings do not contradict our posi-tion. Certainly we are sympathetic to his position that no external measure in the logical (to us physical) or social sphere is absolutely dependent on the other and that cognition in the various domains does not inexorably march toward final form irrespective of environmental provisions of content.

Loevinger (1976) brought together work from many sources, especially work of the psychoanalytically-oriented ego psychologists and some of the work of Piaget. In a scholarly and germinal manner, she set psychology into its historical psychophilosophical roots and framework.

Our efforts and Loevinger's overlap as attempts to integrate the work of the psychoanalysts with that of Piaget. However, our basic techniques and final objectives differ from hers. We use the clinical interview, while she used sentence completion tests. Both of us felt that we found in certain adults reflections of stages of ego development of the child as postulated primarily by psychoanalytically oriented ego psychologists. Loevinger, however, while recognizing a symbiotic stage in ego development, did not find evidence of that stage in adults, while we do, that is, in our symbolic characters. Further, she made finer distinctions in her adult groups than we make. For instance, she distinguished the impulsive from the opportunistic which we do not. She distinguished five other stages or substages—conformist, conscientious-conformist, conscientious, individualistic, autonomous, and integrated in that order. We see her stages as reflecting distinctive and abiding personality traits that are more often associated with one of our character structures than with another or with one personality type than another. However, we do not see her stages as constituting primary levels of organization as we believe our character structures are.

Frank and Quinlan (1976) found that delinquent behavior corresponded to Loevinger's stage concepts. In their 66 delinquent and nondelinquent adolescent black and Puerto Rican inner city girls, however, they also found relative absence of Loevinger's conformist stage while the substage below (e.g., struggle for impulse control and desire for respectability) and above (self-conscious) was evidenced. To explain their findings, they suggested that it might be an artifact of their using an oral test or that ego development and delinquency is different in nonwhites. An alternate explanation is that Loevinger's conformist stage reflects a personality trait that is closer to more mature function than Loevinger's next stage, the self-conscious stage.

Loevinger stated she did not wish to set up a new school, but to bring together works from many sources, especially the psychoanalytic work on ego psychology, into a subdiscipline of psychology which uses its own methodologies. Like her, we attempt to integrate knowledge from diverse sources and are especially influenced by the findings and theory of psychoanalysis.

However, we differ from Loevinger in our basic goal. Generally, we would support the formation of a new school of psychology, the basis of which would be the Piagetian model. We favor theory-based psychology, not a method-based psychology. We are in hopes that the Piagetian paradigm will be the organizer around which both classical psychological methods and clinical treatment and investigation methods will be employed and that this model will bear fruit just as, for many years, the psychoanalytic model has.

We did not encounter Riesman, Glazer, and Denney's (1950) work until very late in the writing of this manuscript. It is for this reason that we see the overlap of our characterology and his as confirmatory. Heavily influenced by Eric Fromm's characterology, Riesman and his coauthors drew upon population studies to formulate a division of adult character into inner-directed, other-directed, and tradition-directed. His inner-directed character who has a "gyroscope" set by his parents is similar to our operational character. His other-directed, who is peer-oriented and has a "radar" device, corresponds very closely to our intuitive character. Riesman's tradition-directed character does not have the complexity of our symbolic character, but shares basic properties. At the descriptive level, Riesman, Glazer, and Denney and we are very close. However, we differ in some of the salient factors of parenting that mediate development of the different character types. We think of character types as more separable then he proposes. Nevertheless, given certain distinctions between the two characterologies, the similarities of description are striking. Finally, it is entirely reasonable that Riesman's proposal that the typical character type for certain phases of population growth is correct, with the tradition-directed (symbolic) being called for during a period of high growth potential, the inner-directed (operational) serving the transitional period, and the other-directed (intuitive) fitting the period of incipient decline.

Chapter 12

THEORETICAL, DIAGNOSTIC, AND THERAPEUTIC EFFECTS OF THE MODEL

This is a book for clinicians, clinicians brought up on the psychoanalytic model, who have seen its usefulness, have watched the development of object relations theories with interest, who might consider a new model if it provided them with a better way of organizing their clinical experience and pointed to applications in treatment.

The system we propose is holistic and parsimonious, dividing the data into but three groupings, each grouping characterized by one social cognitive style and its intertwined social investment. By seeing the symbolic character's presenting with social cognition and investments of the intuitive, operational, or some mixture of the two and having a more basic social cognitive organization and investment of his own allows the system to embrace incompatibilities or exceptions in existing typologies, e.g., persons who have both impulsive and compulsive tendencies. Our model's strongest arguments are the totality of embrace, the simplicity, and that the two basic parameters and secondary criteria are logically meaningful to each other and make their appearance together in any given individual in the pschotherapeutic setting.

We encourage the clinicians reading this book to set aside temporarily their own theoretical framework and their preferred typology to see if their patients may be classified as we suggest, and to see if there is a natural coherence and relative exclusiveness of the basic parameters and secondary criteria of each of the three character syndromes. We think they will find this system generally dissects sharply one type of patient from another, and that once the dissection is made that each new finding in a patient readily fits into the already collected data that supports the patient's character diagnosis.

The value of this text and our work would suffice if some clinicians' understanding of our typology were the only yield. Once having embraced our model, however, some theoretical, therapeutic, and research implications follow. These are the subject of this chapter.

For example, adoption of the Piagetian developmental system as a theoretical base for understanding character development confronts us with a timing conflict between the developmental stages described by Piaget and those reconstructed by psychoanalysts. The reconstruction upon which we wish to focus is the psychoanalytic one that the oral triad—dependency-independency, trust-distrust, and social reality testing problems, found as part of the syndrome of infantile personality, or other pregenital syndromes—is derived principally from the oral period, the first year of life (Erikson, 1950; Kernberg, 1972; Zetzel, 1970). Taking into account Piaget's findings, it is likely that the factors of the oral triad are not within a child's understanding even in a rudimentary way prior to 18 months or 2 years of age and they are not really dealt with before age 7 or 8, if then.

In keeping with the time frame set by their psychoanalytic predecessors, Mahler (1968) and Kernberg (1972) have suggested relationships between adult pregenital syndromes and the oral period. Mahler proposed that borderlines take origin from her "hatching" phase, age 6 to 12 months, and narcissistic personalities from her "practicing" phase, age 12 to 18 months. Kernberg proposed that acute schizophrenia takes origin from his Stage II which begins around the 4th to the 12th week, and borderline from his Stage III which is from 6 to 18 months.

These theoretical considerations lead to application in both treatment and research. Volkan (1976) in his treatment of psychotic, borderline, and narcissistic patients conceptualized his approach in accordance with Kernberg's timetable of development. Gamer, Gallant and Gruenbaum (1976) investigated 1-year-olds' development toward object permanence, expecting to see impairment (which they did not find) in those whose mothers were schizophrenic. Apparently they had assumed that the reality testing problems encountered in schizophrenia are related to the first 12 months of life, rather than to a later period.

The timing conflict between psychoanalysis and our adaptation of the Piagetian system is in terms of interpretation, not in terms of findings. As may be noted in Chapters 3 and 4, there is considerable agreement between Mahler, Piaget, and Spitz about certain aspects of the child's development during the first year of life: that he is completely dependent on his caretaker; that starting from an undifferentiated state, he begins to distinguish his caretaker as an object, a beginning of reality testing; that differentiation of object from self is unlikely during the first 12 months; and that his development or construction of person object representations (at this stage it is likely that person as a social being and person as a thing are indistinguishable) precedes his development of thing-object representations. It is probable that if the mother reliably, repeatedly gratifies a child when he is in need, he will have some sense that things will work out or that the familiar is good or safe, something that could be called basic trust (Erikson, 1950). But how a 1-year-old, let alone a 6-month-old, without a concept of self or object, understands this is a question. Likewise, while there is no argument that a child is absolutely dependent on his mother during the first year of life, more so than at any other time, does he know that? There is little meaning to dependency without some concept of external objects. So, any sense of needing to be with, or to be ministered to by an external object is unlikely to be present even in a rudimentary way before Stage 4, around the end of the first year of life. Dependency as a preconcept could be expected to be much more a factor after 18 months to 2 years of age when a child has begun to differentiate self- from object-representation, when mental image (thought) and perception separate. The seeds of dependency-independency, trust-distrust, or reality testing are present or being formed during the first year. However, the flowering of these kinds of functions must take place after object and self are somewhat separate, that is, from 18 months to 7 years of age, or later.

Prior to 18 months, perception and thought are not differentiated, hence, a child is still hallucinating. Although object and self are somewhat separate after 18 months, the essence of self, object, part object, and symbol or sign are not understood until after 4, while values or attributes of objects or events are not grasped until after 7. So development of reality testing at 1 year of age is just beginning. Furthermore, while a child is dependent from the beginning, his awareness (conscious or unconscious) of his dependency cannot begin until he has some notion of his self-representation as separate from an object representation upon which he is dependent. He continues to be highly dependent for a number of years, certainly until he can make it to school or to the playground and back. Trust appears to be a function of dependency. The concept that one can depend on an object is trust. To have an abstract concept of dependency or trust as an attribute of an object seems unlikely much before 7 or 8 any more than one can understand quantities before that age. Since person-cognitive development in regard to physical attributes precedes thing-cognitive development, it is possible (though unlikely) that trust or dependency, attributes which involve persons and not things, could be understood early, perhaps as early as 5 or 6. It is unlikely, how-

unlikely, however, that they would be understood in a holistic way much before that and very likely not until considerably later. An intuitive-stage child knows if a person is giving him what he wants at the moment, not whether he can trust him generally or that he needs to depend on him. As far as being trustworthy, a child who does not see any great distinction between lies, mistakes, fantasy, play, and facts is not expected to be trustworthy. Stealing and lying prior to 7 is within normal limits.

Consider the understanding of dependency or trust that is possible for the 2- to 4-year-old, one who is in the Symbolic Stage. During that stage, a symbol is not fully separate from the thing it represents. Various views of a thing are seen as separate things. A thing or a person is not united into one object; parts of a thing or person define the thing or person as being different. Trustworthy to a symbolic-stage child must be part of the object, just as Lucienne's bathing suit is a part of Lucienne, sharp is part of a particular scissors and obedience is part of a father. Similarly, there may be a depending-on-mother and a not-depending-on-mother, all as separate representations.

If we take into account Piaget's time table of development of cognitive structures, we can absorb Mahler's and Spitz's findings (see Chap. 3). However, even allowing for possible premature development of person cognition (probably unlikely in the social sphere per se, in fact contradicted by Wolfson's 1972 findings) compared to thing cognition, the style of social cognition (including embrace of concepts of dependency and trust) found in symbolic characters is not likely to take place prior to age 2 and probably persists as the style of functioning at least until 3 or 4. Correspondingly the style of social cognition found in intuitive characters is not likely evidenced prior to age 3 or 4 and could be expected to persist at least until age 6 or 7.

So, a patient who manifests significant problems with social reality testing, dependency, and trust is exhibiting a level of function which is normal much later than the first year of life.

This is not to say that the mother-child relationship for the first 12 to 18 months may not set tones, form a base for developing trust or mistrust and in fact have far-reaching effects, even impair the whole procedure of development. Rather, our point is that just because the child is completely dependent and he learns to postpone a bit (in a sense, trust) does not mean that he has any concept consciously or unconsciously that he is dependent on or needs objects or knows that he can or cannot rely on them.* Persistence of primitive constructs of trust and dependency at least as late as the intuitive stage as parts of normal development makes it inconsistent to attribute such primitive expressions to earlier phases of development.

Trust or dependency are likely constructed along with other part-objects, for example, Lucienne's dress, or other attributes, such as Lucienne's littleness and Jacqueline's bigness. During the Intuitive Stage, both the attribute, little, and the object, dress, are first seen as somewhat separate from Lucienne. At around this time, it could be expected that dependency and trust are beginning to be understood as separate from certain adults. At the same time, when the dress becomes an object in its own right, the attribute, little, while separate from the object, is still bound to the event that is in view. Accordingly, other attributes such as dependency (that one needs another to take care of him) and trust (that one can rely on someone else) can be expected to be bound to the situation in view. For a child to develop an understanding that he can rely on someone, that is, trust them in a general sense in spite of disappointments, he likely must be 7- or 8-years-old. He must be in the Concrete Operational Period. Prior to then, he does not fully see another's point of view. He has not separated out

---

*Klein's (1948) concept of the depressive position, a stage of fused depression-paranoia, is likely the experience of a child during this early period when he is in distress, just as it may be postulated he experiences fused symbiotic bliss when he is pleased. Also in keeping with our view, is Zetzel's (1966) contention that depression is not possible, as such, prior to some development of ego boundaries.

his own point of view nor does he have any notion of his own long-term or repeat interests. He cannot coordinate various dimensions. It is reasonable that he would not be able to conceptualize his generally needing to have someone else around to take care of him (dependency-independency) or of his generally believing that people (his caretakers) are likely to take care of him when he needs care (trust-distrust) as soon as, let alone sooner than, he would understand littleness-bigness as it applies to people.

Studies of social cognition provide fragmentary confirmation of the timing of development that we propose. Most of the social cognitive data have been gathered in the laboratory and are dependent on the child-subject's verbalization, nonspontaneous verbalization at that. As a consequence, it is likely that the child understands identity and trust somewhat earlier than he demonstrates it in the experimental laboratory; however, not as early as psychoanalytic theory would have it.

When children are examined in a laboratory setting their concepts of identity of persons rest on part-objects until very late in their development. Not until 6 or 7 is a child reasonably certain that the gender of another child (in a photograph) cannot be changed by changing his or her hair or clothes (Kohlberg, 1966). Six- to seven-year-olds first recognize themselves as human and as male or female largely based on names, physical appearance and behavior (Guardo & Bohan, 1971). Although after 8 or 9, names, physical characteristics, and behavior remain important, more covert and personalized differences in feelings and attitudes begin to contribute to this sense of identity. Wolfson (1972) found that a majority of eight- to ten-year-olds generally justified their future continued sameness, their identity, pointing out that their actions, roles, or social validation (e.g., I will still be my mother's daughter) will be the same. If they contended they would be different when they were older, they used the same kinds of justifications. Selman (1976) reported that on verbal measures a child does not fully understand the meaning of trust until he is 10 or 12.

Taking into account Piaget's observations moves up the timetable of development. It once again establishes the oedipal time period—that is, the Intuitive Stage, age 5 to 7 or so—as being of very special importance in psychological function.

Perhaps most powerful in our understanding of patients has been the recognition of the symbolic character, one of whose primary concerns is tangible, assured, though not necessarily constant connection to another human being. Also, modification of treatment of symbolic patients follows once it is understood that feeling connected is critical for these patients' sense of well-being and their function. One symbolic patient was depressed, agitated, anorexic, and insomniac. She had been treated as an involutional melancholiac, but was intolerant of antidepressants. When allowed to tell her story, she made it clear that she was not an involutional melancholiac who had a history of phobias, but a woman who had been phobic much of her life and whose phobias and depression were closely tied to her loss of human connections. Without understanding that personal contact is very important for symbolic characters, such statements as, "I'm not as scared if I hear footsteps overhead, as [occurs] in my friend's apartment," would have been missed by us. This woman, while unable to sleep alone in her own house, was able to sleep in her neighbor's home, something that an involutional melancholiac is unable to do. After she realized that there was often not a live person on television, "Just a tape being played," she could not sleep alone at home. Before that she could sleep if she kept her television turned on.

We became alert to the kinds of events, often breaks in attachments, that precipitate a symbolic character's symptomatology. The patient last cited lost a number of human connections. She had lived with her parents until their deaths, 15 years prior to her seeking psychiatric treatment. When they died, she had other attachments which took their place, particularly her father's dog and a neighbor who was a friend of her parents. This neighbor, whose daughter died shortly before our patient's parents died, became a symbiotic partner for our patient. At the time therapy began, it was likely our patient would lose her symbiotic partner-neighbor (due to illness). For 30 years, the patient worked with the same friendly, accepting fellow employees. For various reasons this group broke up. The patient's heart disease prohibited her from working and later from participating in a club that had been important to her. The patient had had diverse attachments which broke for various reasons.

All these breaks in attachment were instrumental in the patient's increased anxiety and depression. Such losses are disturbing to anyone; however, keeping such connections had enabled this patient to function. Breaches in the connections were her undoing. A person with a different character structure can be expected to be vulnerable to other types of stress or to be responsive in a different manner to losses.

Not only does assimilation of the basic parameters of the three syndromes increase our ability to tune in on factors that might have gone unnoticed, but it also directs our treatment approach. In the patient just discussed, in a major way, treatment consisted of mending hook-ups and facilitating new links.

Using an energic model, such as the psychoanalytic one, especially taking into account the phenomenon of transference, it is theoretically possible to modify anything. The only limiting factor is one's technique. In our system, there are certain structures in the adult that we feel cannot be altered. Treatment in this system becomes repairing, sometimes modifying small pieces of structures, but not a true restructuring. The knowledge of character structure aids in overall strategy and sets limits. Knowing that connecting and identity is important for a symbolic character and assuming he will not be able to transform into another structure in any way that would benefit him, then the aim is to assist him in finding suitable connections and supports for his identity and in offering the therapist for both functions.

We have worked long and hard with intuitive characters, but have not seen them become operational (at one time, we had thought that effecting such a change was our task). In one patient, several interventions appeared to modify her approach. Her fee was reduced to allow her to take some steps toward her long-term financial well-being. Her fee was then increased when she decided to spend her money on current luxury. We think our intervention was instrumental in her subsequent stabilizing and vastly improving her economic condition. To some extent, the therapist had offered her protective (noncorrupt) parenting in the financial aspect of her life. Subsequently, she functioned well in her own behalf in her investments, but often struggled with the temptation to sell her holdings and flee a current uncomfortable situation. Frugality or saving for a rainy day was never an automatic, integral part of her character.

Some intuitive patients, when their belief in immanent justice is brought to their attention, are able to use this knowledge (usually as a corrective device) at times. So far, we have not seen such insight become automatic.

Intuitive or symbolic characters being transformed into operationals is the implied goal of some therapists. We remain unconvinced that such structural change results even from Volkan's (1976) ambitious treatment approach in which he proposed that transference psychosis be allowed to develop. It appears to us that just as our patients continue with attachment behavior at the conclusion of their treatment, his patient's needs for symbiotic attachment were met in more symbolic, less socially aberrant or painful ways (e.g., religion), but were still in evidence. In contrast to Volkan, Kohut's (1977) treatment goal calls for reparation of the self, not for risky analysis of all accessible structures. However, he is also more optimistic than we are regarding the benefits derived from analysis of defects of the nuclear-self.

In an operational character who undergoes psychoanalysis, regression allows him to correct certain approaches or expectations which he manifests toward current figures, but which were residual from childhood. While there is some structural change, the basic form of ego or superego does not change; rather, some changes in content or some loosening of structure takes place. An operational character does not become an intuitive character or vice versa. It is rather that an operational character's or an intuitive character's mechanisms may not be as rapidly and frequently operative after therapy and that each may recognize and take a somewhat relaxed view toward their mechanisms. For example, referring to his undoing goodhumoredly, one obsessive-compulsive noted, "There I go cancelling out again." To some extent this is what is hoped for in a not too sociopathic intuitive character who uses denial, projection, and externalization with great facility. An objective of treatment is that he not always use such defenses automatically, that he recognize his use of them at times, that he not feel too criminal about use of such operations, and that some of the time he should be able to acknowledge blame. We have seen massive reorganizations in certain symbolic characters who shifted between constricted obsessive behavior and flamboyant hysterical, psychotic behavior. However, these patients have remained symbolic.

As we interpret treatment in this model, we are limited by the equilibrated character structure. However, if we were able to change a person's character structure, who is to say which character structure is best? Is the social world really a trustworthy place? Should an intuitive or symbolic character learn to trust the social world? Should an operational learn to distrust? The answer, of course, lies in learning whom to trust. It would help an intuitive character if he could recognize a trustworthy person or a reliable system when he was confronted with one, just as it would help him if he learned not to flit from person to person or situation to situation, unable to recognize or stay with more reliable sources of supply that have modest, but obvious defects. It is possible to assist an intuitive to do this to some extent, but changes, when effected, appear not to be integral to his function. They are more like compensating devices that are added on to his automatic systems. His basic wiring remains unchanged. As we mentioned, operationals may learn to distrust at times, but those who tend to overtrust will readily slip back into such a stance.

If it were possible, should part-to-part reasoning of the symbolic character be prevented? Keying off a stray triggering experience into a live memory of 30 years ago may cause severe pain and disturbed function. On the other hand, poetry, literature, and new forms of art likely rest on such leaps in thinking. Certainly, the zealot who is a symbolic character, who experiences both intense pain or gratification from his close associates, at times can also effect major changes in society for good or evil. Also, the symbolic character who defines his structure and goals in terms of the needs of his surroundings may serve society very well and be extremely adaptive even though he forsakes considerable personal realization in the process.

In a changing environment the intuitive character may be the most adaptive of all. The operational character, in spite of being the most "mature" character structure, may be quite unadaptive to change in the rules and may be at the very least a fool as he follows his code. It seems inevitable that people think of the operational character as better, since he makes use of functions drawn from a more advanced developmental stage. This is unfortunate since neither in terms of adaptability, creativity, wisdom nor plain likability is he necessarily any better or worse than the other two. Or, as a friend of ours said, even an operational character may be able to have fun or be creative, etc. (Edwin F. Alston, personal communication 1977).

So minor structural change seems desirable and possible; major structural change is not the therapeutic task even if it could be done. The therapeutic task, as always, is reduction of pain and improvement of function. Here the system that is more accurate than the others, in the long run, will prove most helpful.*

An essential focus of this book is theory. The book contributes to psychological theory by adapting Piaget's model to current knowledge of dynamic psychiatry. As has been stressed,

*For a more thorough explication of the treatment approach which derives from this model, see Ahern (1978).

whatever theoretical model is employed is of great importance for both further knowledge and application. The ability to apply and adhere to a scientific model was of singular significance in the work of both Freud and Piaget. Our hope is that the adapted Piagetian model proposed herein will help extend knowledge and facilitate practice. In this model, we see the budding of a coherent and structural general psychology, which is based on Piaget's psychological theory, which provides a framework for including psychoanalytic clincial findings and knowledge of content, and which embraces normal and abnormal function.

REFERENCES

Ahern, M. *A differential context approach to treatment based on a social cognitive model of character structure.* Sacramento, Ca.: Unpublished Doctoral Dissertation, Institute for Clinical Social Work, Society for Clinical Social Work, 1978.

Ainsworth, M. D. S. Object relations, dependency, and attachment: A theoretical view of the infant-mother relationship. *Child Development,* 1969, *40,* 969–1025.

Appel, Y. H. *Maternal efforts at socialization: A developmental study.* Paper presented at the Seventh Annual International Interdisciplinary Conference on Piagetian Theory and the Helping Professions, University of Southern California, Los Angeles, Jan. 28, 1977.

Aronfreed, J. Moral development from the standpoint of a general psychological theory. In T. Lickona (Ed.), *Moral development and behavior.* New York: Holt, 1976.

Bandura, A., & McDonald, F. J. The influence of social reinforcement and the behavior models in shaping children's moral judgments. *Journal of Abnormal and Social Psychology,* 1963, *67,* 274–281.

Basch, M. F. Developmental psychology and explanatory theory in psychoanalysis. *The Annual of Psychoanalysis,* 1977, *5,* 229–263.

Bavelas, J. B. *Personality: Current theory and research.* Monterey, Ca.: Brooks/Cole, 1978.

Becker, W. Consequences of different kinds of parental discipline. In M. L. Hoffman & L. W. Hoffman (Eds.), *Review of Child Development Research,* Vol. I. New York: Russell Sage Foundation, 1964.

Bell, S. The development of the concept of the object as related to infant-mother attachment. *Child Development,* 1970, *41,* 291–311.

Bem, D. J., & Allen, A. On predicting some of the people some of the time: The search for cross-situational consistencies in behavior. *Psychological Review,* 1974, *82,* 506–520.

Blanck, G., & Blanck, R. *Ego psychology: Theory and practice.* New York: Columbia University Press, 1974.

Blank, H. R. Dreams of the blind. *Psychoanalytic Quarterly,* 1958, *27,* 158–174.

Blatt, S. J., & Wild, C. M. *Schizophrenia: A developmental analysis.* New York: Academic, 1976.

Bovet, M. Piaget's theory of cognitive development and individual differences. In B. Inhelder & H. H. Chipman (Eds.), *Piaget and his school: A reader in developmental psychology.* New York: Springer-Verlag, 1976.

Bowers, K. S. Situationism in psychology: An analysis and a critique. *Psychological Review,* 1973, *80,* (5), 307–336.

Bowlby, J. Forty-four juvenile thieves: Their characters and home life. *International Journal of Psychoanalysis,* 1944, *25,* 107–128.

Bowlby, J. *Attachment and loss,* Vol. I. New York: Basic Books, 1969.

Brock, C. T., & Del Giudice, C. Stealing and temporal orientation. *Journal of Abnormal and Social Psychology,* 1963, *66,* 91–94.

Bursten, B. The manipulative personality. *AMA Archives of General Psychiatry,* 1972, *26,* (4), 318–321.

Burton, R. V. Honesty and dishonesty. In T. Lickona (Ed.), *Moral development and behavior.* New York: Holt, 1976.

Cameron, N. *The psychology of behavior disorders.* Boston: Houghton-Mifflin, 1947.

Case, R. Structure and strictures: Some limitations on the course of cognitive growth. *Cognitive Psychology,* 1974, *6,* 544–574.

Chandler, M. J. Egocentrism and antisocial behavior: The assessment and training of social perspective-taking skills. *Developmental Psychology,* 1973, *9,* 326–332.

Chandler, M. J. Social cognition: A selective review of current research. In W. F. Overton & J. M. Gallagher (Eds.), *Knowledge and development,* Vol. I. New York: Plenum Press, 1977.

Damon, W. *The social world of the child.* San Francisco: Jossey-Bass, 1977.

Décarie, T. G. *Intelligence and affectivity in early childhood.* New York: International Universities Press, 1965. Translation by E. P. Brandt & L. W. Brandt.

Deutsch, H. Some forms of emotional disturbance and their relationship to schizophrenia. *Psychoanalytic Quarterly,* 1942, *11,* 301–321.

Erikson, E. *Childhood and society.* New York: Norton, 1950.

Escalona, S. K. Patterns of infantile experience and the developmental process. *Psychoanalytic Study of the Child,* 1963, *18,* 197–244.

Fenichel, O. *Psychoanalytic theory of neurosis.* New York: Norton, 1945.

Flavell, J. H. *The developmental psychology of Jean Piaget.* New York: Van Nostrand, 1963.

Flavell, J. H. *The development of role-taking and communication skills in children.* New York: Wiley, 1968.

Fraiberg, S. Parallel and divergent patterns in blind and sighted infants. *The Psychoanalytic Study of the Child,* 1968, *23,* 264–300.

Frank, S. & Quinlan, D. Ego development and female delinquency: A cognitive-developmental approach. *Journal of Abnormal Psychology,* 1976, *85,* 505–510.

Freedman, D. G. *Human infancy: An evolutionary perspective.* Hillsdale, N.J.: Lawrence Erlbaum, 1974.

Freud, A. *The ego and the mechanisms of defense.* New York: International Universities Press, 1946.

Freud, A., & Dann, S. An experiment in group upbringing. *Psychoanalytic Study of the Child,* 1951, *6,* 127–168.

Freud, S. *New introductory lectures on psychoanalysis.* New York: Norton, 1933. Translation by W. J. H. Sprott.

Freud, S. *A general introduction to psychoanalysis.* Garden City, N.Y.: Garden City Publishing, 1943. Translation by J. Riviere.

Freud, S. Character and anal eroticism. *Collected papers II.* London: Hogarth Press, 1953a (originally written in 1908). Translation by J. Riviere.

Freud, S. Notes upon a case of obsessional neurosis. *Collected papers III.* London: Hogarth Press, 1953b (originally written in 1909). Translation by A. Strachey & J. Strachey.

Freud, S. *The ego and the id.* London: Hogarth Press, 1957. Translation by J. Riviere.

Friedman, L. Trends in the psychoanalytic theory of treatment. *Psychoanalytic Quarterly,* 1978, *47,* 524–567.

Gamer, E., Gallant, D., & Gruenbaum, H. An evaluation of 1-year-olds on a test of object permanence. *AMA Archives of General Psychiatry,* 1976, *33,* 311–317.

Garbarino, J., & Bronfenbrenner, U. The socialization of moral judgment and behavior in cross-cultural perspective. In T. Lickona (Ed.), *Moral development and behavior*. New York: Holt, 1976.

Gardner, H. *The quest for the mind*. New York: Alfred A. Knopf, 1973.

Gellman, E., & Formaneck, R. *Young children's criteria for gender classification*. Paper presented at the Seventh Annual Symposium of the Jean Piaget Society, Philadelphia, Pa., May, 1977.

Geschwind, N. Specializations of the human brain. *Scientific American*, 1979, *241*, 180–199.

Ginsburg, H., & Opper, S. *Piaget's theory of intellectual development, an introduction*. Englewood Cliffs, N.J.: Prentice-Hall, 1969.

Glueck, S., & Glueck, E. *Unraveling juvenile delinquency*. New York: Commonwealth Fund, 1950.

Golding, S. L. Flies in the ointment: Methodological problems in the analysis of the percentage of variance due to persons and situations. *Psychological Bulletin*, 1975, *82*, 278–288.

Gough, H. G. A sociological theory of psychopathy. *American Journal of Sociology*, 1948, *53*, 359–366.

Gough, H. G., & Peterson, D. R. The identification and measurement of predispositional factors in crime and delinquency. *Journal of Consulting Psychology*, 1952, *16*, 207–212.

Gould, R. *Child studies through fantasy*. New York: Quadrangle, 1972.

Guardo, C. J., & Bohan, J. B. Development of a sense of self-identity in children. *Child Development*, 1971, *42*, 1909–1921.

Gunderson, J. G., & Singer, M. T. Defining borderline patients: An overview. *American Journal of Psychiatry*, 1975, *132*, (1), 1–10.

Hall, C., & Lindzey, G. *Theories of personality*. New York: Wiley, 1957.

Hanford, H. A. *The impact of piagetian theory on problems of mental health*. Paper presented at the Fifth Annual Symposium of the Jean Piaget Society, Philadelphia, Pa., June 13–14, 1975.

Hartmann, H., Kris, E., & Lowenstein, R. M. Papers on psychoanalytic psychology. In *Psychological Issues*, G. S. Klein, Editor, Vol. 4, No. 2, Monograph 14. New York: International Universities Press, 1964.

Hill, L. B. *Psychotherapeutic intervention in schizophrenia*. Chicago: University of Chicago Press, 1955.

Hogan, R. Moral conduct and moral character: A psychological perspective. *Psychological Bulletin*, 1973, *79*, 217–232.

Inhelder, B., & Piaget, J. *The growth of logical thinking from childhood to adolescence*. New York: Basic Books, 1958. Translation by A. Parsons & S. Milgram.

Inhelder, B., & Piaget, J. *The early growth of logic in the child*. New York: Norton, 1969. Translation by E. Lunzer & D. Papert.

Inhelder, B., Sinclair, H., & Bovet, M. *Learning and the development of cognition.* Cambridge, Mass.: Harvard University Press, 1974.

Johanssen, G. Visual motor perception. *Scientific American,* June, 1975, *232,* 76–88.

Kagan, J. The three faces of continuity in human development. In D. Goslin (Ed.), *Handbook of socialization theory and research.* Chicago: Rand McNally, 1969.

Kernberg, O. A psychoanalytic classification of character pathology. *Journal of the American Psychoanalytic Association,* 1970, *18,* 800–822.

Kernberg, O. Early ego integration and object relations. *Annals New York Academy of Sciences,* 1972, *193,* 233–247.

Klein, M. Mourning and its relationship to manic-depressive states. In *Contributions to psychoanalysis, 1921–1945.* London: Hogarth Press, 1948.

Kohlberg, L. A. The development of children's orientation toward a moral order: Sequence in the development of moral thought. *Vita Humana,* 1963a, *6,* 11–33.

Kohlberg, L. A. Moral development and identification. In H. Stevenson (Ed.), *Child Psychology, 1963 Yearbook of National Society for Study of Education,* Chicago: University of Chicago Press, 1963b.

Kohlberg, L. A. Development of moral character and moral ideology. In M. L. Hoffman & L. W. Hoffman (Eds.), *Review of Child Development Research, 1,* 383–432. New York, Russel Sage Foundation, 1964.

Kohlberg, L. A. A cognitive-developmental analysis of children's sex-role concepts and attitudes. In E. Maccoby (Ed.), *The development of sex differences.* Stanford, Ca.: Stanford University Press, 1966.

Kohlberg, L. A. Moral Stages and Moralization: The Cognitive-Developmental Approach. In T. Lickona (Ed.), *Moral development and behavior.* New York: Holt, 1976.

Kohut, H. *The restoration of the self.* New York: International Universities Press, 1977.

Kugelmass, S., & Breznitz, S. The development of intentionality in moral judgment in city and kibbutz adolescents. *Journal of Genetic Psychology,* 1967, *3,* 103–111.

Lashley, K. S. In search of the engram. *Symposia of the Society for Experimental Biology* (Great Britain), *Vol. 4: Psychological mechanisms in animal behavior.* Cambridge, England: Cambridge University Press, 1950.

Laurendeau, M., & Pinard, A. *The development of the concept of space in the child.* New York: International Universities Press, 1970.

Lempke, S. P. Identity and conservation: The child's developing conceptions of social and physical transformation. Unpublished Doctoral Dissertation, University of California, Berkeley, 1973.

Lickona, T. Research on Piaget's theory of moral development. In T. Lickona (Ed.), *Moral development and behavior.* New York: Holt, 1976.

Lidz, T. *The origin and treatment of schizophrenic disorders.* New York: Basic Books, 1973.

Liebert, R. M., & Poulos, R. W. Television as a moral teacher. In T. Lickona (Ed.), *Moral development and behavior.* New York: Holt, 1976.

Link, N. F., Scherer, S. E., & Byrne, P. N. Moral judgment and moral conduct in the psychopath. *Canadian Psychiatric Association Journal,* 1977, *22,* 341–346.

Liu, C. The influence of cultural background on the moral judgments of children. In an unpublished doctoral dissertation, Columbia University, 1950, cited by T. Lickona (Ed.), *Moral development and behavior.* New York: Holt, 1976.

Loevinger, J. with the assistance of A. Blasi. *Ego development: Conceptions and theories.* San Francisco: Jossey-Bass, 1976.

Luria, A. R. In Cole, M. (Ed.): *Cognitive development, Its cultural and social foundation.* Cambridge, Mass.: Harvard University Press, 1976. Translation by M. Lopez-Morillas & L. Solotoroff.

Mahler, M. S. (in collaboration with M. Furer). *On human symbiosis and the vicissitudes of individuation. Vol. I: Infantile Psychosis,* New York: International Universities Press, 1968.

Mahler, M. S., Pine, F., & Bergman, A. *The psychological birth of the human infant: symbiosis and individuation.* New York: Basic Books, 1975.

Maier, H. W. *Three theories of child development.* New York: Harper and Row, 1965.

Malerstein, A. J. Korsakoff's syndrome and resumption of an interrupted task as an index of initiative. *The Journal of Nervous and Mental Disease,* 1969, *148,* 506–514.

Malerstein, A. J., & Ahern, M. M. Piaget's stages of cognitive development and adult character structure. *American Journal of Psychotherapy,* 1979, *33,* 107–118.

Millar, S. *The psychology of play.* Baltimore, Md.: Penguin Books, 1968.

Mussen, P. The roots of prosocial behavior in children. Paper presented at the Seventh Interdisciplinary Conference on Piagetian Theory and the Helping Professions, Univ. of So. Calif., Los Angeles, Jan. 28, 1977.

Neale, J. M. Egocentrism in institutionalized and non-institutionalized children. *Child Development,* 1966, *37,* 97–101.

Piaget, J. La pensée symbolique et la pensée l'enfant. *Archiv de psychologie,* 1923, *18,* 273–304.

Piaget, J. *The moral judgment of the child.* New York: The Free Press, 1965a (originally published in 1932). Translation by M. Gabain.

Piaget, J. Principle factors determining intellectual evolution from childhood to adult life. In *Factors determining human behavior* (Report of the

Harvard Tercentary Conference of Arts and Sciences), Cambridge, Mass.: Harvard University Press, 1937.

Piaget, J. *The origins of intelligence in children.* New York: Norton, 1963 (originally published in the U.S. by International Universities Press in 1952). Translation by M. Cook.

Piaget, J. *The construction of reality in the child.* New York: Basic Books, 1954. Translation by M. Cook.

Piaget, J. *Play, dreams, and imitation in childhood.* (Trans. C. Gattegno & F. M. Hodgson). New York: Norton, 1962a.

Piaget, J. The relation of affectivity to intelligence in the mental development of the child. *Bulletin of the Menninger Clinic,* 1962b, *26,* 129–137.

Piaget, J. *The child's conception of number.* New York: Norton, 1965b.

Piaget, J. *Six psychological studies.* D. Elkind (Ed.), New York: Vintage Books, 1968. Translation by A. Tenzer.

Piaget, J. Intellectual development from adolescence to adulthood. *Human Development,* 1972, *15,* 1–12.

Piaget, J. *The child and reality.* New York: Grossman, 1973. Translation by A. Rosin.

Piaget, J., & Inhelder, B. *The psychology of the child.* New York: Basic Books, 1969. Translation by H. Weaver.

Pribram, K. H., Nuwer, M., & Baron, R. J. The holographic hypothesis of memory structure in brain and perception. In R. C. Atkinson, D. H. Krantz, R. C. Luce, & P. Suppes (Eds.) *Contemporary development in mathematical psychology.* San Francisco: Freeman, 1974.

Rapaport, D. Some metapsychological considerations concerning activity and passivity. In M. Gill (Ed.), *Collected Papers of David Rapaport.* New York: Basic Books, 1967.

Reich, A. Narcissistic object choice in women. *Journal of the American Psychoanalytic Association,* 1953, *1,* 22–44.

Reich, W. *Character analysis.* New York: Orgone Institute Press, 1949.

Riesman, D. (in collaboration with), Glazer, N., & Denney, R. *The Lonely Crowd.* New Haven, Conn.: Yale University Press, 1950.

Rosenhan, D. L., Moore, B. S., & Underwood, B. The social psychology of moral behavior. In T. Lickona (Ed.), *Moral development and behavior.* New York: Holt, 1976.

Rubin, K. H. Egocentrism in childhood: A unitary construct? *Child Development,* 1973, *44,* 102–110.

Saltzstein, H. D. Social influence and moral development: A perspective on the role of parents and peers. In T. Lickona (Ed.), *Moral development and behavior.* New York: Holt, 1976.

Sameroff, A. J., & Zax, M. In search of schizophrenia: Young offspring of schizophrenic women. In L. C. Wynne (Ed.), *The nature of schizophrenia.* New York: Wiley, 1978.

Sarbin, T. R. Role theory. In G. Lindzey (Ed.), *Handbook of social psychology*. Reading, Mass.: Addison-Wesley, 1954.

Selman, R. L. Social-cognitive understanding: a guide to educational practice. In T. Lickona (Ed.), *Moral developmental behavior*. New York: Holt, 1976.

Selman, R. L. The relation of role-taking to the development of moral judgment in children. *Child Development*, 1971, *42*, 79–91.

Simpson, E. L. A holistic approach to moral development and behavior. In T. Lickona (Ed.), *Moral development and behavior*. New York: Holt, 1976.

Slipp, S. The symbiotic survival pattern: A relational theory of schizophrenia. *Family Process*, 1973, *12*, (4), 377–398.

Snyder, S. H. The opiate receptor and morphine-like peptides in the brain. *American Journal of Psychiatry*, 1978, *135*, 645–652.

Spitz, R. Anaclitic depression. *Psychoanalytic Study of the Child*, 1946, *2*, 313–342.

Spitz, R. (in collaboration with W. G. Cobliner). *The first year of life*. New York: International Universities Press, 1965.

Sullivan, H. S. *The interpersonal theory of psychiatry*. New York: Norton, 1953.

Sullivan, F. V., & Hunt, D. E. Interpersonal and objective decentering as a function of age and social class. *Journal of Genetic Psychology*, 1967, *110*, 199–210.

Turiel, E. Conflict and transition in adolescent moral development. *Child Development*, 1974, *45*, 14–29.

Turiel, E. Distinct conceptual development domains: Social convention and morality. In M. P. Jones (Series Ed.), *Nebraska Symposium on Motivation*, Vol. 25 (*Current Theory and Research in Motivation*). Lincoln, Neb.: University of Nebraska Press, 1977.

Ugurel-Semin, R. Moral behavior and moral judgment of children. *Journal of Abnormal and Social Psychology*, 1952, *47*, 463–474.

Vaillant, G. E. The maturation of defense mechanisms over the adult life cycle —A forty-year Study. Paper presented at the Northern California Psychiatric Society, C.M.E. Program, San Francisco, Calif., January 27, 1979.

Volkan, V. D. *Primitive internalized object relations: A clinical study of schizophrenic, borderline, and narcissistic patients*. New York: International Universities Press, 1976.

Wagner, S. The construction of correspondences and compositions relative to the resistence of chains. Paper given by the author at the Fifth Annual Symposium of the Jean Piaget Society, Philadelphia, Pa., June 1975.

Weiner, M. L. *The cognitive unconscious: A piagetian approach to psychother-apy.* Davis, Ca.: International Psychological Press, 1975.

Weiss, J. The integration of defenses. *International Journal of Psychoanalysis,* 1967, *48,* 520–524.

Wolff, P. Developmental psychologies of Jean Piaget and psychoanalysis. *Psychological Issues,* Vol II, (1), Monograph 5. New York: International Universities Press, 1960.

Wolfson, A. Aspects of the development of identity concepts. Unpublished Doctoral Dissertation, University of California, Berkeley, 1972.

Wynne, L. C., Singer, M. T., & Toohey, M. L. Communication of the adoptive parents of schizophrenics. *Annual Review of the Schizophrenic Syndrome,* 1976–7, *5,* 528–559.

Yarrow, M. R., Scott, P. M., & Waxler, C. A. Learning concern for others. *Developmental Psychology,* 1973, *8,* 240–260.

Zetzel, E. R. The predisposition to depression. *Canadian Psychiatric Association Journal,* 1966, *127,* S236–S249.

Zetzel, E. R. *The capacity for emotional growth.* New York: International Universities Press, 1970.

Zetzel, E. R. A developmental approach to the borderline patient. *American Journal of Psychiatry,* 1971, *127,* 867–871.

NAME INDEX

SUBJECT INDEX